VAULT

VAULTCOMICS.COM

DAMIAN A. WASSEL
PUBLISHER

ADRIAN F. WASSEL
EDITOR-IN-CHIEF

NATHAN C. GOODEN
ART DIRECTOR

TIM DANIEL
EVP BRANDING/DESIGN

KIM McLEAN
VP OF MARKETING

DAVID DISSANAYAKE
DIRECTOR OF PR & RETAILER RELATIONS

IAN BALDESSARI
OPERATIONS MANAGER

DAMIAN A. WASSEL, SR.
PRINCIPAL

WRITTEN BY
ALEX PAKNADEL

ILLUSTRATED BY
MARTIN SIMMONDS

COLORED BY
DEE CUNNIFFE

LETTERS BY
TAYLOR ESPOSITO

TARA FERGUSON · WHITE NOISE MARKETING

SPECIAL THANKS:
ARTYOM TRAKHANOV · RUSSIAN TRANSLATION
ANT MERCER

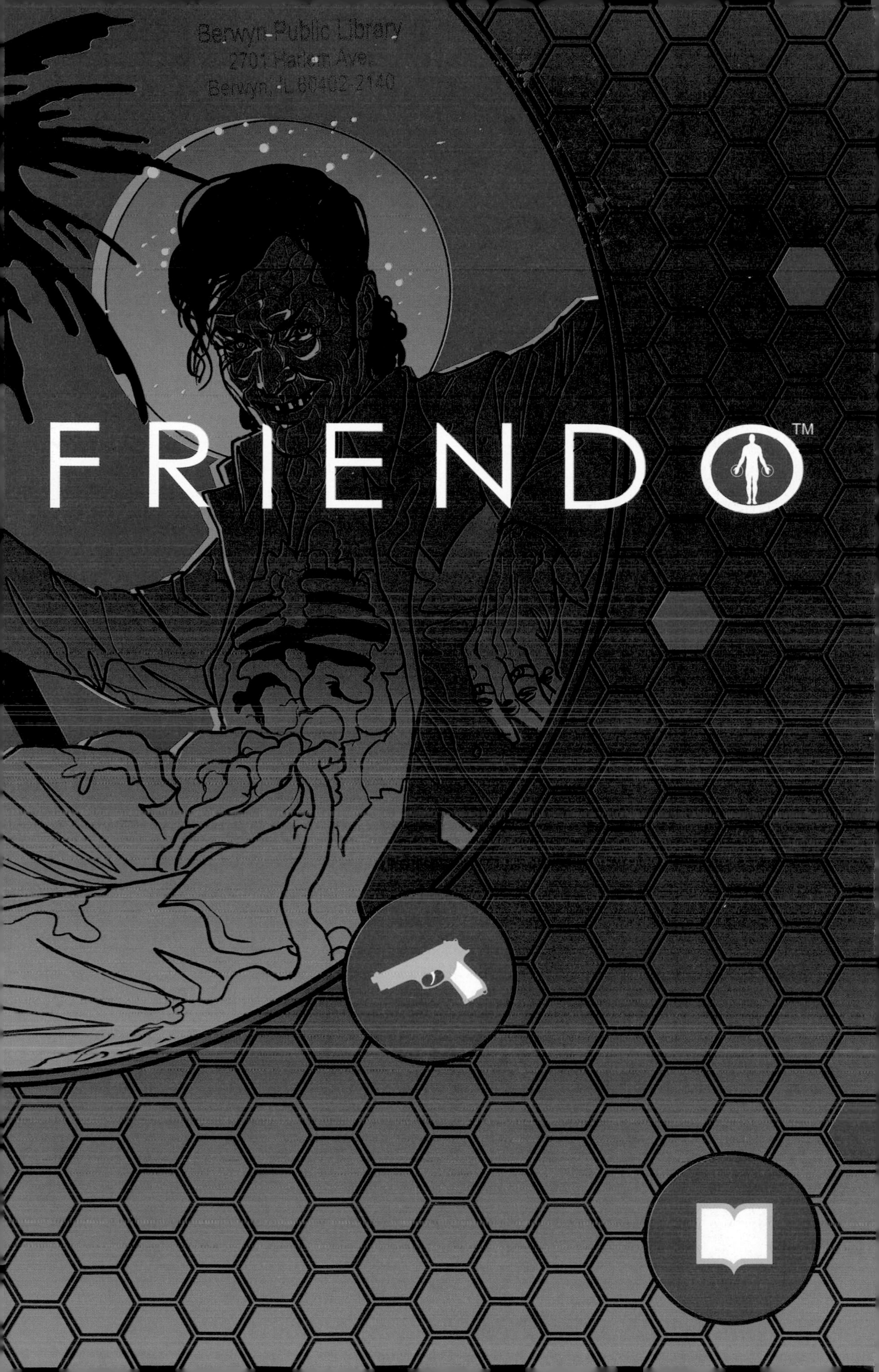
FRIENDO™

ONE

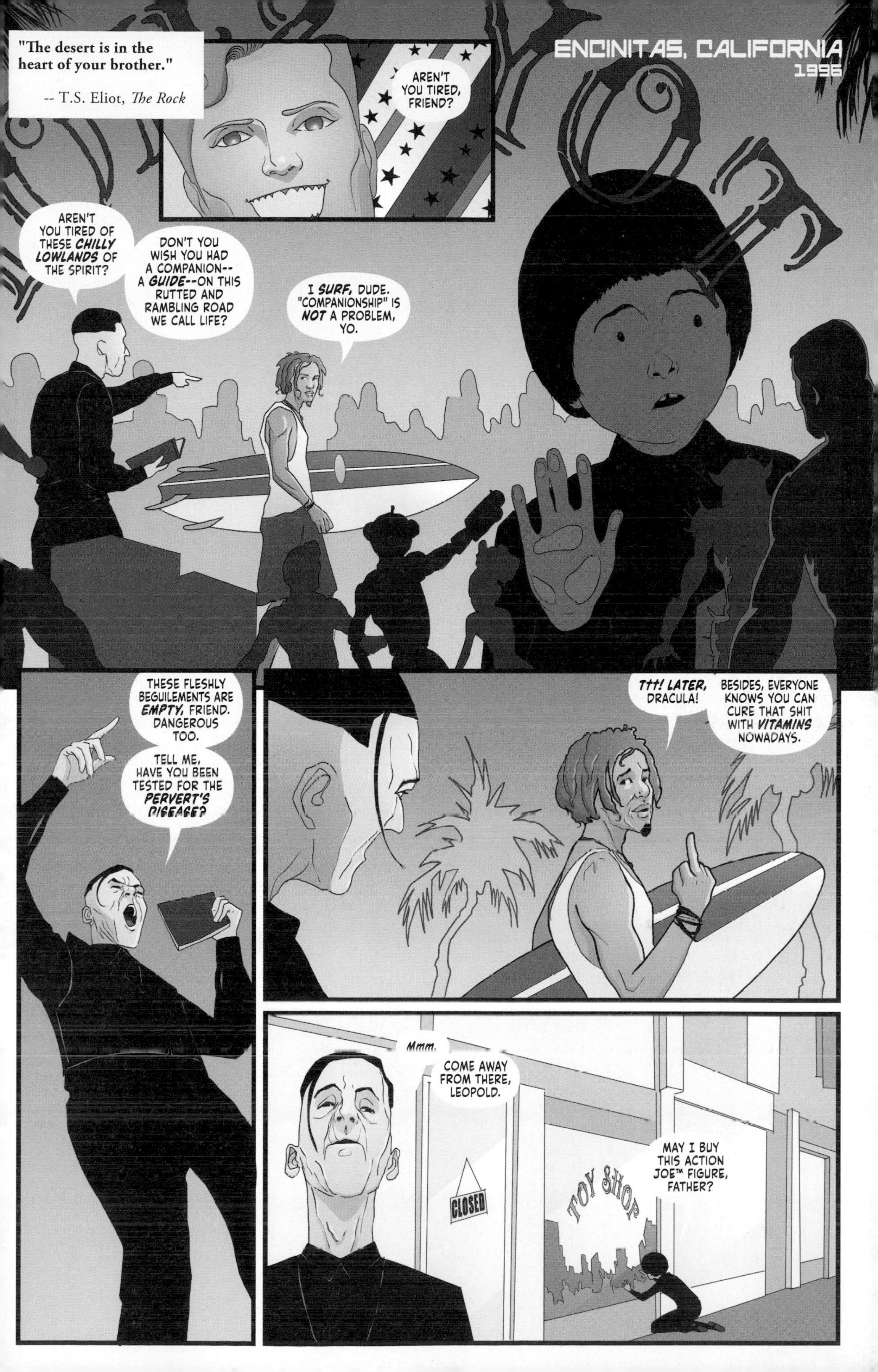
"The desert is in the heart of your brother."
-- T.S. Eliot, *The Rock*
ENCINITAS, CALIFORNIA
1996
AREN'T YOU TIRED, FRIEND?
AREN'T YOU TIRED OF THESE CHILLY LOWLANDS OF THE SPIRIT?
DON'T YOU WISH YOU HAD A COMPANION-- A GUIDE--ON THIS RUTTED AND RAMBLING ROAD WE CALL LIFE?
I SURF, DUDE. "COMPANIONSHIP" IS NOT A PROBLEM, YO.
THESE FLESHLY BEGUILEMENTS ARE EMPTY, FRIEND. DANGEROUS TOO.
TELL ME, HAVE YOU BEEN TESTED FOR THE PERVERT'S DISEASE?
TTT! LATER, DRACULA!
BESIDES, EVERYONE KNOWS YOU CAN CURE THAT SHIT WITH VITAMINS NOWADAYS.
Mmm.
COME AWAY FROM THERE, LEOPOLD.
CLOSED
TOY SHOP
MAY I BUY THIS ACTION JOE™ FIGURE, FATHER?

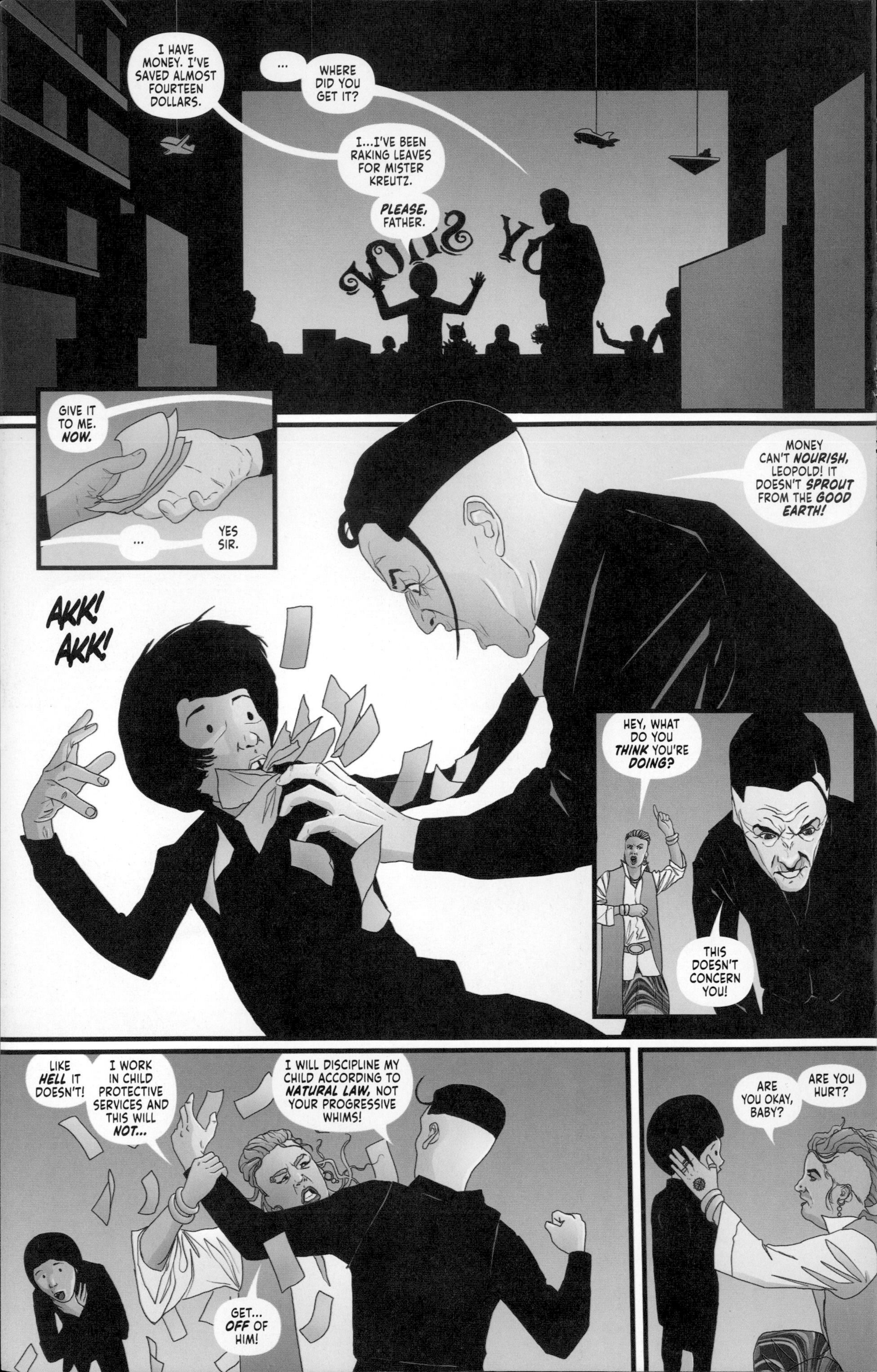

I HAVE MONEY. I'VE SAVED ALMOST FOURTEEN DOLLARS.
...
WHERE DID YOU GET IT?
I...I'VE BEEN RAKING LEAVES FOR MISTER KREUTZ.
PLEASE, FATHER.
GIVE IT TO ME. NOW.
...
YES SIR.
MONEY CAN'T NOURISH, LEOPOLD! IT DOESN'T SPROUT FROM THE GOOD EARTH!
AKK! AKK!
HEY, WHAT DO YOU THINK YOU'RE DOING?
THIS DOESN'T CONCERN YOU!
LIKE HELL IT DOESN'T!
I WORK IN CHILD PROTECTIVE SERVICES AND THIS WILL NOT...
I WILL DISCIPLINE MY CHILD ACCORDING TO NATURAL LAW, NOT YOUR PROGRESSIVE WHIMS!
GET... OFF OF HIM!
ARE YOU OKAY, BABY?
ARE YOU HURT?

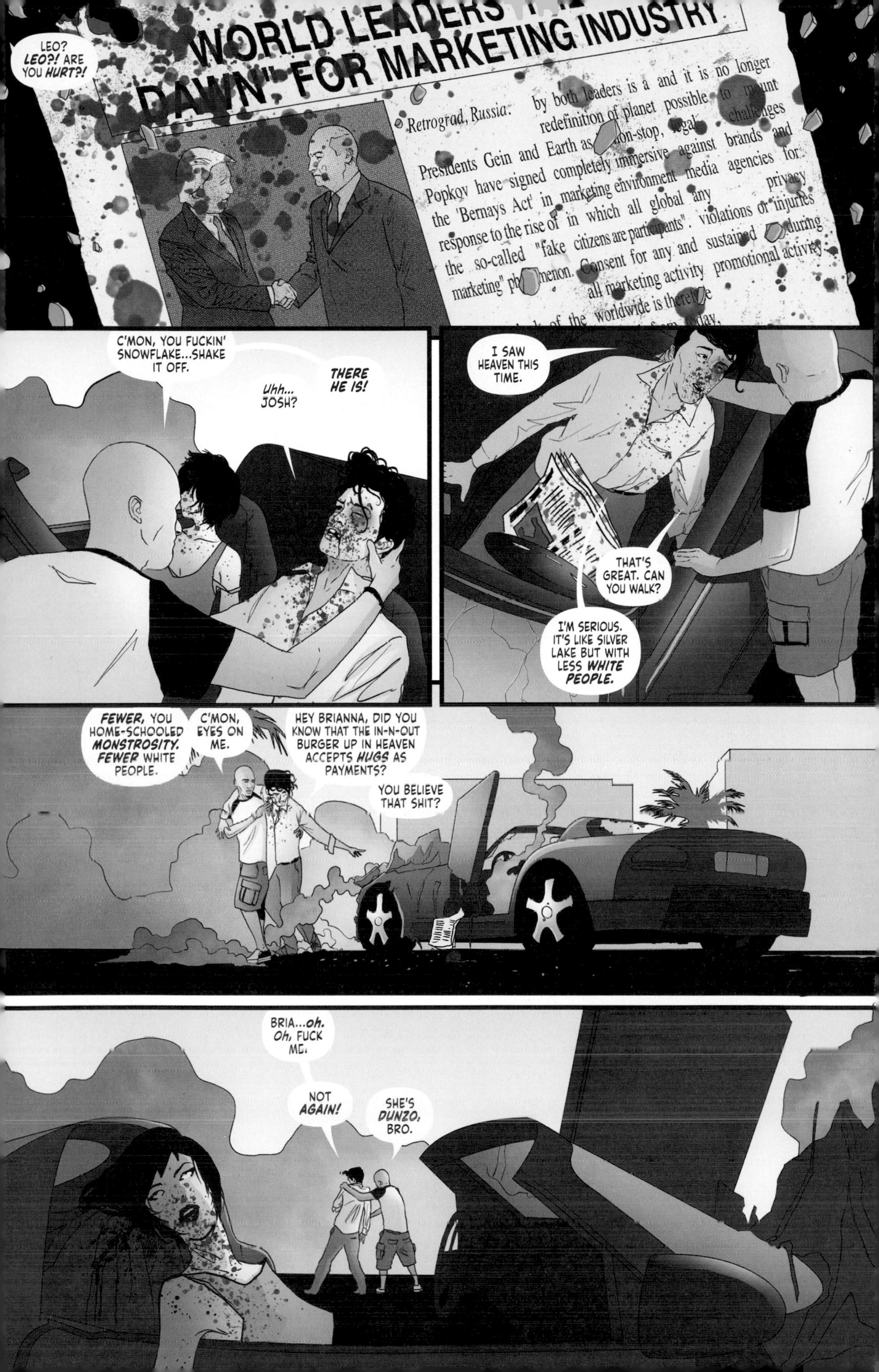

WORLD LEADERS
"DAWN" FOR MARKETING INDUSTRY
Retrograd, Russia.
LEO? LEO?! ARE YOU HURT?!
C'MON, YOU FUCKIN' SNOWFLAKE...SHAKE IT OFF.
Uhh... JOSH?
THERE HE IS!
I SAW HEAVEN THIS TIME.
THAT'S GREAT. CAN YOU WALK?
I'M SERIOUS. IT'S LIKE SILVER LAKE BUT WITH LESS WHITE PEOPLE.
FEWER, YOU HOME-SCHOOLED MONSTROSITY. FEWER WHITE PEOPLE.
C'MON, EYES ON ME.
HEY BRIANNA, DID YOU KNOW THAT THE IN-N-OUT BURGER UP IN HEAVEN ACCEPTS HUGS AS PAYMENTS?
YOU BELIEVE THAT SHIT?
BRIA...oh. Oh, FUCK ME.
NOT AGAIN!
SHE'S DUNZO, BRO.

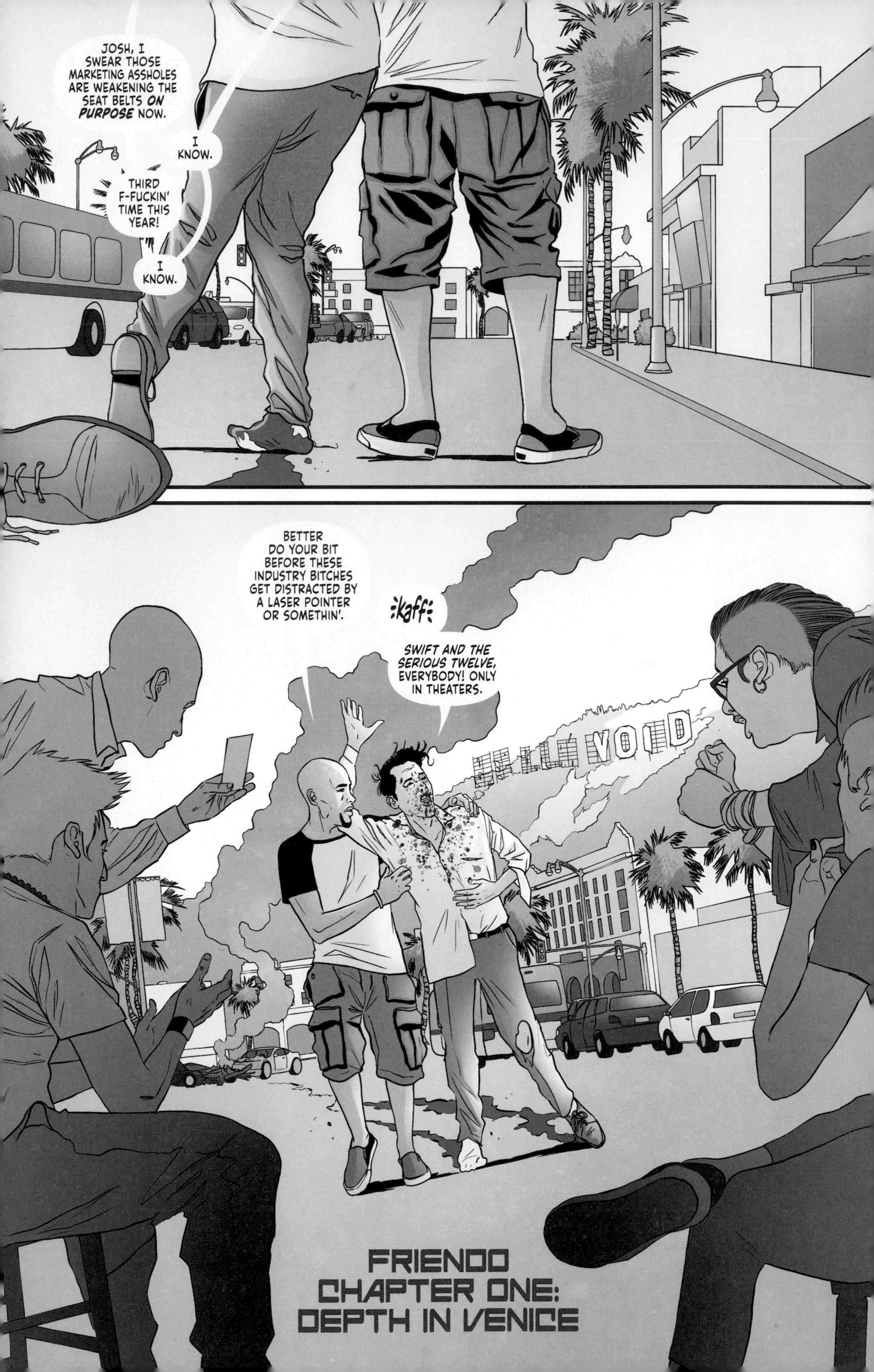

JOSH, I SWEAR THOSE MARKETING ASSHOLES ARE WEAKENING THE SEAT BELTS ***ON PURPOSE*** NOW.
I KNOW.
THIRD F-FUCKIN' TIME THIS YEAR!
I KNOW.
BETTER DO YOUR BIT BEFORE THESE INDUSTRY BITCHES GET DISTRACTED BY A LASER POINTER OR SOMETHIN'.
KAFF
SWIFT AND THE SERIOUS TWELVE, EVERYBODY! ONLY IN THEATERS.
VOID
FRIENDO
CHAPTER ONE:
DEPTH IN VENICE

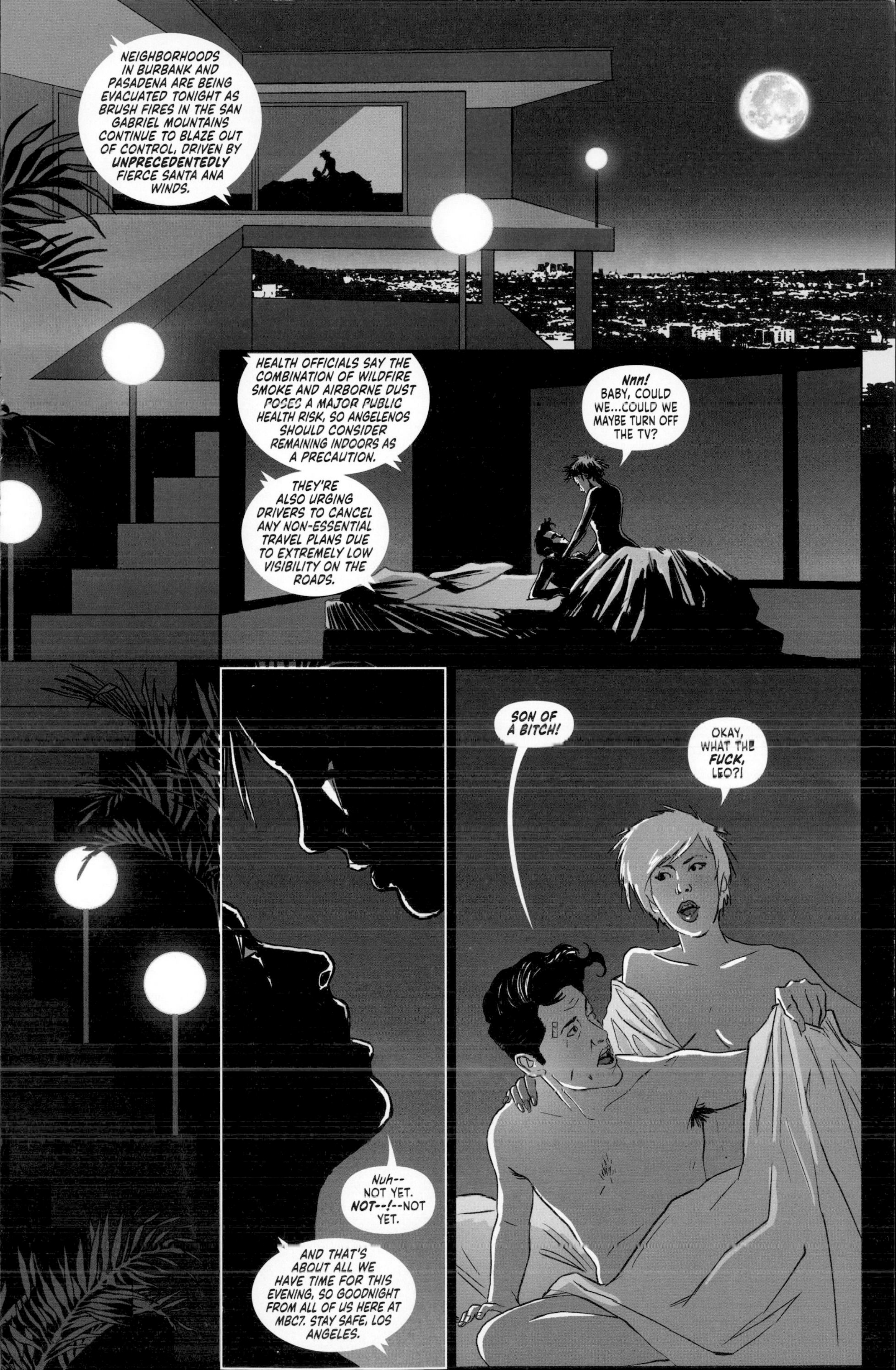
NEIGHBORHOODS IN BURBANK AND PASADENA ARE BEING EVACUATED TONIGHT AS BRUSH FIRES IN THE SAN GABRIEL MOUNTAINS CONTINUE TO BLAZE OUT OF CONTROL, DRIVEN BY UNPRECEDENTEDLY FIERCE SANTA ANA WINDS.
HEALTH OFFICIALS SAY THE COMBINATION OF WILDFIRE SMOKE AND AIRBORNE DUST POSES A MAJOR PUBLIC HEALTH RISK, SO ANGELENOS SHOULD CONSIDER REMAINING INDOORS AS A PRECAUTION.
THEY'RE ALSO URGING DRIVERS TO CANCEL ANY NON-ESSENTIAL TRAVEL PLANS DUE TO EXTREMELY LOW VISIBILITY ON THE ROADS.
Nnn! BABY, COULD WE...COULD WE MAYBE TURN OFF THE TV?
Nuh-- NOT YET. NOT--!--NOT YET.
AND THAT'S ABOUT ALL WE HAVE TIME FOR THIS EVENING, SO GOODNIGHT FROM ALL OF US HERE AT MBC7. STAY SAFE, LOS ANGELES.
SON OF A BITCH!
OKAY, WHAT THE FUCK, LEO?!

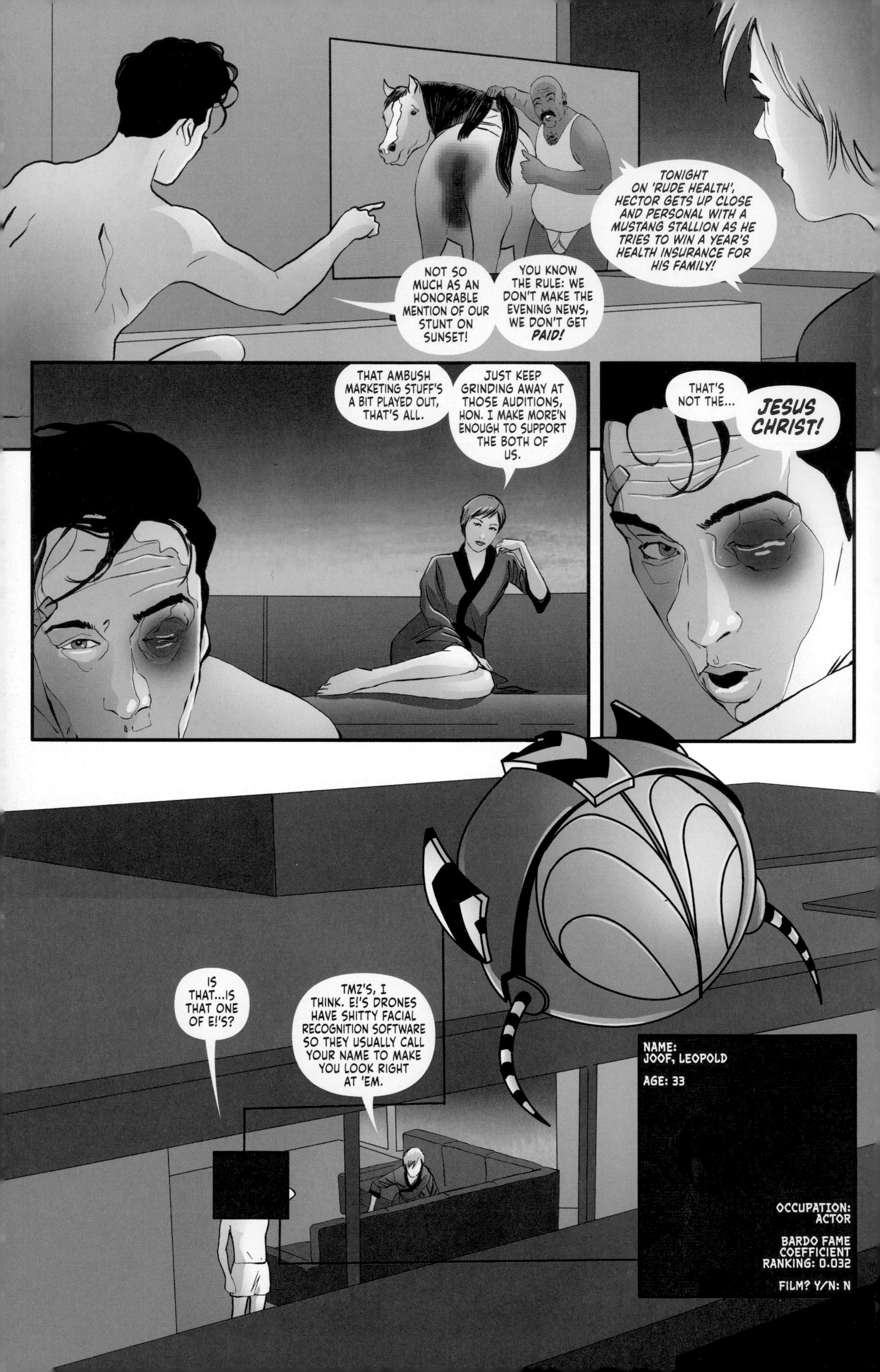
TONIGHT ON 'RUDE HEALTH', HECTOR GETS UP CLOSE AND PERSONAL WITH A MUSTANG STALLION AS HE TRIES TO WIN A YEAR'S HEALTH INSURANCE FOR HIS FAMILY!
NOT SO MUCH AS AN HONORABLE MENTION OF OUR STUNT ON SUNSET!
YOU KNOW THE RULE: WE DON'T MAKE THE EVENING NEWS, WE DON'T GET PAID!
THAT AMBUSH MARKETING STUFF'S A BIT PLAYED OUT, THAT'S ALL.
JUST KEEP GRINDING AWAY AT THOSE AUDITIONS, HON. I MAKE MORE'N ENOUGH TO SUPPORT THE BOTH OF US.
THAT'S NOT THE...
JESUS CHRIST!
IS THAT...IS THAT ONE OF E!'S?
TMZ'S, I THINK. E!'S DRONES HAVE SHITTY FACIAL RECOGNITION SOFTWARE SO THEY USUALLY CALL YOUR NAME TO MAKE YOU LOOK RIGHT AT 'EM.
NAME:
JOOF, LEOPOLD
AGE: 33
OCCUPATION:
ACTOR
BARDO FAME
COEFFICIENT
RANKING: 0.032
FILM? Y/N: N

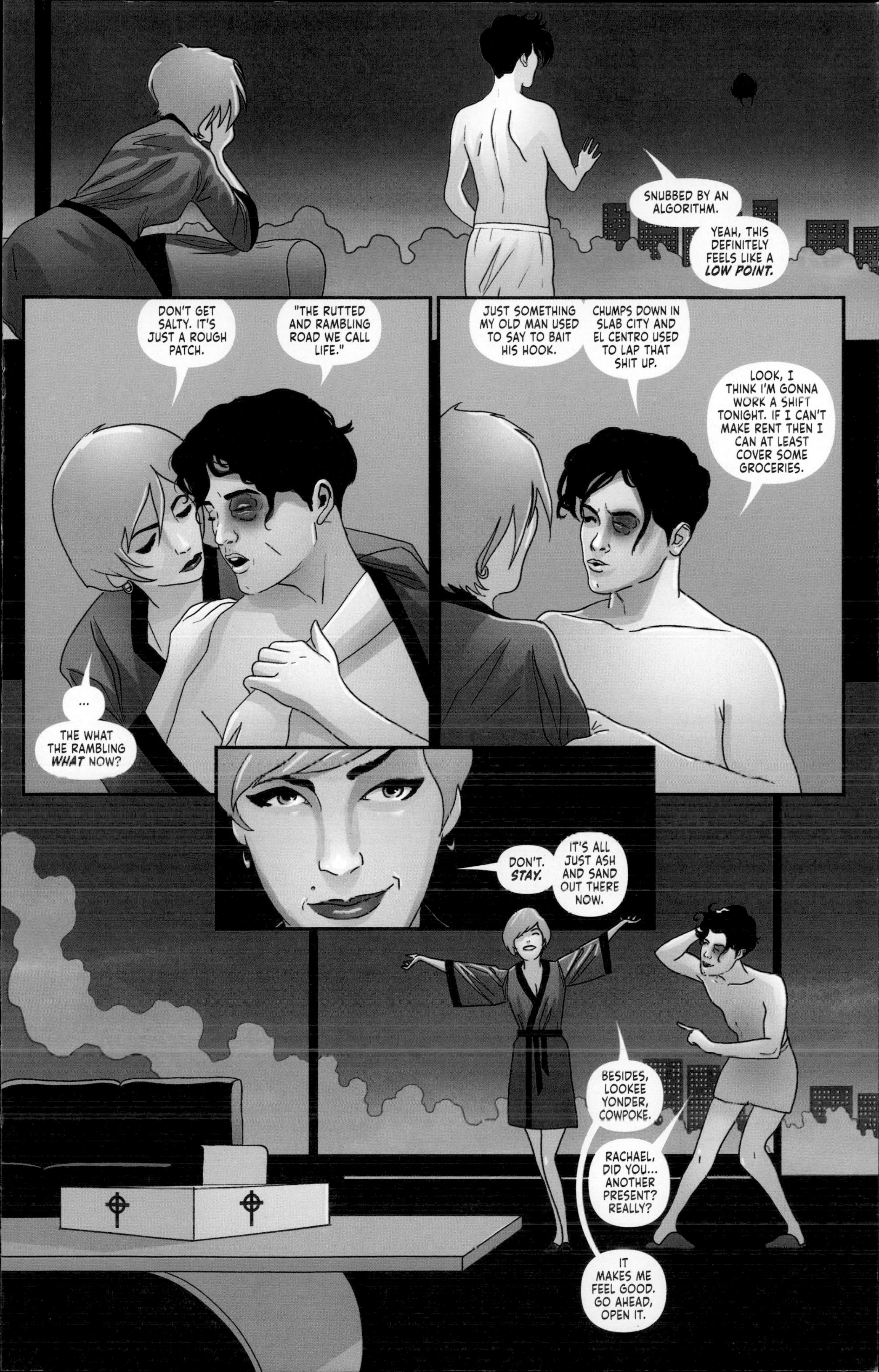
SNUBBED BY AN ALGORITHM.
YEAH, THIS DEFINITELY FEELS LIKE A ***LOW POINT.***
DON'T GET SALTY. IT'S JUST A ROUGH PATCH.
"THE RUTTED AND RAMBLING ROAD WE CALL LIFE."
...
THE WHAT THE RAMBLING ***WHAT*** NOW?
JUST SOMETHING MY OLD MAN USED TO SAY TO BAIT HIS HOOK.
CHUMPS DOWN IN SLAB CITY AND EL CENTRO USED TO LAP THAT SHIT UP.
LOOK, I THINK I'M GONNA WORK A SHIFT TONIGHT. IF I CAN'T MAKE RENT THEN I CAN AT LEAST COVER SOME GROCERIES.
DON'T. ***STAY.***
IT'S ALL JUST ASH AND SAND OUT THERE NOW.
BESIDES, LOOKEE YONDER, COWPOKE.
RACHAEL, DID YOU... ANOTHER PRESENT? REALLY?
IT MAKES ME FEEL GOOD. GO AHEAD, OPEN IT.

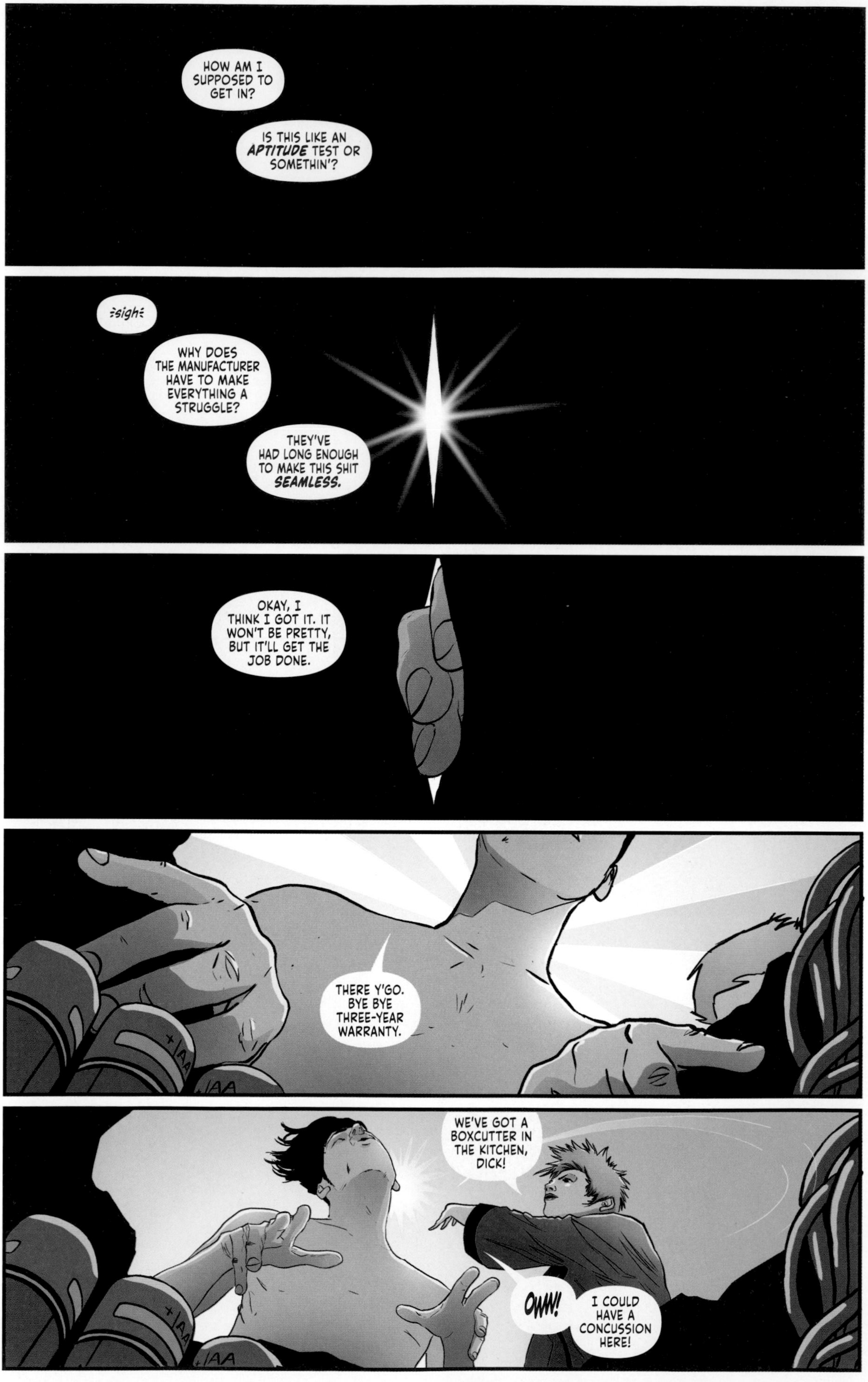
HOW AM I SUPPOSED TO GET IN?
IS THIS LIKE AN *APTITUDE* TEST OR SOMETHIN'?
≈sigh≈
WHY DOES THE MANUFACTURER HAVE TO MAKE EVERYTHING A STRUGGLE?
THEY'VE HAD LONG ENOUGH TO MAKE THIS SHIT *SEAMLESS.*
OKAY, I THINK I GOT IT. IT WON'T BE PRETTY, BUT IT'LL GET THE JOB DONE.
THERE Y'GO. BYE BYE THREE-YEAR WARRANTY.
WE'VE GOT A BOXCUTTER IN THE KITCHEN, DICK!
OWW!
I COULD HAVE A CONCUSSION HERE!

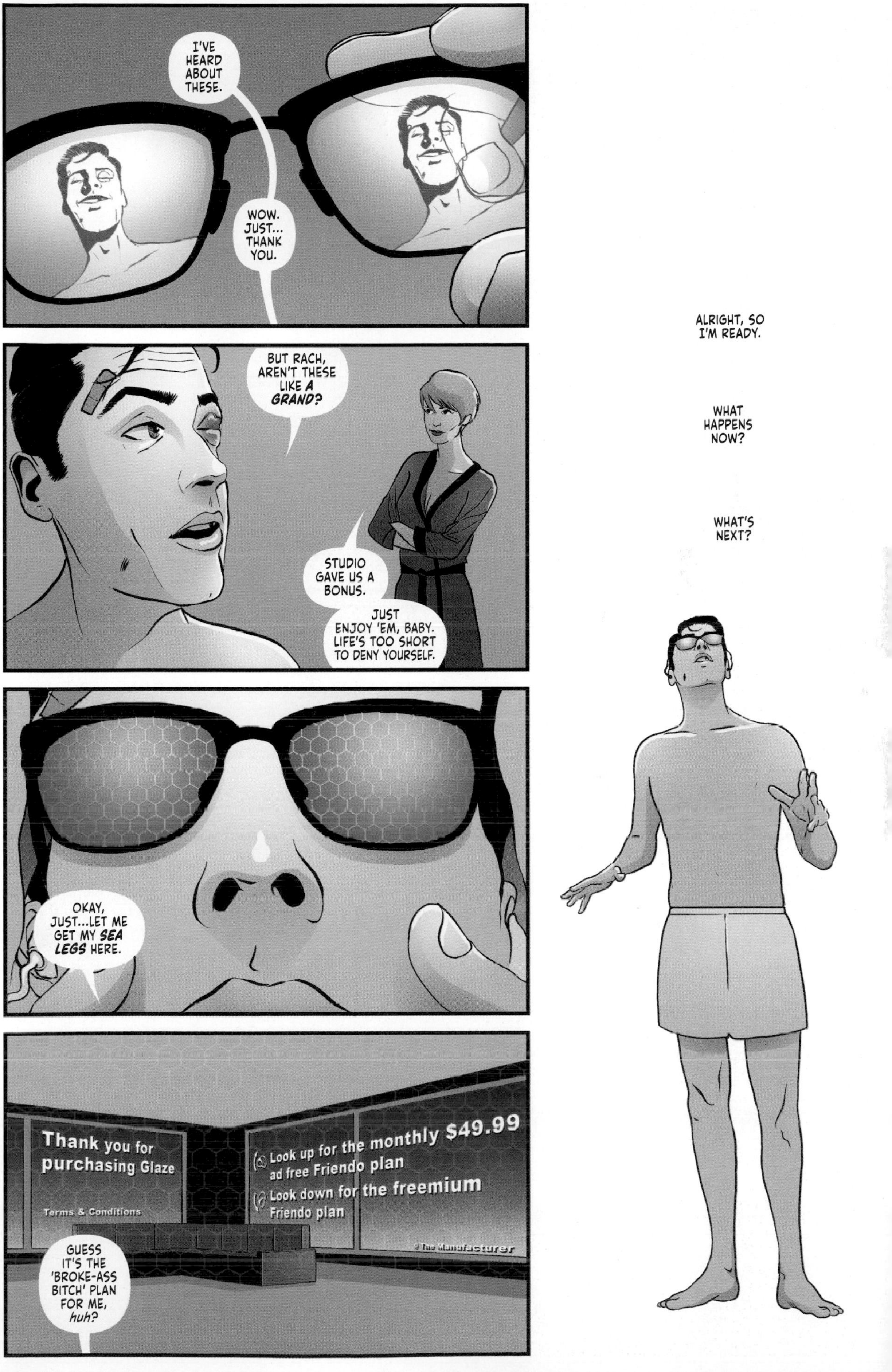
I'VE HEARD ABOUT THESE.
WOW. JUST... THANK YOU.
BUT RACH, AREN'T THESE LIKE *A GRAND?*
STUDIO GAVE US A BONUS.
JUST ENJOY 'EM, BABY. LIFE'S TOO SHORT TO DENY YOURSELF.
OKAY, JUST...LET ME GET MY *SEA LEGS* HERE.
Thank you for purchasing Glaze
Terms & Conditions
Look up for the monthly $49.99 ad free Friendo plan
Look down for the freemium Friendo plan
© The Manufacturer
GUESS IT'S THE 'BROKE-ASS BITCH' PLAN FOR ME, *huh?*
ALRIGHT, SO I'M READY.
WHAT HAPPENS NOW?
WHAT'S NEXT?

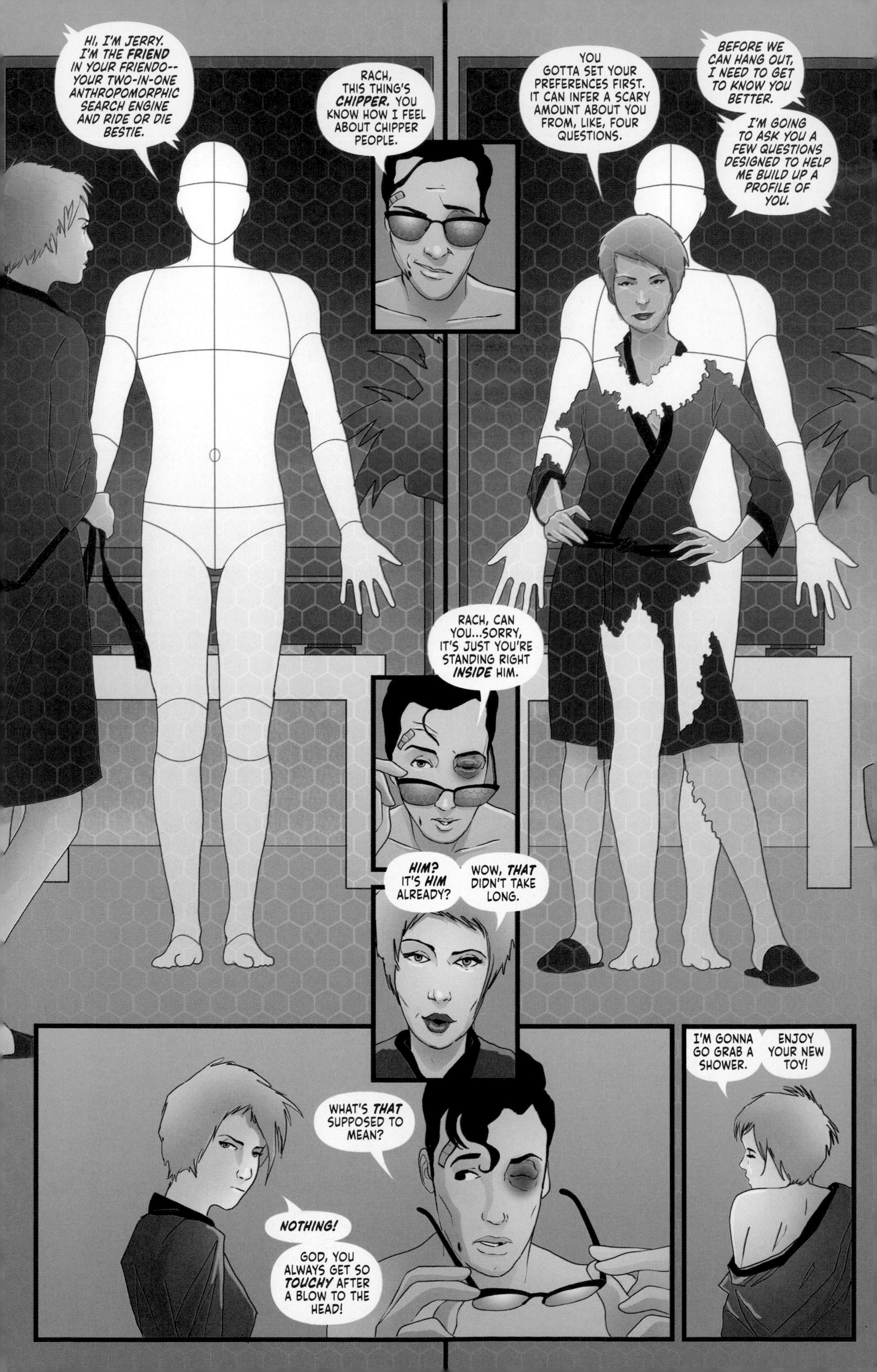
HI, I'M JERRY. I'M THE FRIEND IN YOUR FRIENDO-- YOUR TWO-IN-ONE ANTHROPOMORPHIC SEARCH ENGINE AND RIDE OR DIE BESTIE.
RACH, THIS THING'S CHIPPER. YOU KNOW HOW I FEEL ABOUT CHIPPER PEOPLE.
YOU GOTTA SET YOUR PREFERENCES FIRST. IT CAN INFER A SCARY AMOUNT ABOUT YOU FROM, LIKE, FOUR QUESTIONS.
BEFORE WE CAN HANG OUT, I NEED TO GET TO KNOW YOU BETTER.
I'M GOING TO ASK YOU A FEW QUESTIONS DESIGNED TO HELP ME BUILD UP A PROFILE OF YOU.
RACH, CAN YOU...SORRY, IT'S JUST YOU'RE STANDING RIGHT INSIDE HIM.
HIM? IT'S HIM ALREADY?
WOW, THAT DIDN'T TAKE LONG.
WHAT'S THAT SUPPOSED TO MEAN?
NOTHING!
GOD, YOU ALWAYS GET SO TOUCHY AFTER A BLOW TO THE HEAD!
I'M GONNA GO GRAB A SHOWER.
ENJOY YOUR NEW TOY!

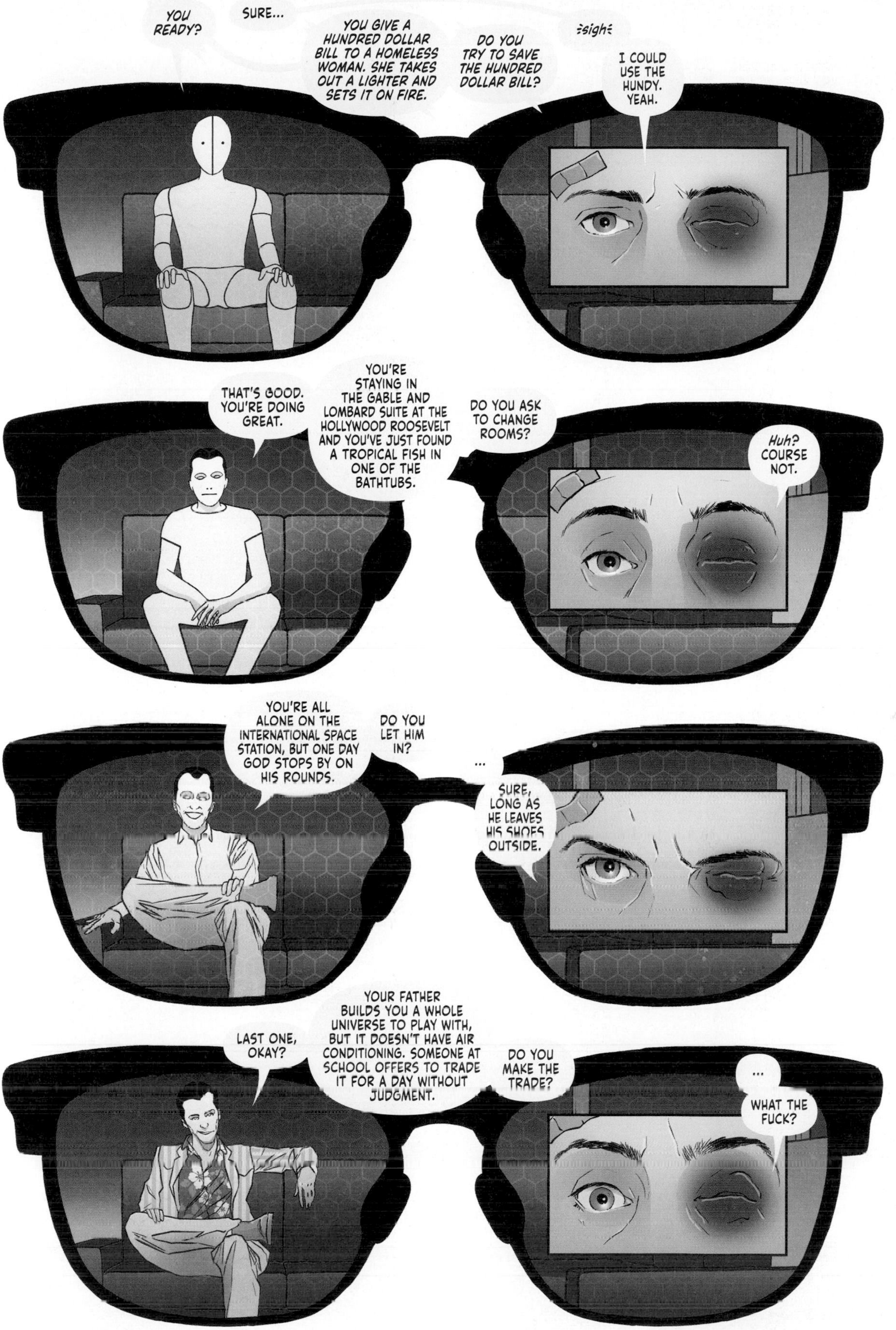
YOU READY?
SURE...
YOU GIVE A HUNDRED DOLLAR BILL TO A HOMELESS WOMAN. SHE TAKES OUT A LIGHTER AND SETS IT ON FIRE.
DO YOU TRY TO SAVE THE HUNDRED DOLLAR BILL?
=sigh=
I COULD USE THE HUNDY. YEAH.
THAT'S GOOD. YOU'RE DOING GREAT.
YOU'RE STAYING IN THE GABLE AND LOMBARD SUITE AT THE HOLLYWOOD ROOSEVELT AND YOU'VE JUST FOUND A TROPICAL FISH IN ONE OF THE BATHTUBS.
DO YOU ASK TO CHANGE ROOMS?
Huh? COURSE NOT.
YOU'RE ALL ALONE ON THE INTERNATIONAL SPACE STATION, BUT ONE DAY GOD STOPS BY ON HIS ROUNDS.
DO YOU LET HIM IN?
...
SURE, LONG AS HE LEAVES HIS SHOES OUTSIDE.
LAST ONE, OKAY?
YOUR FATHER BUILDS YOU A WHOLE UNIVERSE TO PLAY WITH, BUT IT DOESN'T HAVE AIR CONDITIONING. SOMEONE AT SCHOOL OFFERS TO TRADE IT FOR A DAY WITHOUT JUDGMENT.
DO YOU MAKE THE TRADE?
...
WHAT THE FUCK?

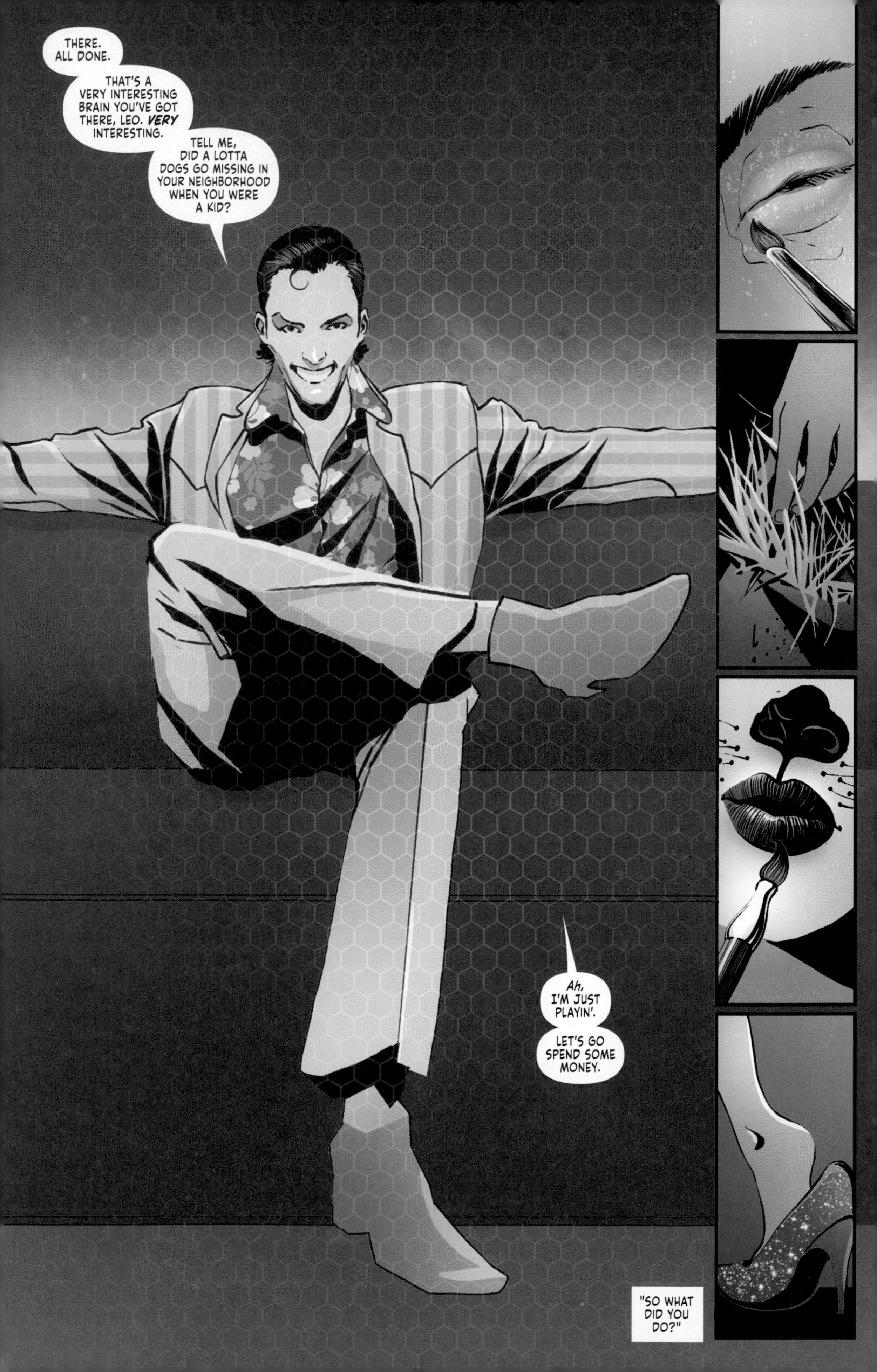
THERE. ALL DONE.
THAT'S A VERY INTERESTING BRAIN YOU'VE GOT THERE, LEO. *VERY* INTERESTING.
TELL ME, DID A LOTTA DOGS GO MISSING IN YOUR NEIGHBORHOOD WHEN YOU WERE A KID?
Ah, I'M JUST PLAYIN'.
LET'S GO SPEND SOME MONEY.
"SO WHAT DID YOU DO?"

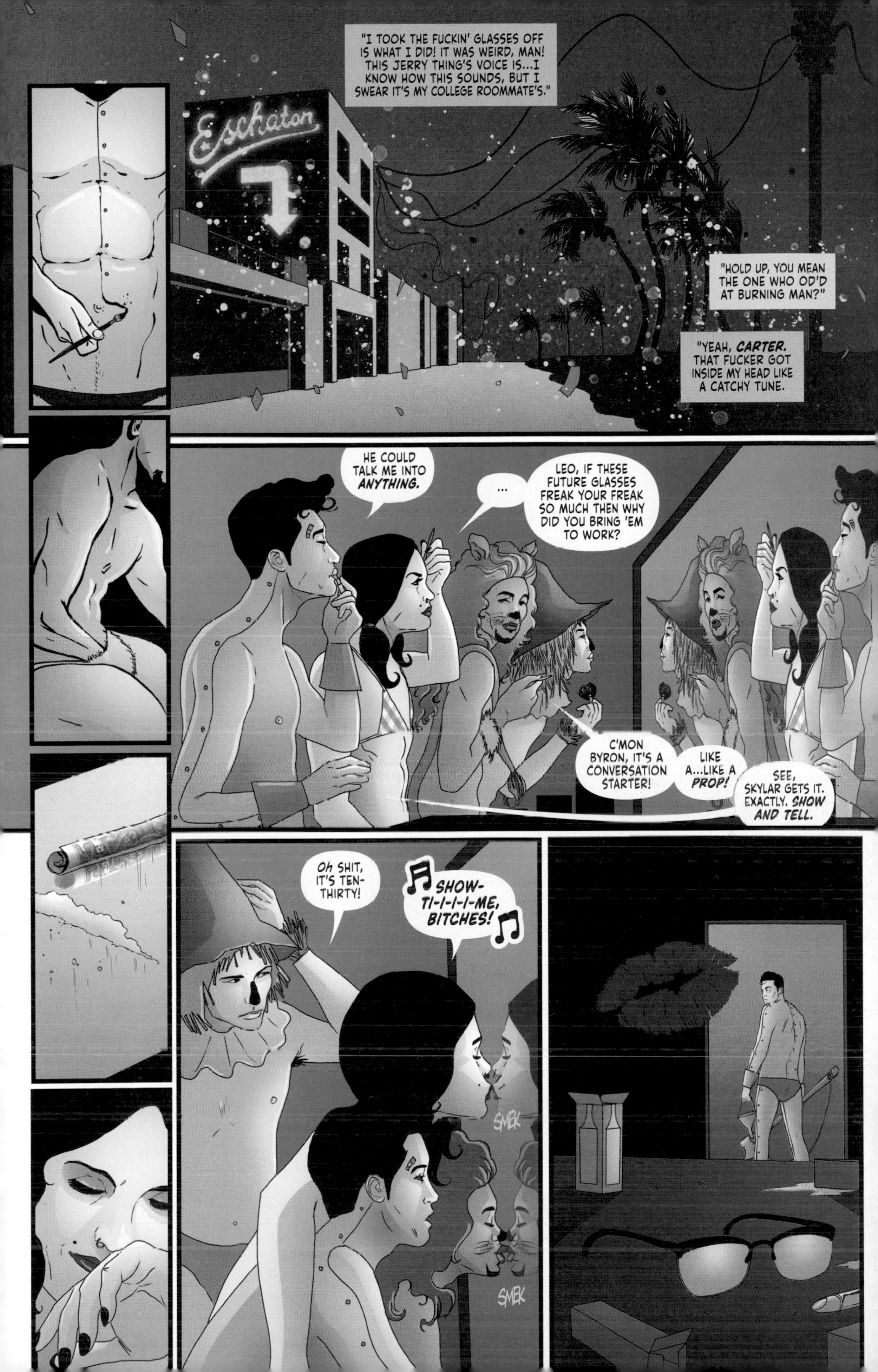
"I TOOK THE FUCKIN' GLASSES OFF IS WHAT I DID! IT WAS WEIRD, MAN! THIS JERRY THING'S VOICE IS...I KNOW HOW THIS SOUNDS, BUT I SWEAR IT'S MY COLLEGE ROOMMATE'S."
Eschaton
"HOLD UP, YOU MEAN THE ONE WHO OD'D AT BURNING MAN?"
"YEAH, CARTER. THAT FUCKER GOT INSIDE MY HEAD LIKE A CATCHY TUNE.
HE COULD TALK ME INTO ANYTHING.
...
LEO, IF THESE FUTURE GLASSES FREAK YOUR FREAK SO MUCH THEN WHY DID YOU BRING 'EM TO WORK?
C'MON BYRON, IT'S A CONVERSATION STARTER!
LIKE A...LIKE A PROP!
SEE, SKYLAR GETS IT. EXACTLY. SHOW AND TELL.
Oh SHIT, IT'S TEN-THIRTY!
SHOW-TI-I-I-I-ME, BITCHES!
SMEK
SMEK

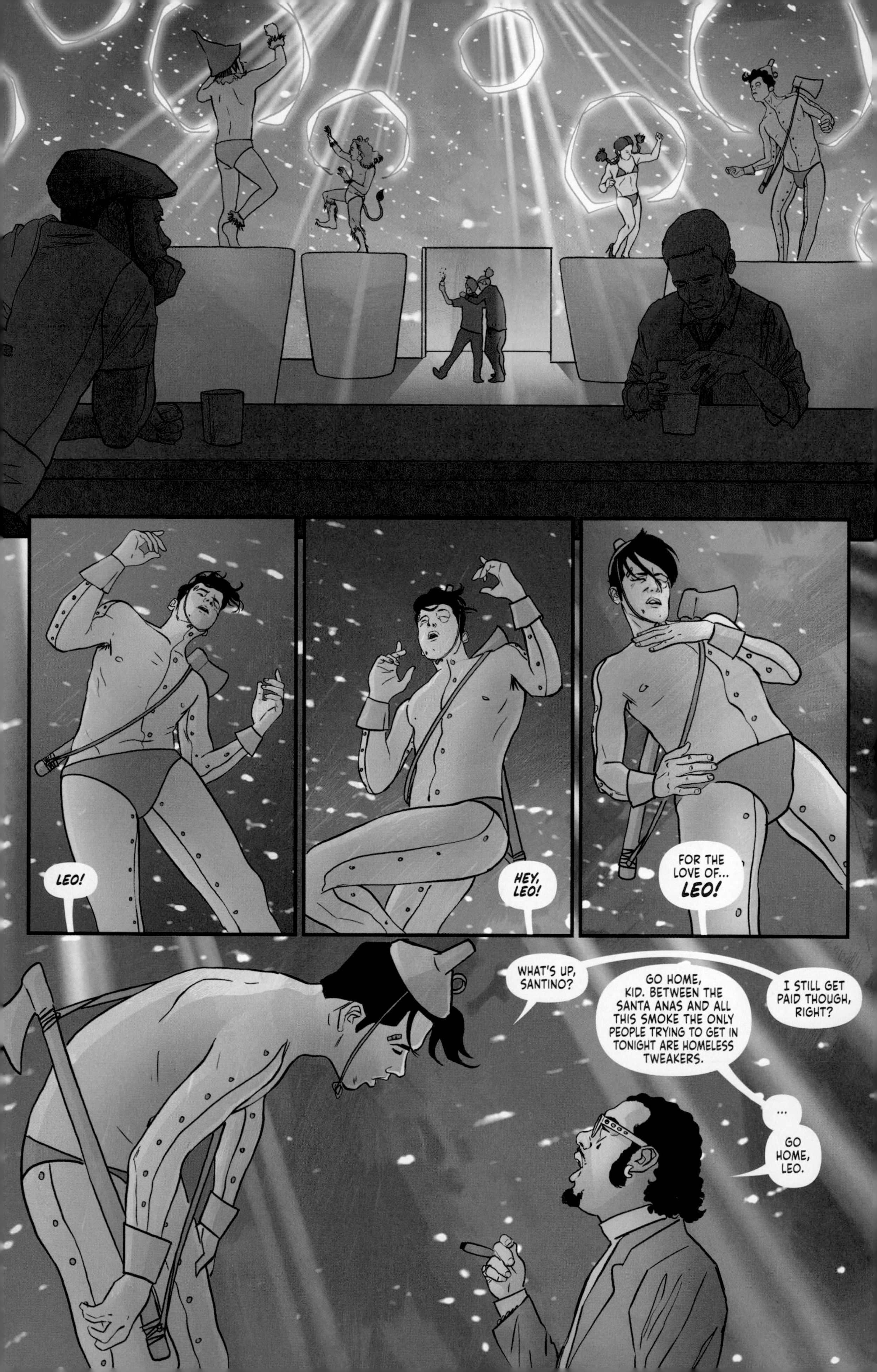
LEO!
HEY, LEO!
FOR THE LOVE OF... LEO!
WHAT'S UP, SANTINO?
GO HOME, KID. BETWEEN THE SANTA ANAS AND ALL THIS SMOKE THE ONLY PEOPLE TRYING TO GET IN TONIGHT ARE HOMELESS TWEAKERS.
I STILL GET PAID THOUGH, RIGHT?
...
GO HOME, LEO.

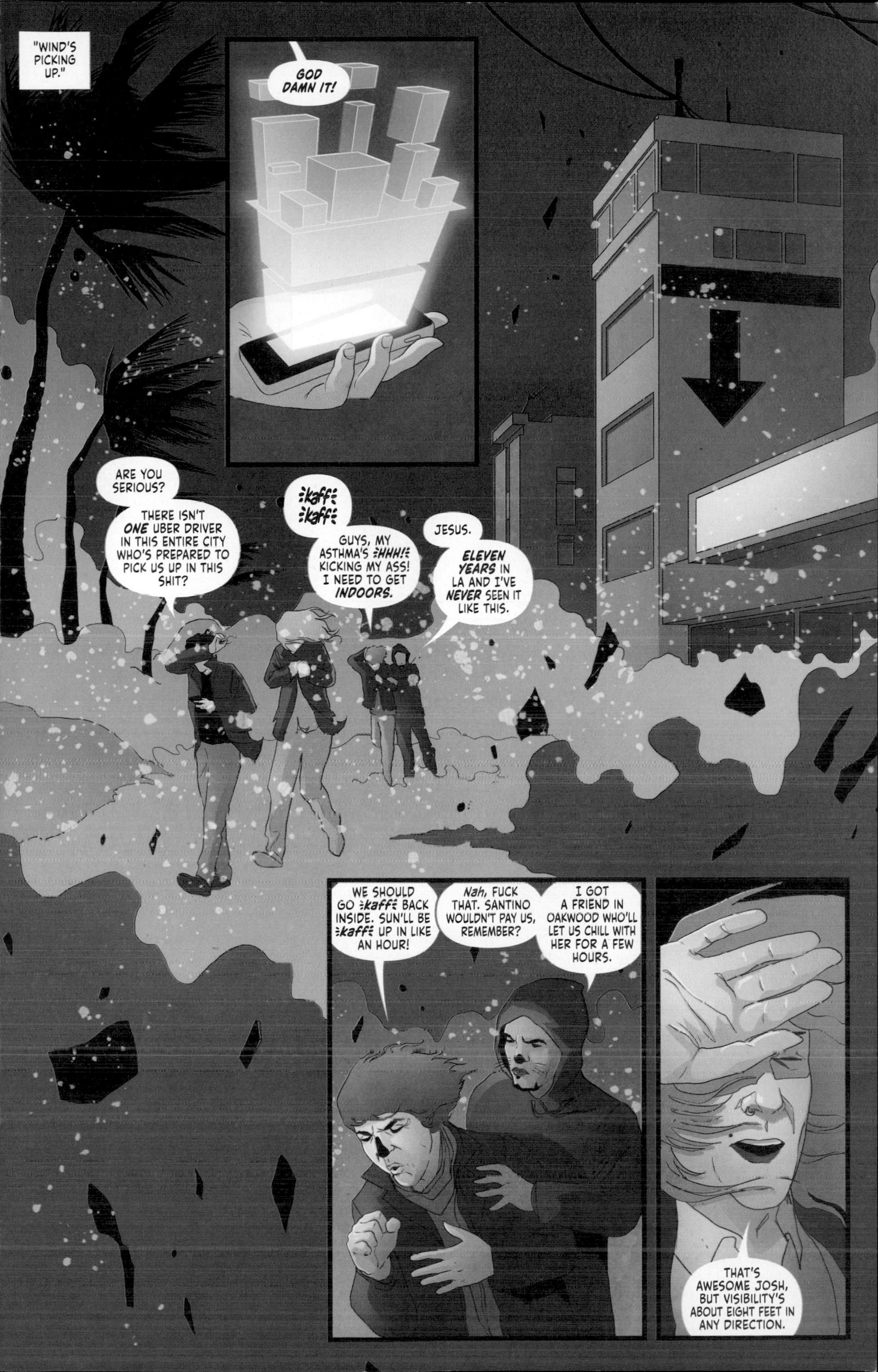
"WIND'S PICKING UP."
GOD DAMN IT!
ARE YOU SERIOUS?
THERE ISN'T ONE UBER DRIVER IN THIS ENTIRE CITY WHO'S PREPARED TO PICK US UP IN THIS SHIT?
kaff kaff
GUYS, MY ASTHMA'S HHH! KICKING MY ASS! I NEED TO GET INDOORS.
JESUS.
ELEVEN YEARS IN LA AND I'VE NEVER SEEN IT LIKE THIS.
WE SHOULD GO kaff BACK INSIDE. SUN'LL BE kaff UP IN LIKE AN HOUR!
Nah, FUCK THAT. SANTINO WOULDN'T PAY US, REMEMBER?
I GOT A FRIEND IN OAKWOOD WHO'LL LET US CHILL WITH HER FOR A FEW HOURS.
THAT'S AWESOME JOSH, BUT VISIBILITY'S ABOUT EIGHT FEET IN ANY DIRECTION.

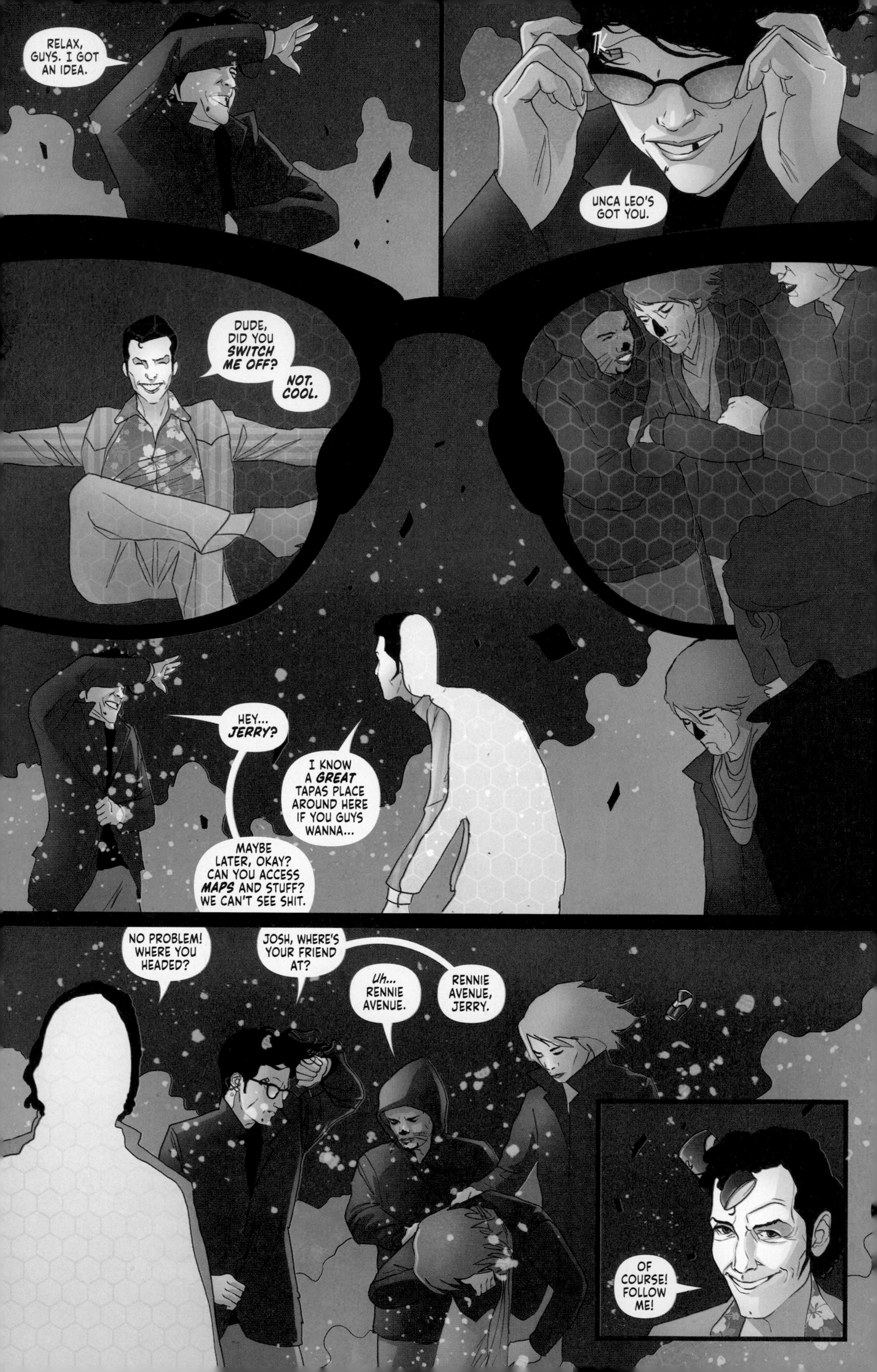
RELAX, GUYS. I GOT AN IDEA.
TK
UNCA LEO'S GOT YOU.
DUDE, DID YOU *SWITCH ME OFF?*
NOT. COOL.
HEY... *JERRY?*
I KNOW A *GREAT* TAPAS PLACE AROUND HERE IF YOU GUYS WANNA...
MAYBE LATER, OKAY? CAN YOU ACCESS *MAPS* AND STUFF? WE CAN'T SEE SHIT.
NO PROBLEM! WHERE YOU HEADED?
JOSH, WHERE'S YOUR FRIEND AT?
Uh... RENNIE AVENUE.
RENNIE AVENUE, JERRY.
OF COURSE! FOLLOW ME!

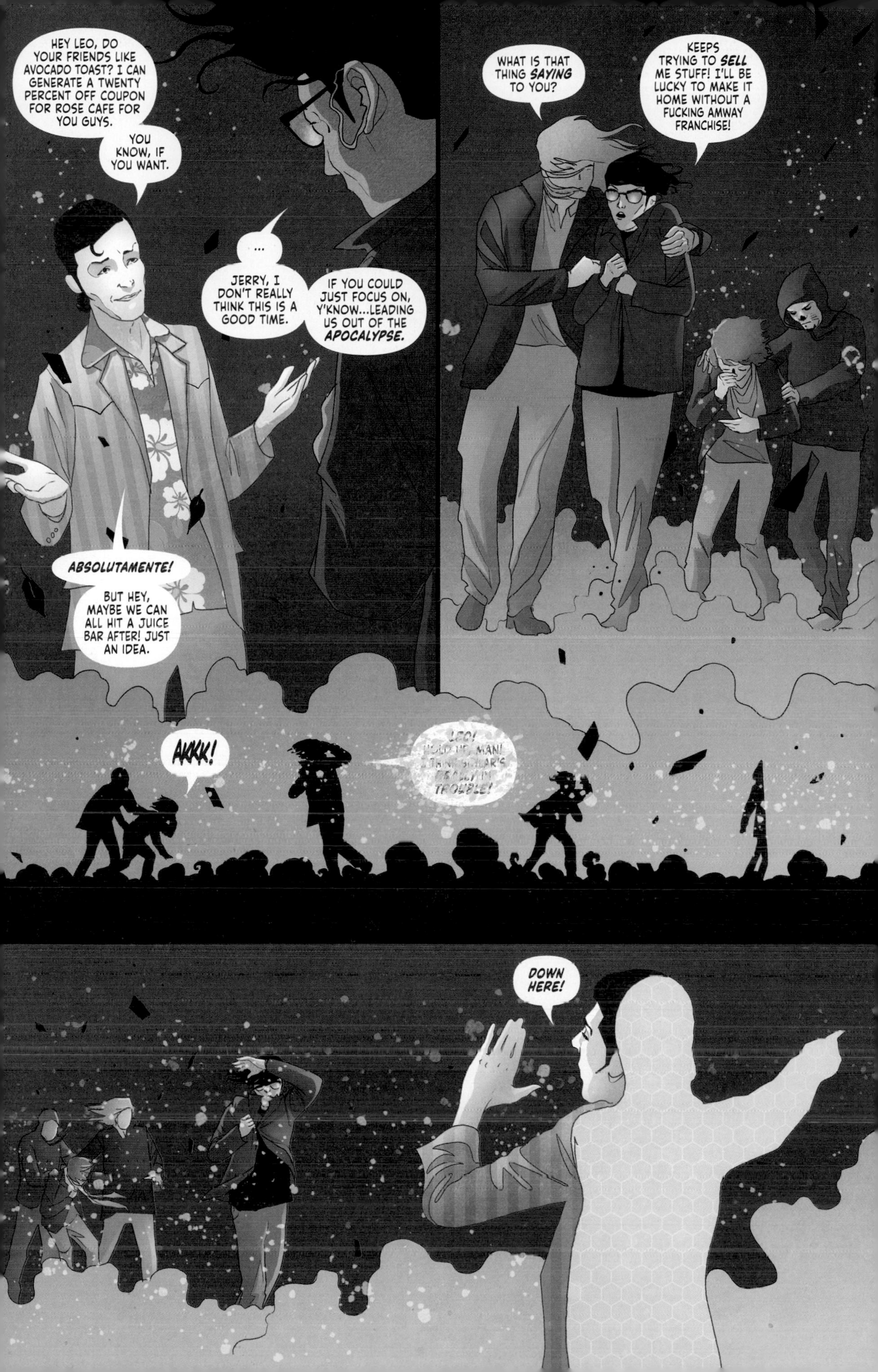
HEY LEO, DO YOUR FRIENDS LIKE AVOCADO TOAST? I CAN GENERATE A TWENTY PERCENT OFF COUPON FOR ROSE CAFE FOR YOU GUYS.
YOU KNOW, IF YOU WANT.
...
JERRY, I DON'T REALLY THINK THIS IS A GOOD TIME.
IF YOU COULD JUST FOCUS ON, Y'KNOW...LEADING US OUT OF THE APOCALYPSE.
ABSOLUTAMENTE!
BUT HEY, MAYBE WE CAN ALL HIT A JUICE BAR AFTER! JUST AN IDEA.
WHAT IS THAT THING SAYING TO YOU?
KEEPS TRYING TO SELL ME STUFF! I'LL BE LUCKY TO MAKE IT HOME WITHOUT A FUCKING AMWAY FRANCHISE!
AKKK!
LEO! HOLD UP, MAN! I THINK SKYLAR'S REALLY IN TROUBLE!
DOWN HERE!

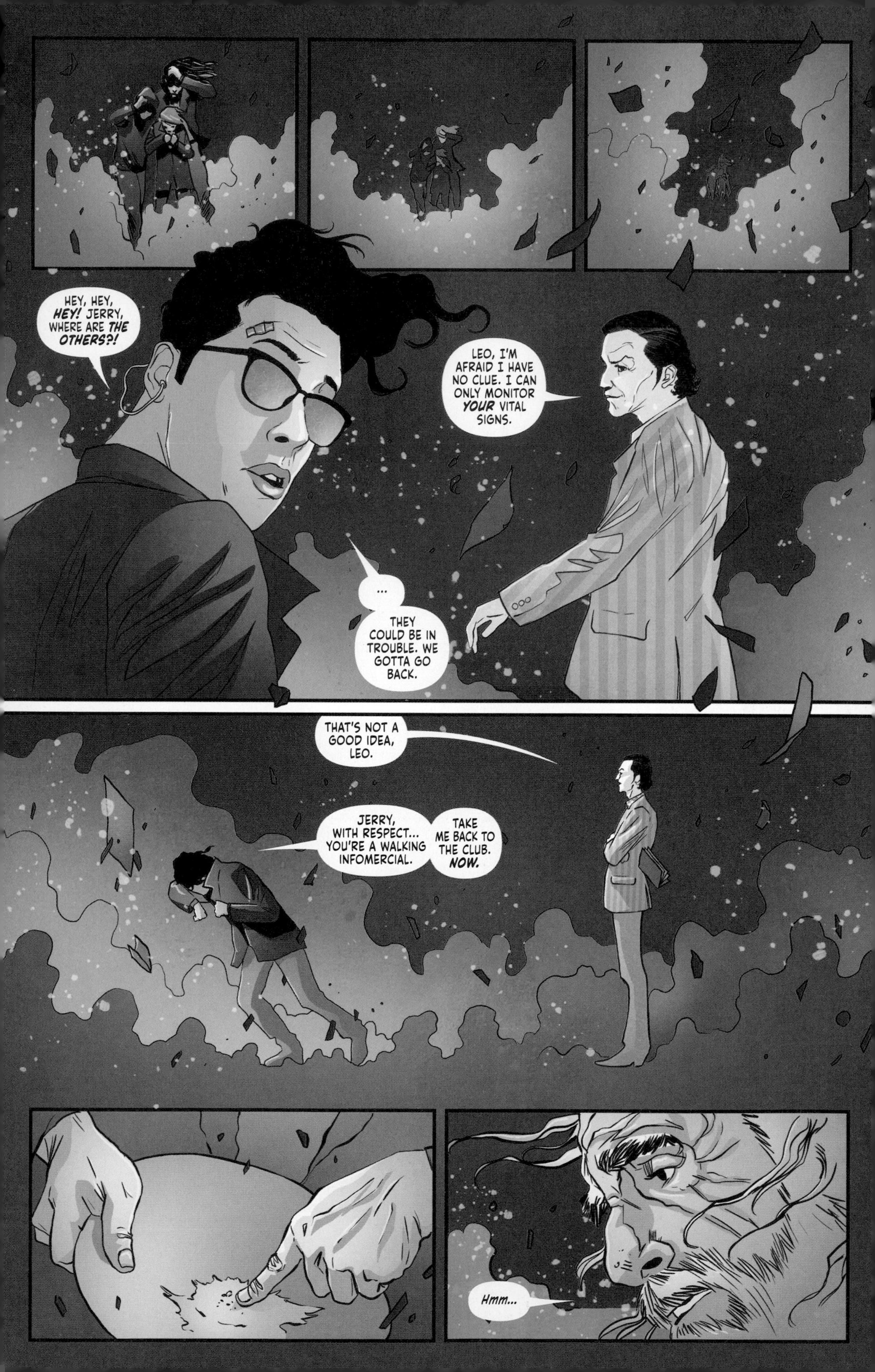
HEY, HEY, HEY! JERRY, WHERE ARE THE OTHERS?!
LEO, I'M AFRAID I HAVE NO CLUE. I CAN ONLY MONITOR YOUR VITAL SIGNS.
...
THEY COULD BE IN TROUBLE. WE GOTTA GO BACK.
THAT'S NOT A GOOD IDEA, LEO.
JERRY, WITH RESPECT... YOU'RE A WALKING INFOMERCIAL.
TAKE ME BACK TO THE CLUB. NOW.
Hmm...

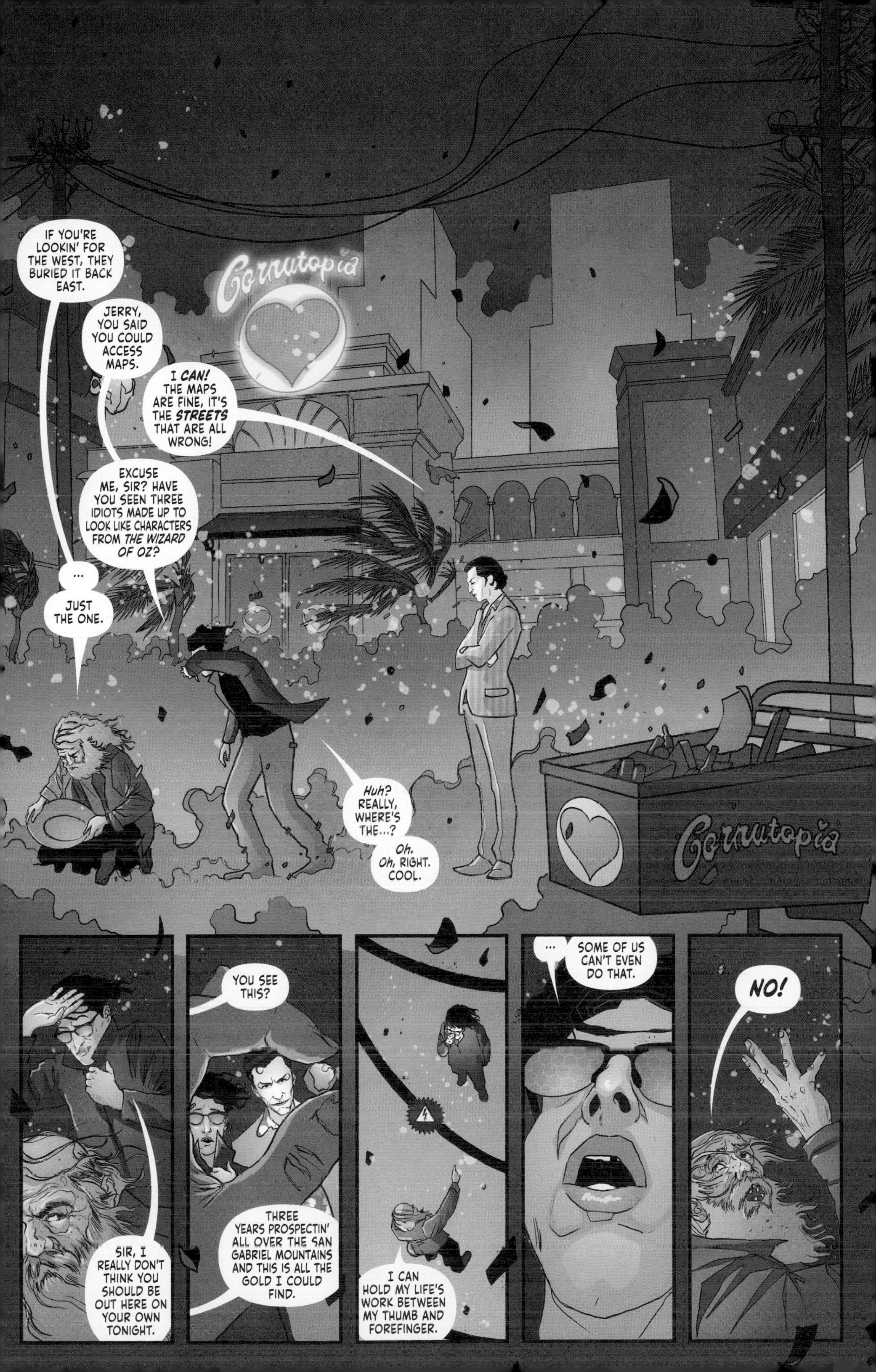
Cornutopia
IF YOU'RE LOOKIN' FOR THE WEST, THEY BURIED IT BACK EAST.
JERRY, YOU SAID YOU COULD ACCESS MAPS.
I *CAN!* THE MAPS ARE FINE, IT'S THE ***STREETS*** THAT ARE ALL WRONG!
EXCUSE ME, SIR? HAVE YOU SEEN THREE IDIOTS MADE UP TO LOOK LIKE CHARACTERS FROM *THE WIZARD OF OZ?*
...
JUST THE ONE.
Huh? REALLY, WHERE'S THE...?
Oh. *Oh,* RIGHT. COOL.
Cornutopia
SIR, I REALLY DON'T THINK YOU SHOULD BE OUT HERE ON YOUR OWN TONIGHT.
YOU SEE THIS?
THREE YEARS PROSPECTIN' ALL OVER THE SAN GABRIEL MOUNTAINS AND THIS IS ALL THE GOLD I COULD FIND.
I CAN HOLD MY LIFE'S WORK BETWEEN MY THUMB AND FOREFINGER.
...
SOME OF US CAN'T EVEN DO THAT.
NO!

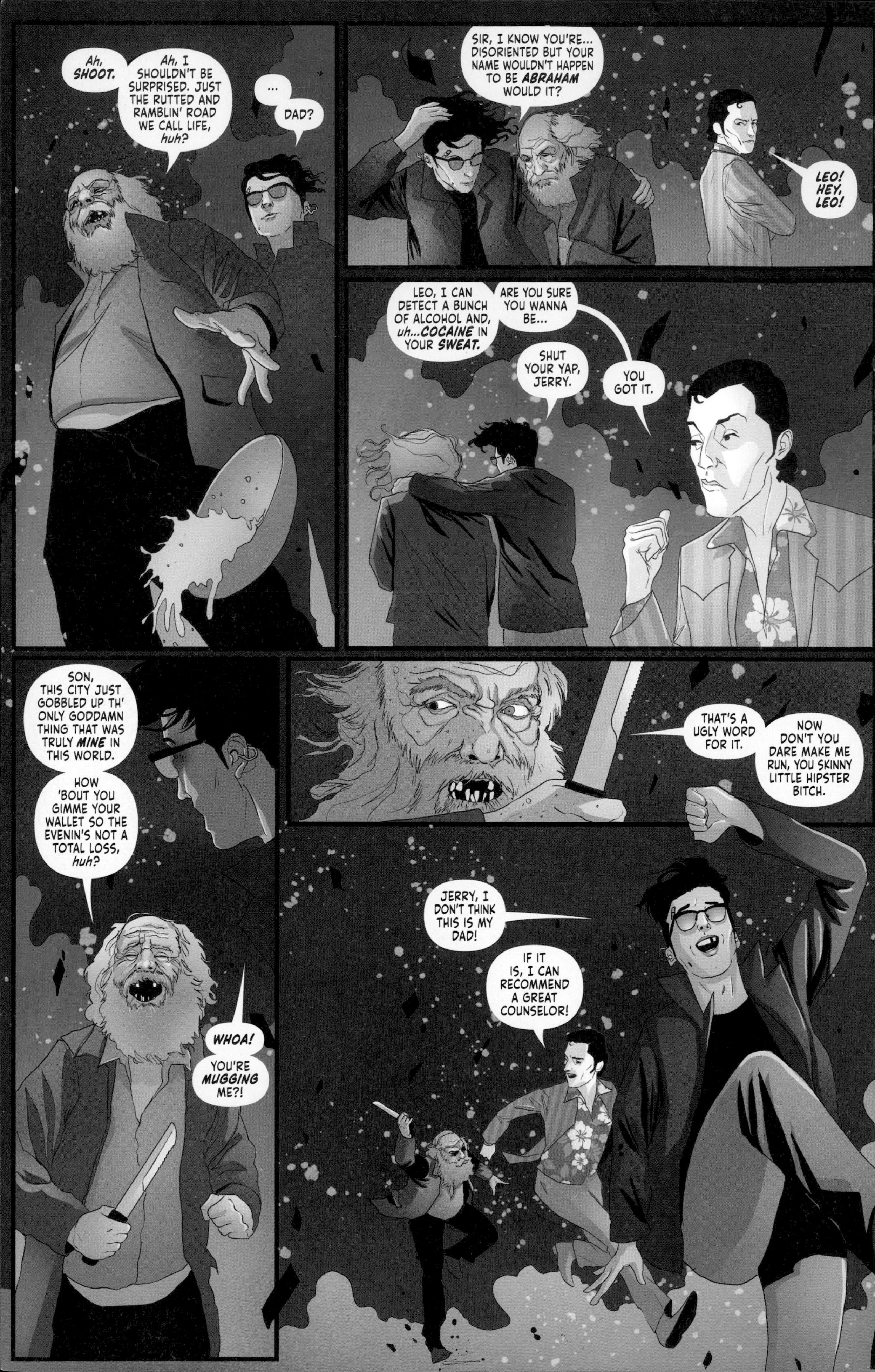

Ah, SHOOT.
Ah, I SHOULDN'T BE SURPRISED. JUST THE RUTTED AND RAMBLIN' ROAD WE CALL LIFE, huh?
...
DAD?
SIR, I KNOW YOU'RE... DISORIENTED BUT YOUR NAME WOULDN'T HAPPEN TO BE ABRAHAM WOULD IT?
LEO! HEY, LEO!
LEO, I CAN DETECT A BUNCH OF ALCOHOL AND, uh...COCAINE IN YOUR SWEAT.
ARE YOU SURE YOU WANNA BE...
SHUT YOUR YAP, JERRY.
YOU GOT IT.
SON, THIS CITY JUST GOBBLED UP TH' ONLY GODDAMN THING THAT WAS TRULY MINE IN THIS WORLD.
HOW 'BOUT YOU GIMME YOUR WALLET SO THE EVENIN'S NOT A TOTAL LOSS, huh?
WHOA!
YOU'RE MUGGING ME?!
THAT'S A UGLY WORD FOR IT.
NOW DON'T YOU DARE MAKE ME RUN, YOU SKINNY LITTLE HIPSTER BITCH.
JERRY, I DON'T THINK THIS IS MY DAD!
IF IT IS, I CAN RECOMMEND A GREAT COUNSELOR!

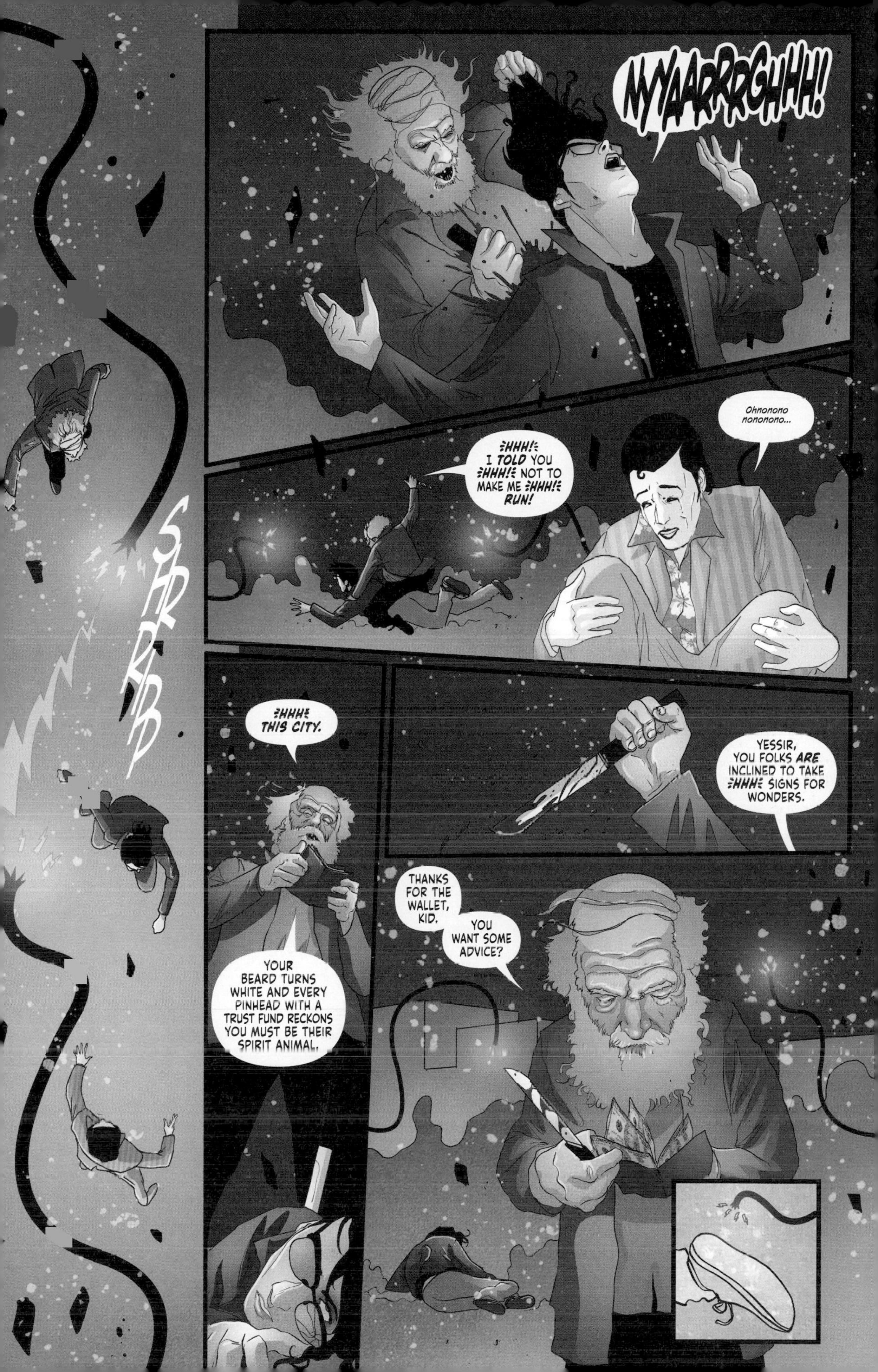
NYAARRRGHHH!
SHRKBB
Ohnonono nononono...
HHH! I TOLD YOU HHH! NOT TO MAKE ME HHH! RUN!
HHH THIS CITY.
YOUR BEARD TURNS WHITE AND EVERY PINHEAD WITH A TRUST FUND RECKONS YOU MUST BE THEIR SPIRIT ANIMAL.
YESSIR, YOU FOLKS ARE INCLINED TO TAKE HHH SIGNS FOR WONDERS.
THANKS FOR THE WALLET, KID.
YOU WANT SOME ADVICE?

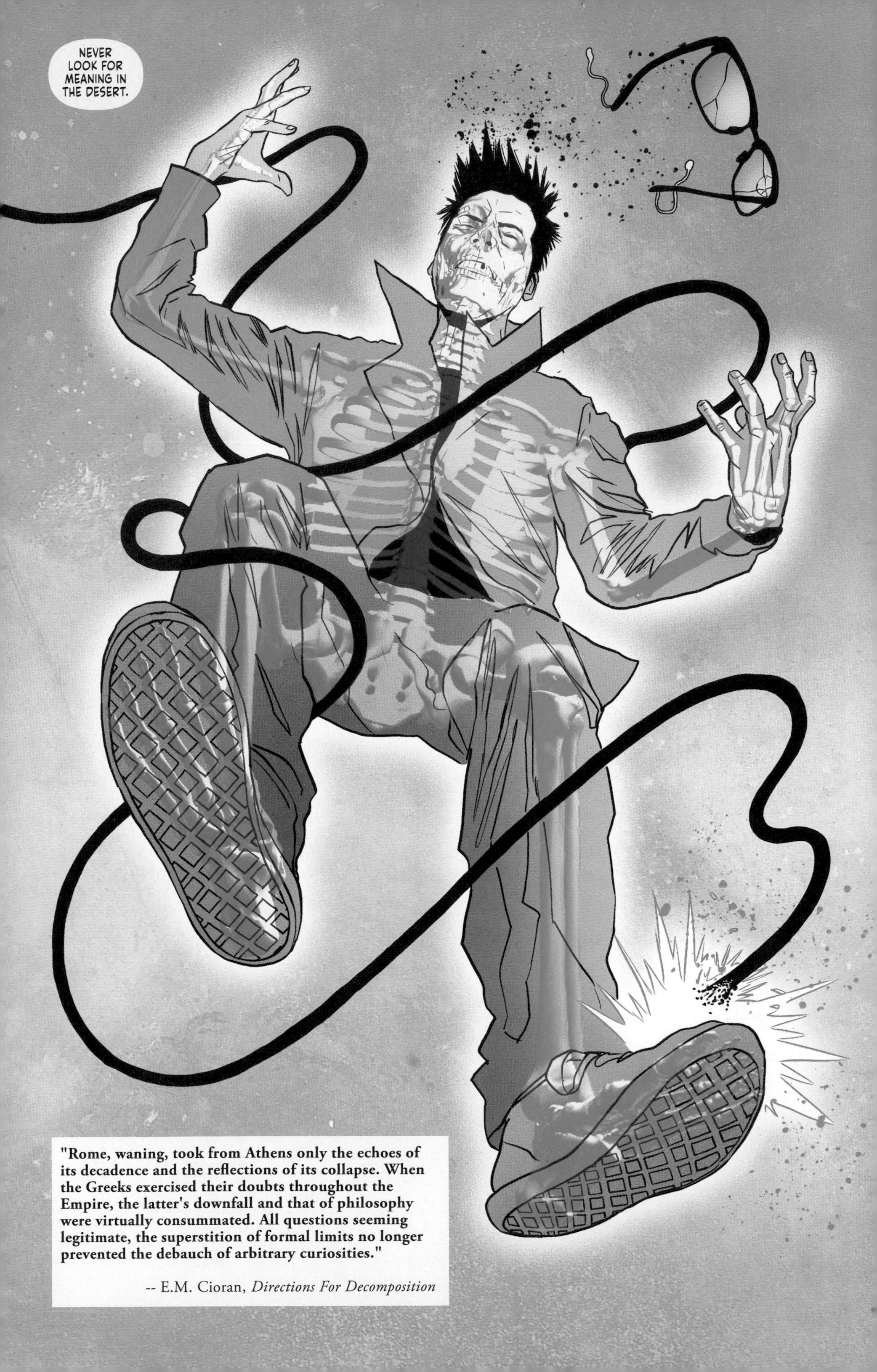
NEVER LOOK FOR MEANING IN THE DESERT.
"Rome, waning, took from Athens only the echoes of its decadence and the reflections of its collapse. When the Greeks exercised their doubts throughout the Empire, the latter's downfall and that of philosophy were virtually consummated. All questions seeming legitimate, the superstition of formal limits no longer prevented the debauch of arbitrary curiosities."
-- E.M. Cioran, *Directions For Decomposition*

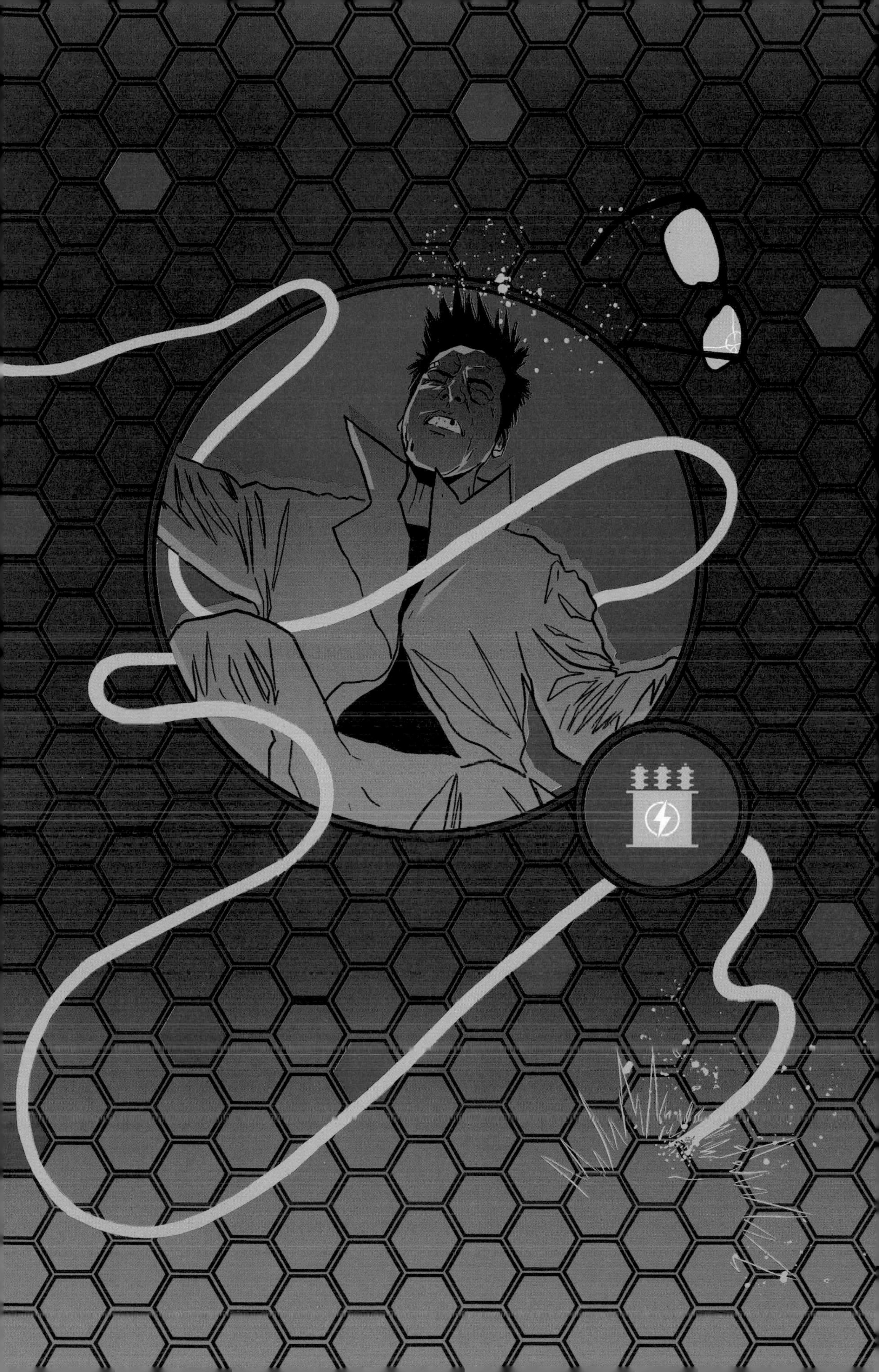

TWO

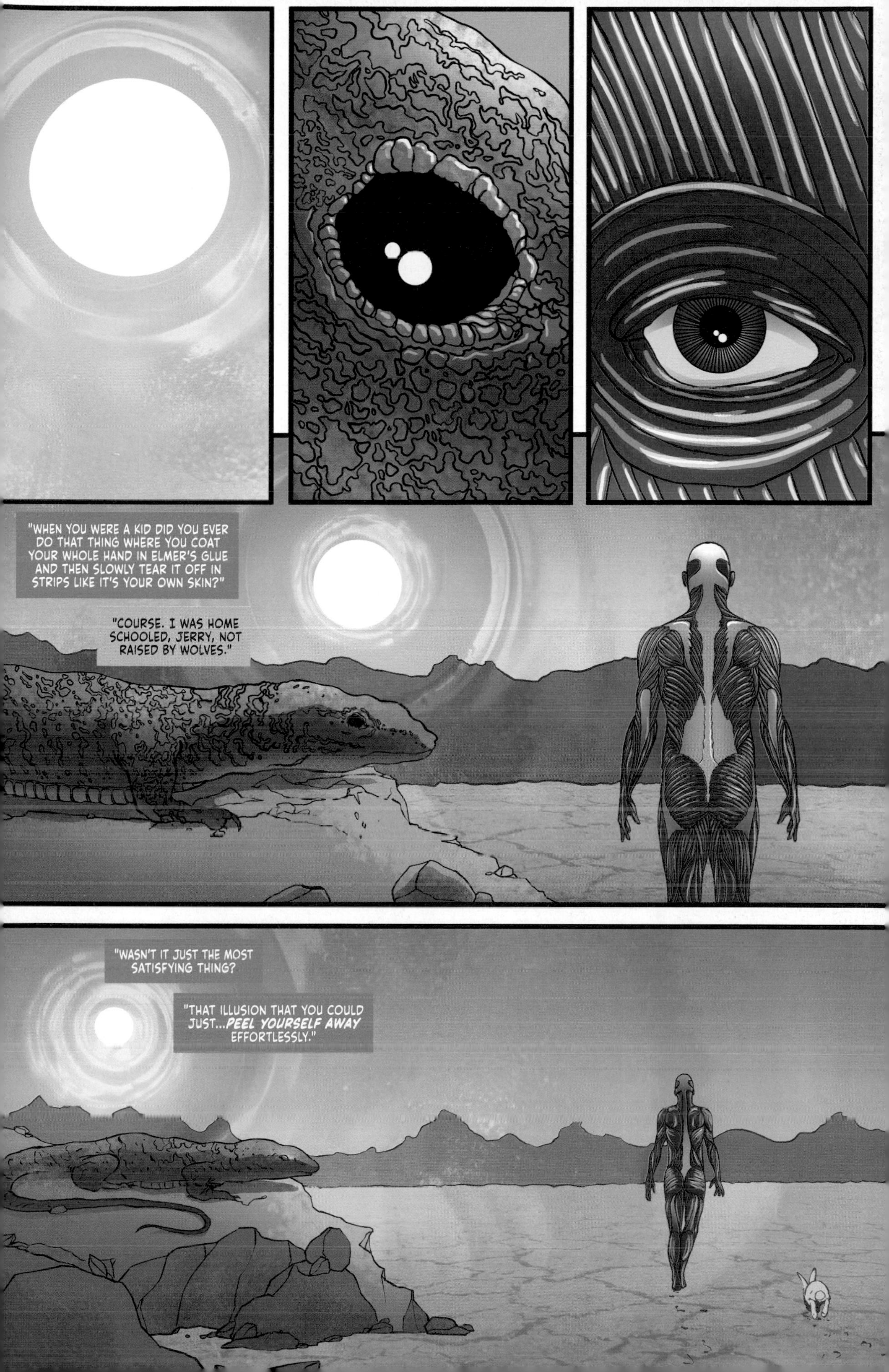
"WHEN YOU WERE A KID DID YOU EVER DO THAT THING WHERE YOU COAT YOUR WHOLE HAND IN ELMER'S GLUE AND THEN SLOWLY TEAR IT OFF IN STRIPS LIKE IT'S YOUR OWN SKIN?"
"COURSE. I WAS HOME SCHOOLED, JERRY, NOT RAISED BY WOLVES."
"WASN'T IT JUST THE MOST SATISFYING THING?
"THAT ILLUSION THAT YOU COULD JUST...PEEL YOURSELF AWAY EFFORTLESSLY."

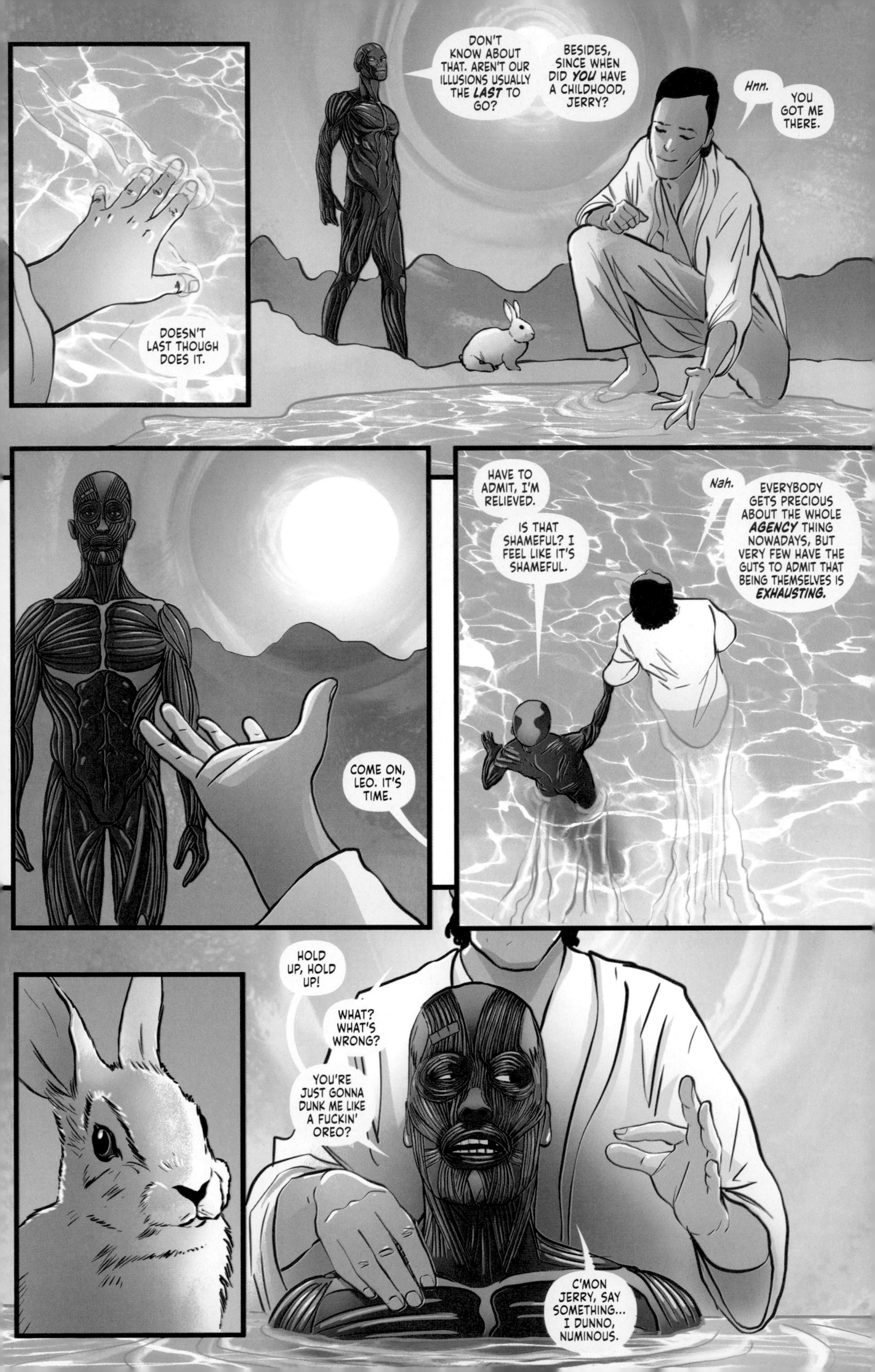
DOESN'T LAST THOUGH DOES IT.
DON'T KNOW ABOUT THAT. AREN'T OUR ILLUSIONS USUALLY THE LAST TO GO?
BESIDES, SINCE WHEN DID YOU HAVE A CHILDHOOD, JERRY?
Hnn.
YOU GOT ME THERE.
COME ON, LEO. IT'S TIME.
HAVE TO ADMIT, I'M RELIEVED.
IS THAT SHAMEFUL? I FEEL LIKE IT'S SHAMEFUL.
Nah.
EVERYBODY GETS PRECIOUS ABOUT THE WHOLE AGENCY THING NOWADAYS, BUT VERY FEW HAVE THE GUTS TO ADMIT THAT BEING THEMSELVES IS EXHAUSTING.
HOLD UP, HOLD UP!
WHAT? WHAT'S WRONG?
YOU'RE JUST GONNA DUNK ME LIKE A FUCKIN' OREO?
C'MON JERRY, SAY SOMETHING... I DUNNO, NUMINOUS.

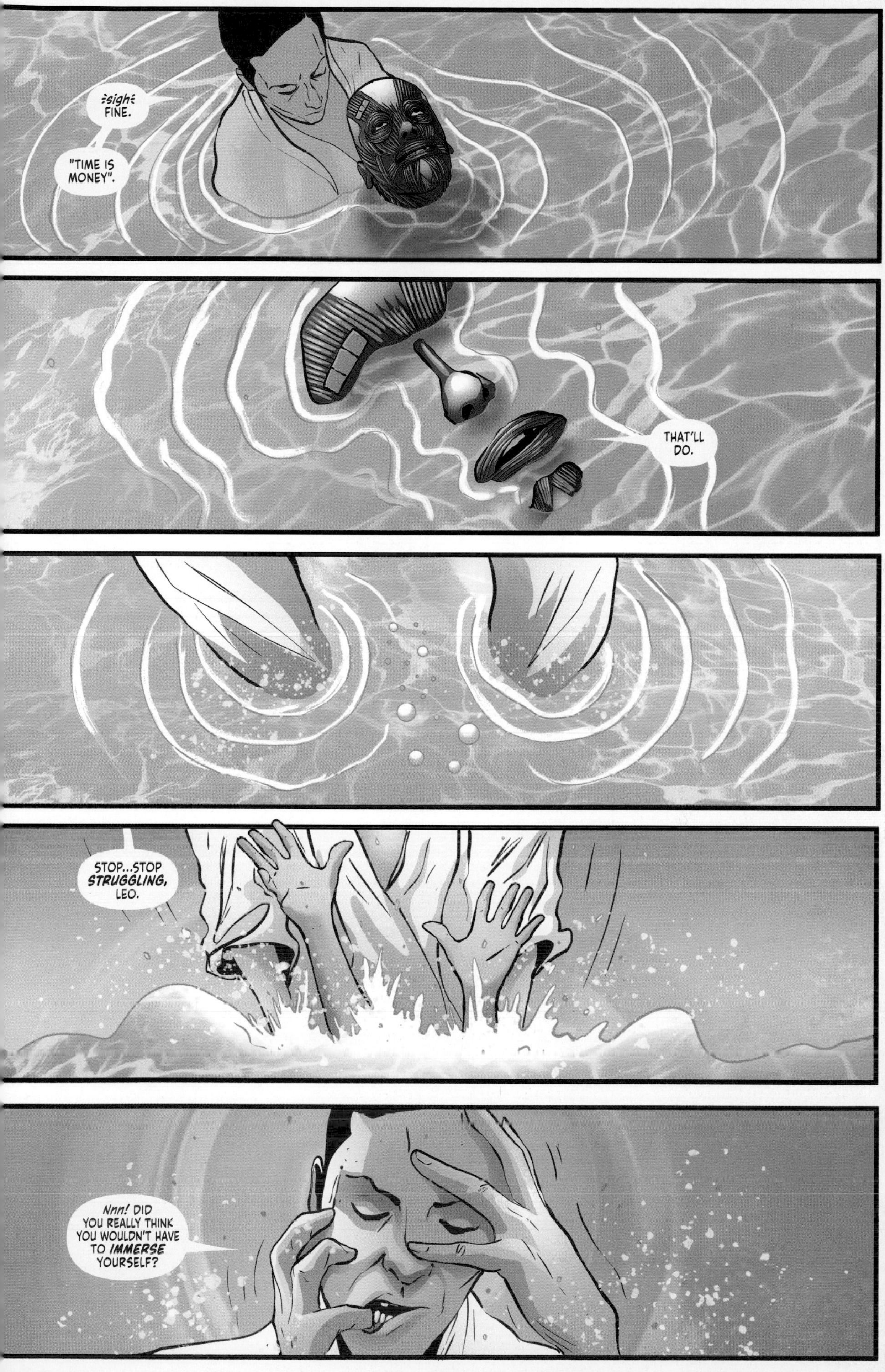

sigh FINE.
"TIME IS MONEY".
THAT'LL DO.
STOP...STOP **STRUGGLING,** LEO.
Nnn! DID YOU REALLY THINK YOU WOULDN'T HAVE TO ***IMMERSE*** YOURSELF?

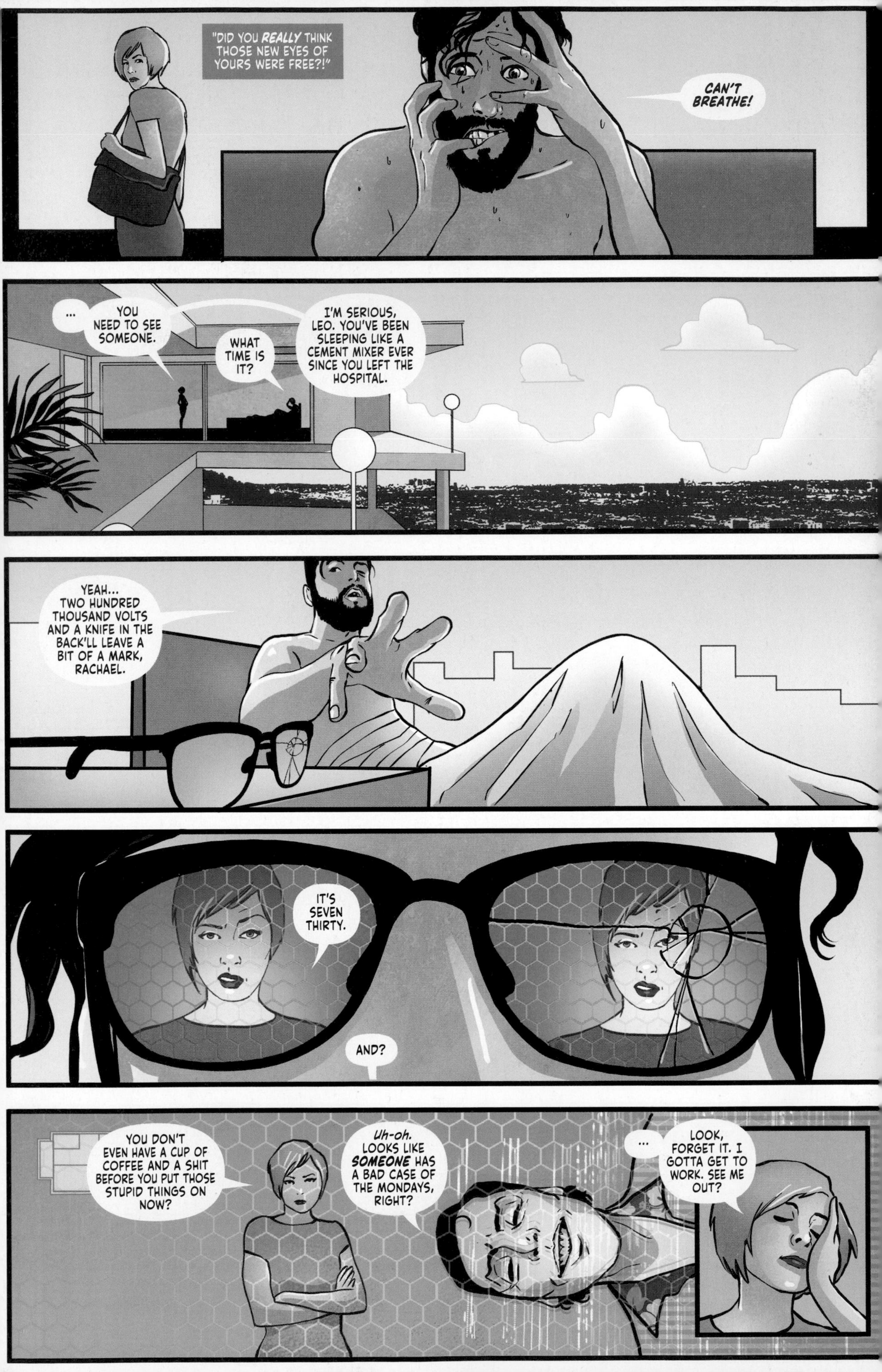
"DID YOU *REALLY* THINK THOSE NEW EYES OF YOURS WERE FREE?!"
CAN'T BREATHE!
...
YOU NEED TO SEE SOMEONE.
WHAT TIME IS IT?
I'M SERIOUS, LEO. YOU'VE BEEN SLEEPING LIKE A CEMENT MIXER EVER SINCE YOU LEFT THE HOSPITAL.
YEAH... TWO HUNDRED THOUSAND VOLTS AND A KNIFE IN THE BACK'LL LEAVE A BIT OF A MARK, RACHAEL.
IT'S SEVEN THIRTY.
AND?
YOU DON'T EVEN HAVE A CUP OF COFFEE AND A SHIT BEFORE YOU PUT THOSE STUPID THINGS ON NOW?
Uh-oh. LOOKS LIKE ***SOMEONE*** HAS A BAD CASE OF THE MONDAYS, RIGHT?
...
LOOK, FORGET IT. I GOTTA GET TO WORK. SEE ME OUT?

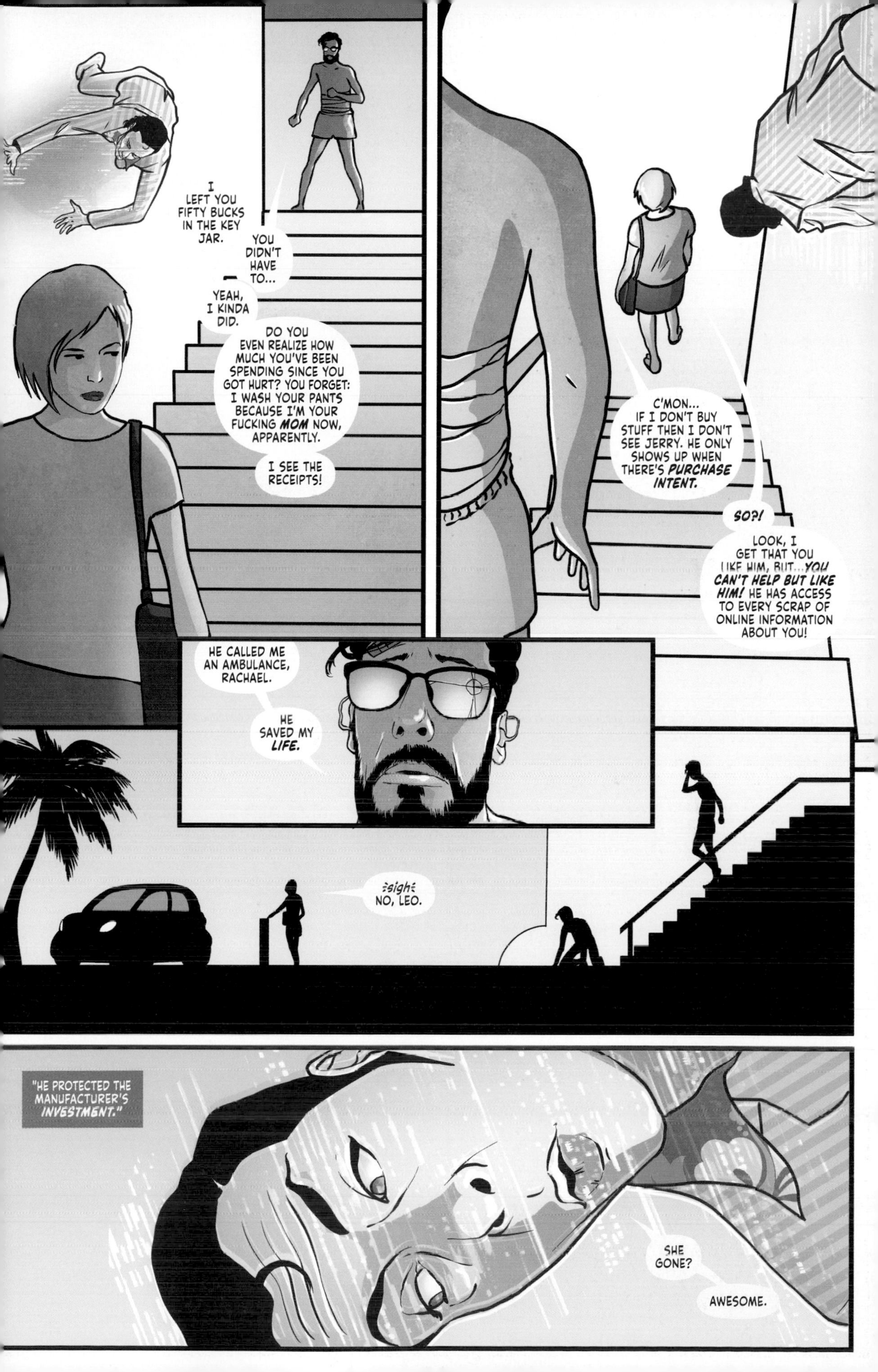
I LEFT YOU FIFTY BUCKS IN THE KEY JAR.
YOU DIDN'T HAVE TO...
YEAH, I KINDA DID.
DO YOU EVEN REALIZE HOW MUCH YOU'VE BEEN SPENDING SINCE YOU GOT HURT? YOU FORGET: I WASH YOUR PANTS BECAUSE I'M YOUR FUCKING MOM NOW, APPARENTLY.
I SEE THE RECEIPTS!
C'MON... IF I DON'T BUY STUFF THEN I DON'T SEE JERRY. HE ONLY SHOWS UP WHEN THERE'S PURCHASE INTENT.
SO?!
LOOK, I GET THAT YOU LIKE HIM, BUT...YOU CAN'T HELP BUT LIKE HIM! HE HAS ACCESS TO EVERY SCRAP OF ONLINE INFORMATION ABOUT YOU!
HE CALLED ME AN AMBULANCE, RACHAEL.
HE SAVED MY LIFE.
sigh NO, LEO.
"HE PROTECTED THE MANUFACTURER'S INVESTMENT."
SHE GONE?
AWESOME.

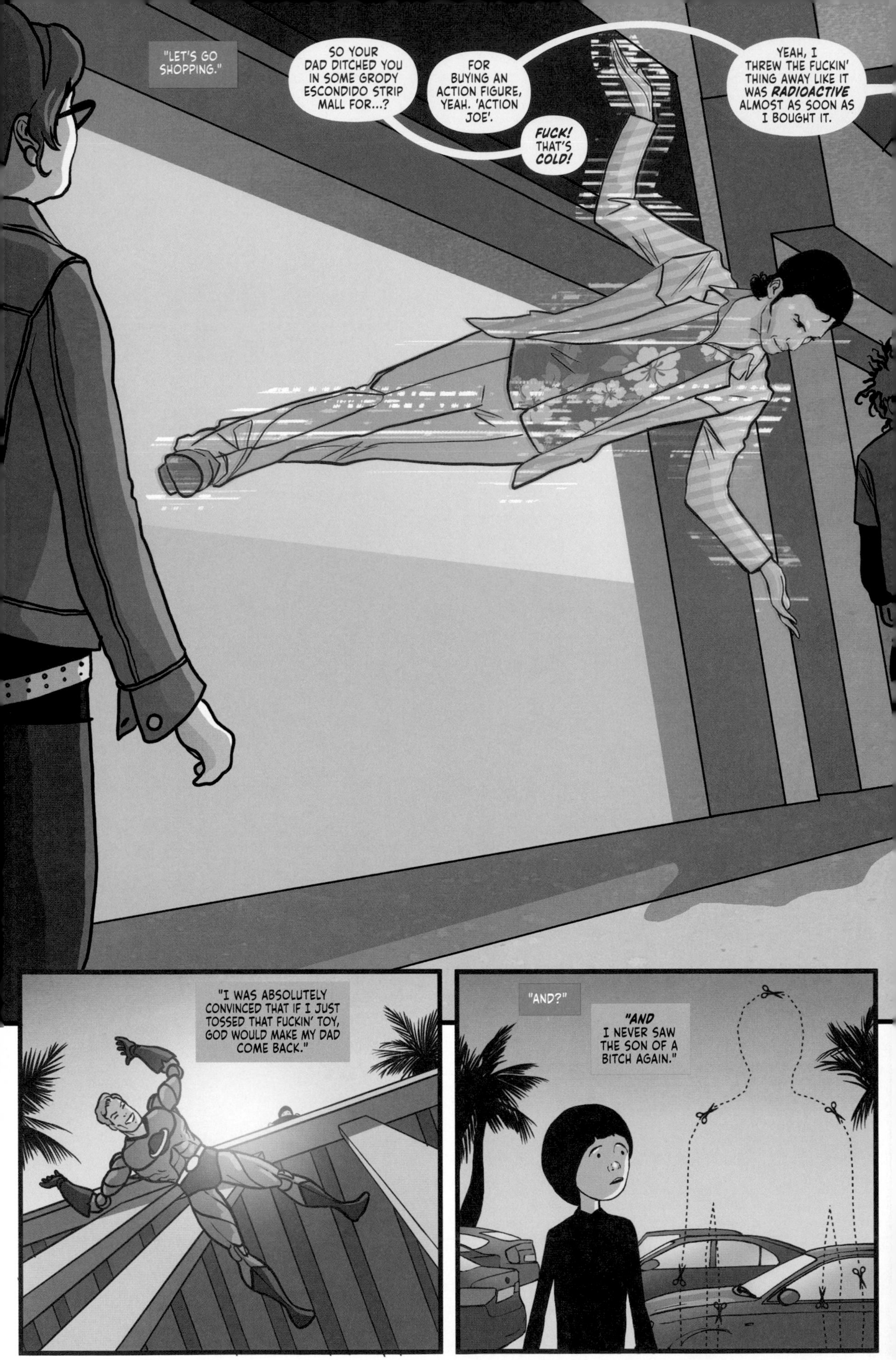
"LET'S GO SHOPPING."
SO YOUR DAD DITCHED YOU IN SOME GRODY ESCONDIDO STRIP MALL FOR...?
FOR BUYING AN ACTION FIGURE, YEAH. 'ACTION JOE'.
FUCK! THAT'S COLD!
YEAH, I THREW THE FUCKIN' THING AWAY LIKE IT WAS RADIOACTIVE ALMOST AS SOON AS I BOUGHT IT.
"I WAS ABSOLUTELY CONVINCED THAT IF I JUST TOSSED THAT FUCKIN' TOY, GOD WOULD MAKE MY DAD COME BACK."
"AND?"
"AND I NEVER SAW THE SON OF A BITCH AGAIN."

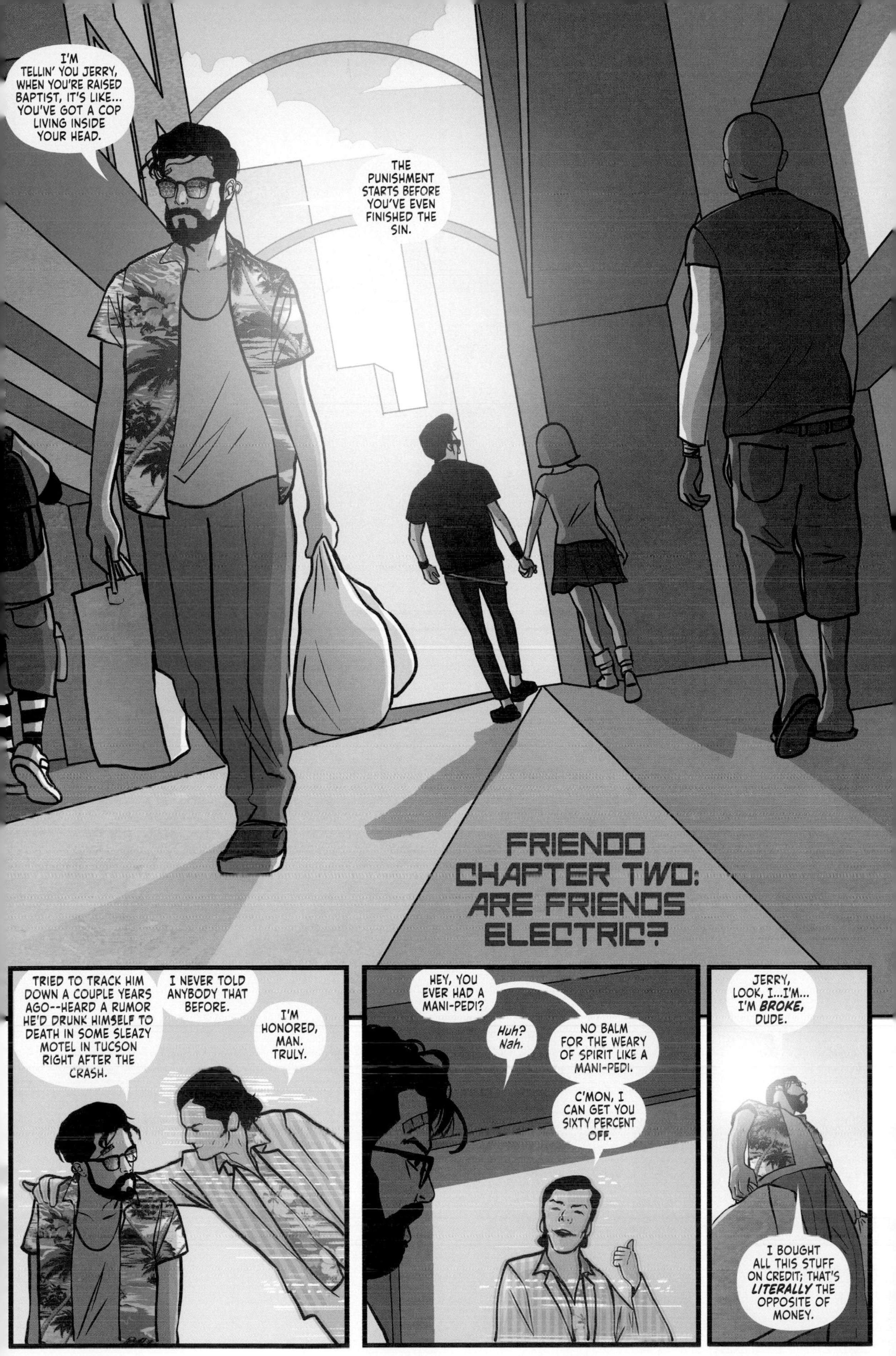
I'M TELLIN' YOU JERRY, WHEN YOU'RE RAISED BAPTIST, IT'S LIKE... YOU'VE GOT A COP LIVING INSIDE YOUR HEAD.
THE PUNISHMENT STARTS BEFORE YOU'VE EVEN FINISHED THE SIN.
FRIENDO CHAPTER TWO: ARE FRIENDS ELECTRIC?
TRIED TO TRACK HIM DOWN A COUPLE YEARS AGO--HEARD A RUMOR HE'D DRUNK HIMSELF TO DEATH IN SOME SLEAZY MOTEL IN TUCSON RIGHT AFTER THE CRASH.
I NEVER TOLD ANYBODY THAT BEFORE.
I'M HONORED, MAN. TRULY.
HEY, YOU EVER HAD A MANI-PEDI?
Huh? Nah.
NO BALM FOR THE WEARY OF SPIRIT LIKE A MANI-PEDI.
C'MON, I CAN GET YOU SIXTY PERCENT OFF.
JERRY, LOOK, I...I'M... I'M ***BROKE,*** DUDE.
I BOUGHT ALL THIS STUFF ON CREDIT; THAT'S ***LITERALLY*** THE OPPOSITE OF MONEY.

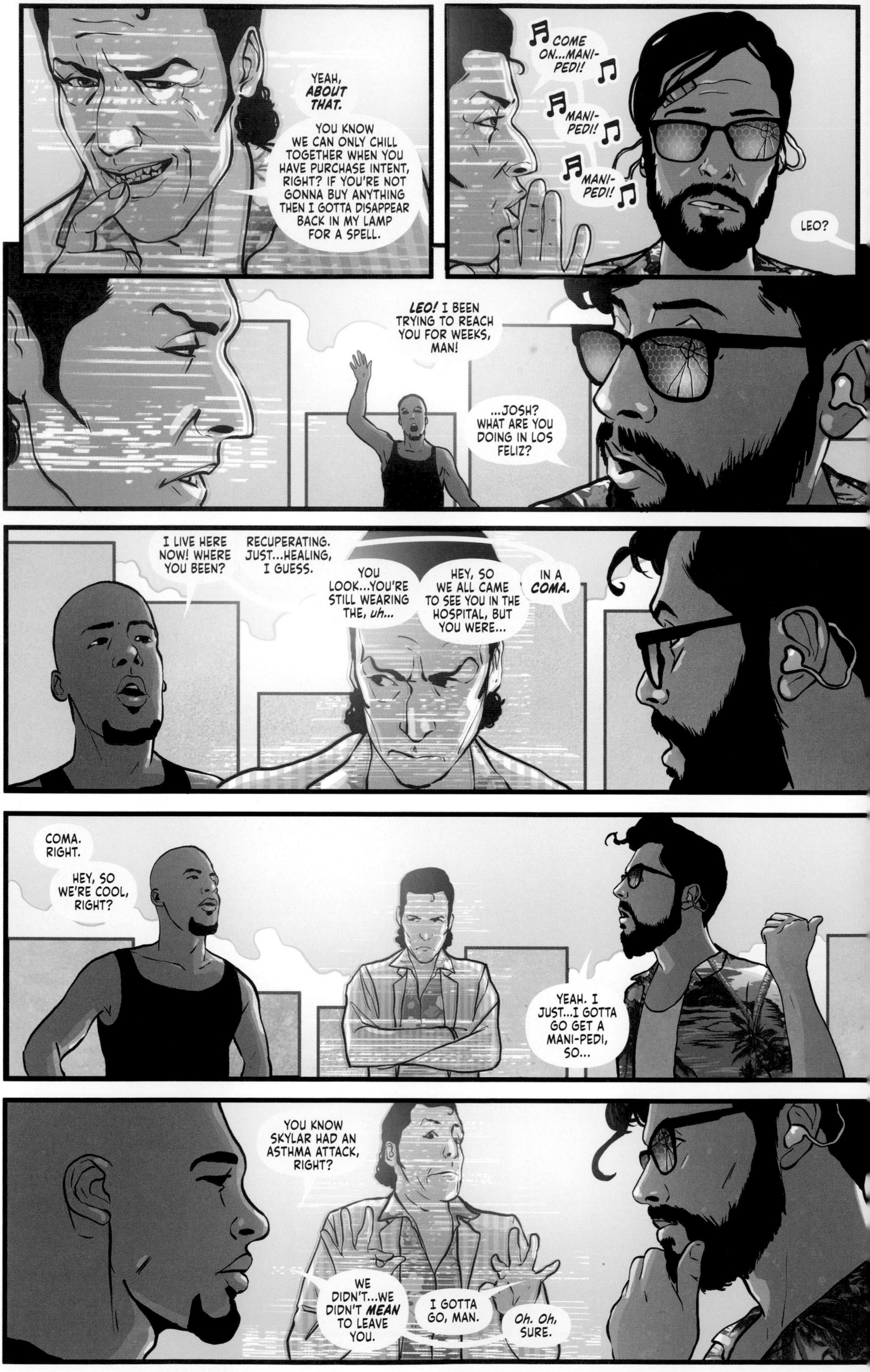
YEAH, ABOUT THAT.
YOU KNOW WE CAN ONLY CHILL TOGETHER WHEN YOU HAVE PURCHASE INTENT, RIGHT? IF YOU'RE NOT GONNA BUY ANYTHING THEN I GOTTA DISAPPEAR BACK IN MY LAMP FOR A SPELL.
♫ COME ON...MANI-PEDI! ♫
♫ MANI-PEDI! ♫
♫ MANI-PEDI! ♫
LEO?
LEO! I BEEN TRYING TO REACH YOU FOR WEEKS, MAN!
...JOSH? WHAT ARE YOU DOING IN LOS FELIZ?
I LIVE HERE NOW! WHERE YOU BEEN?
RECUPERATING. JUST...HEALING, I GUESS.
YOU LOOK...YOU'RE STILL WEARING THE, uh...
HEY, SO WE ALL CAME TO SEE YOU IN THE HOSPITAL, BUT YOU WERE...
IN A COMA.
COMA. RIGHT.
HEY, SO WE'RE COOL, RIGHT?
YEAH. I JUST...I GOTTA GO GET A MANI-PEDI, SO...
YOU KNOW SKYLAR HAD AN ASTHMA ATTACK, RIGHT?
WE DIDN'T...WE DIDN'T MEAN TO LEAVE YOU.
I GOTTA GO, MAN.
Oh. Oh, sure.

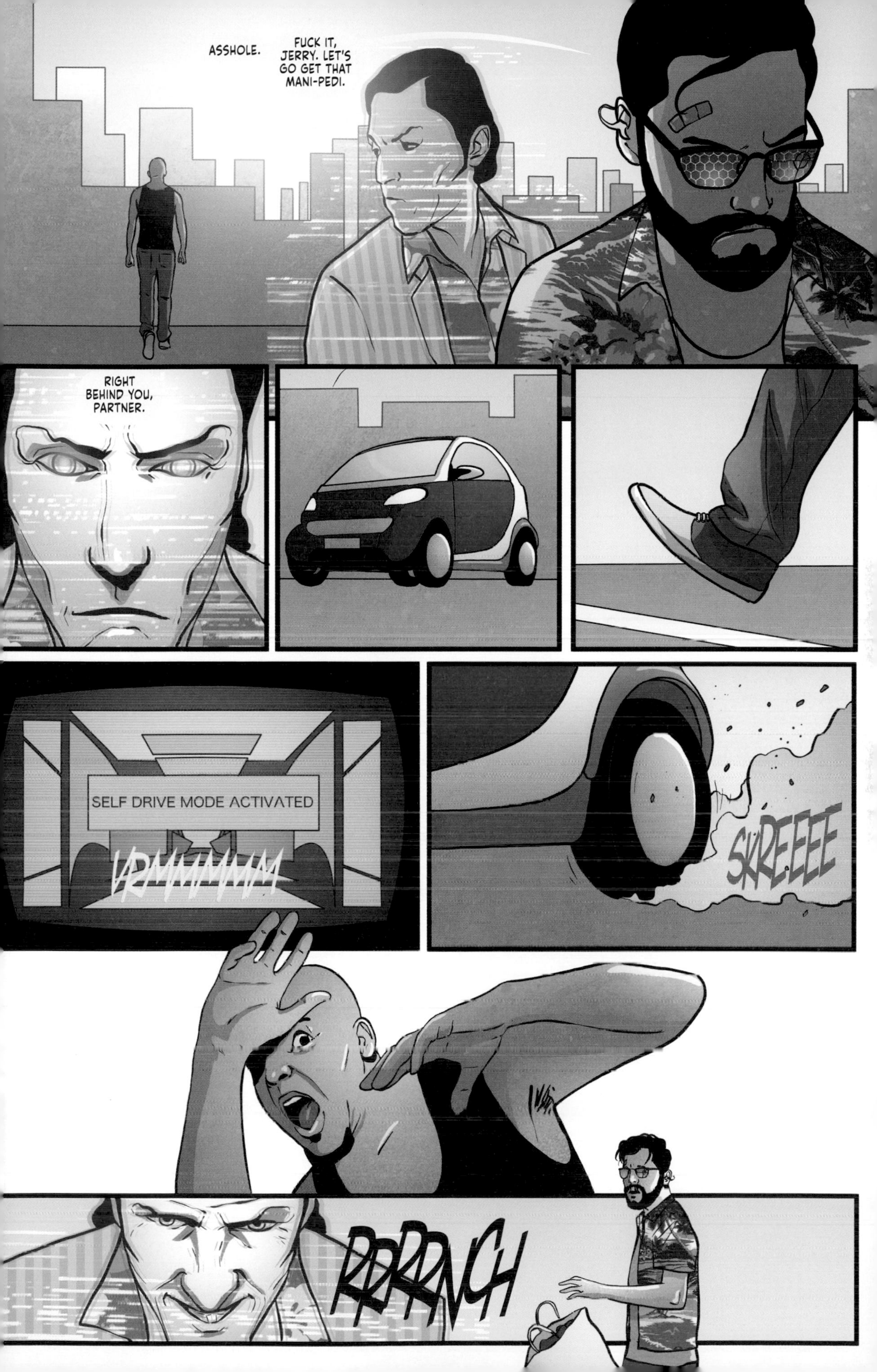
ASSHOLE.
FUCK IT, JERRY. LET'S GO GET THAT MANI-PEDI.
RIGHT BEHIND YOU, PARTNER.
SELF DRIVE MODE ACTIVATED
VRMMMMM
SKREEEE
RRRRNCH

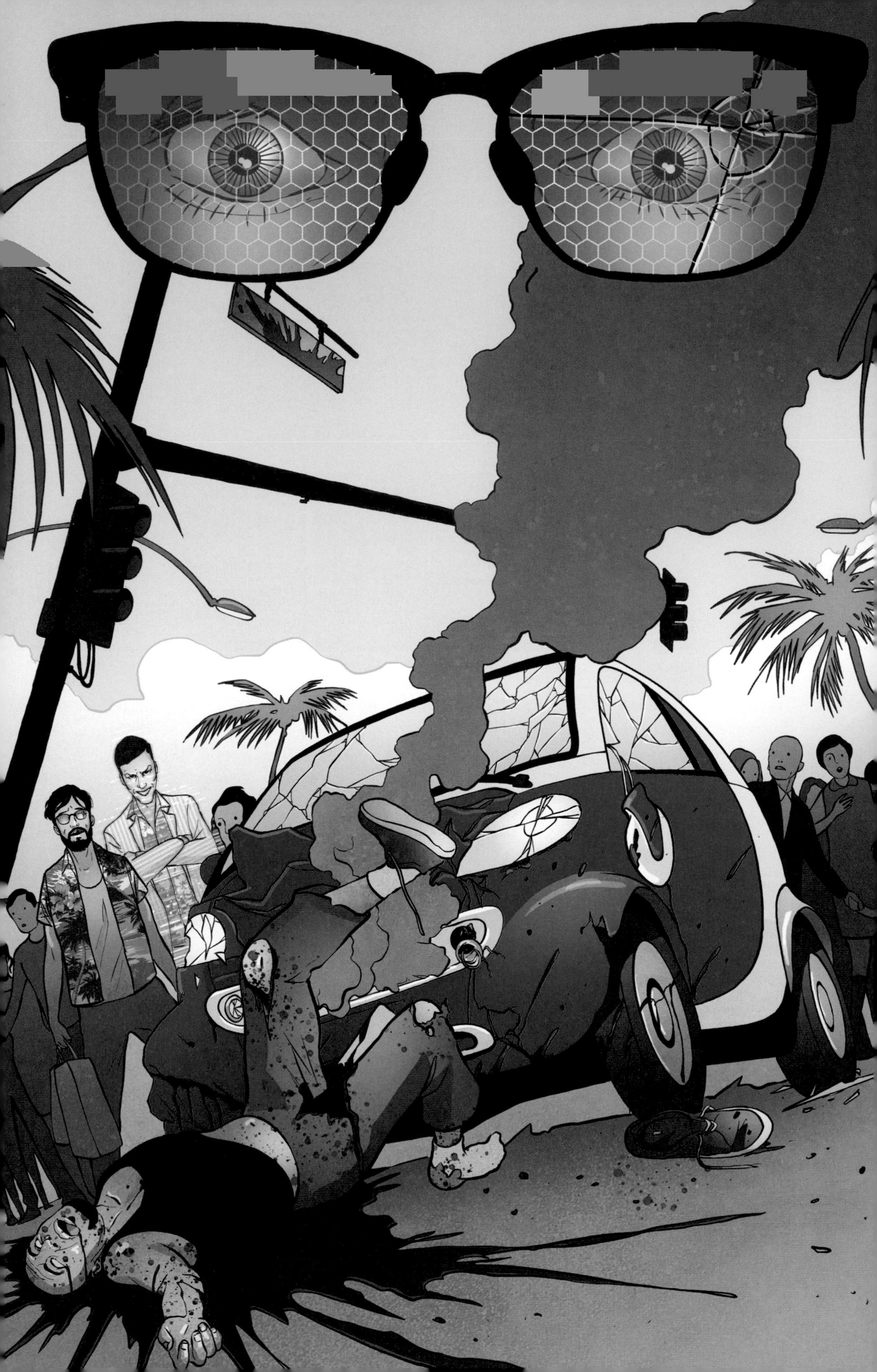

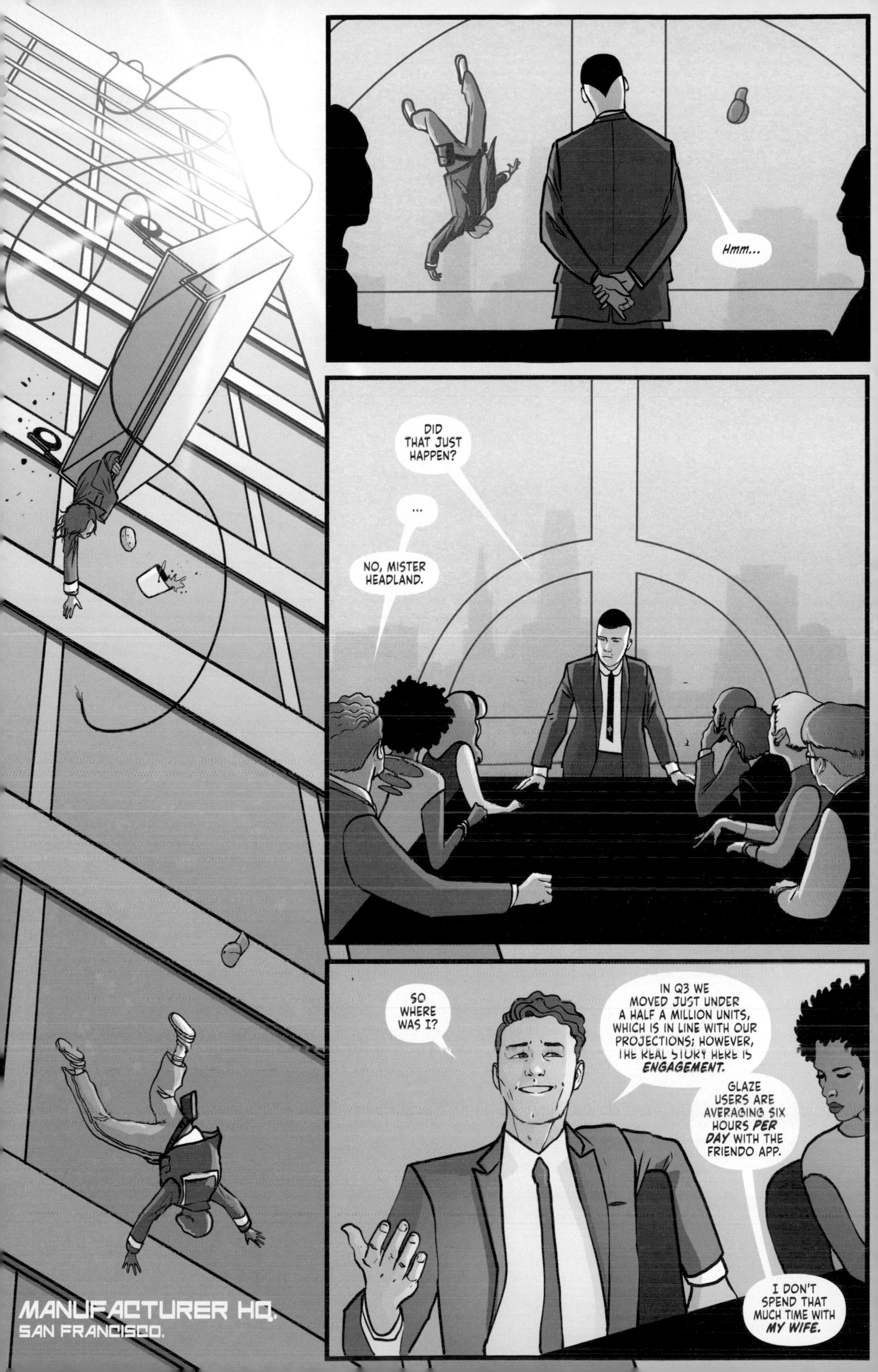
MANUFACTURER HQ.
SAN FRANCISCO.
Hmm...
DID THAT JUST HAPPEN?
...
NO, MISTER HEADLAND.
SO WHERE WAS I?
IN Q3 WE MOVED JUST UNDER A HALF A MILLION UNITS, WHICH IS IN LINE WITH OUR PROJECTIONS; HOWEVER, THE REAL STORY HERE IS *ENGAGEMENT.*
GLAZE USERS ARE AVERAGING SIX HOURS *PER DAY* WITH THE FRIENDO APP.
I DON'T SPEND THAT MUCH TIME WITH *MY WIFE.*

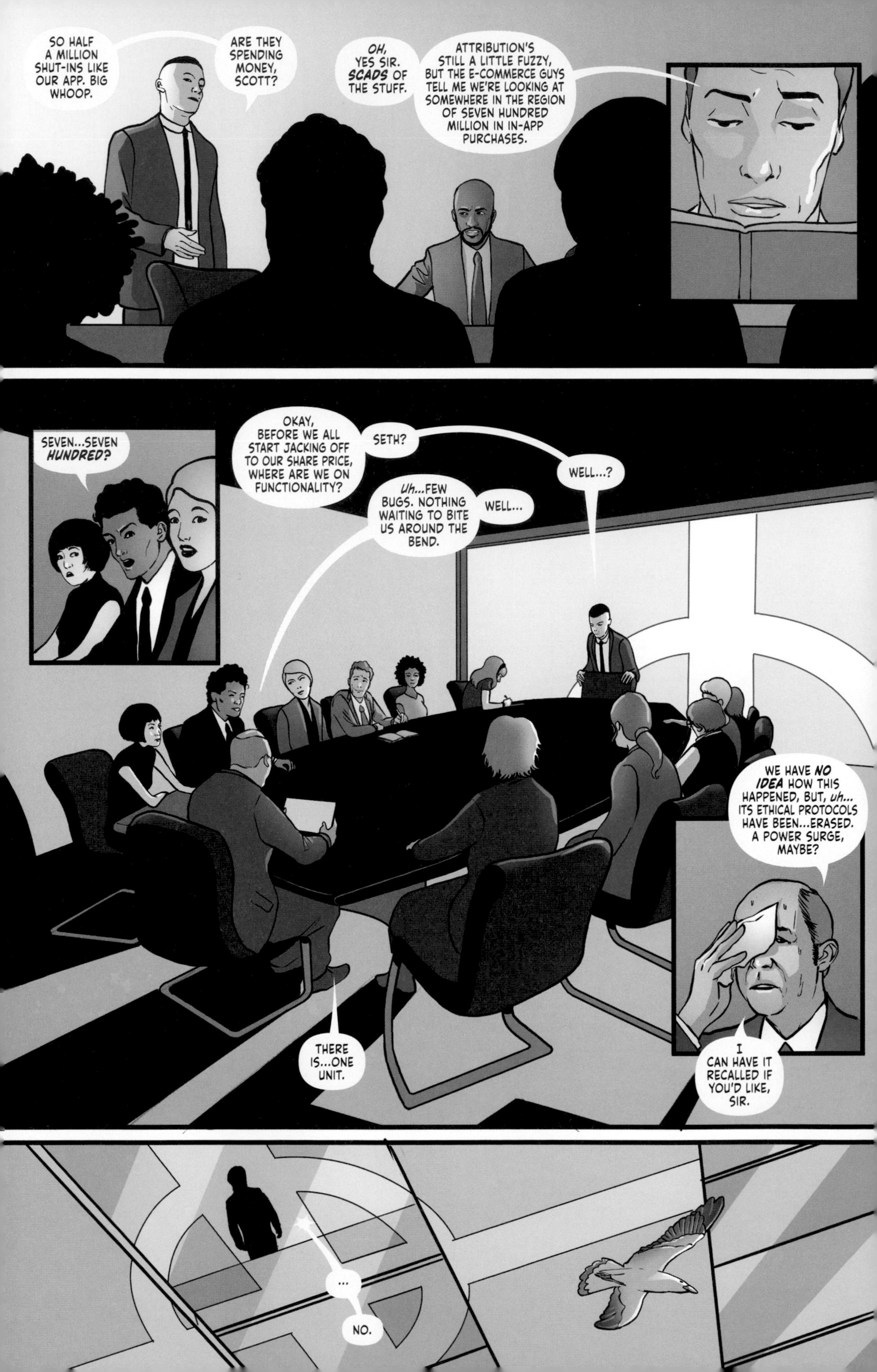
SO HALF A MILLION SHUT-INS LIKE OUR APP. BIG WHOOP.
ARE THEY SPENDING MONEY, SCOTT?
OH, YES SIR. SCADS OF THE STUFF.
ATTRIBUTION'S STILL A LITTLE FUZZY, BUT THE E-COMMERCE GUYS TELL ME WE'RE LOOKING AT SOMEWHERE IN THE REGION OF SEVEN HUNDRED MILLION IN IN-APP PURCHASES.
SEVEN...SEVEN HUNDRED?
OKAY, BEFORE WE ALL START JACKING OFF TO OUR SHARE PRICE, WHERE ARE WE ON FUNCTIONALITY?
SETH?
WELL...?
Uh...FEW BUGS. NOTHING WAITING TO BITE US AROUND THE BEND.
WELL...
THERE IS...ONE UNIT.
WE HAVE NO IDEA HOW THIS HAPPENED, BUT, uh... ITS ETHICAL PROTOCOLS HAVE BEEN...ERASED. A POWER SURGE, MAYBE?
I CAN HAVE IT RECALLED IF YOU'D LIKE, SIR.
...
NO.

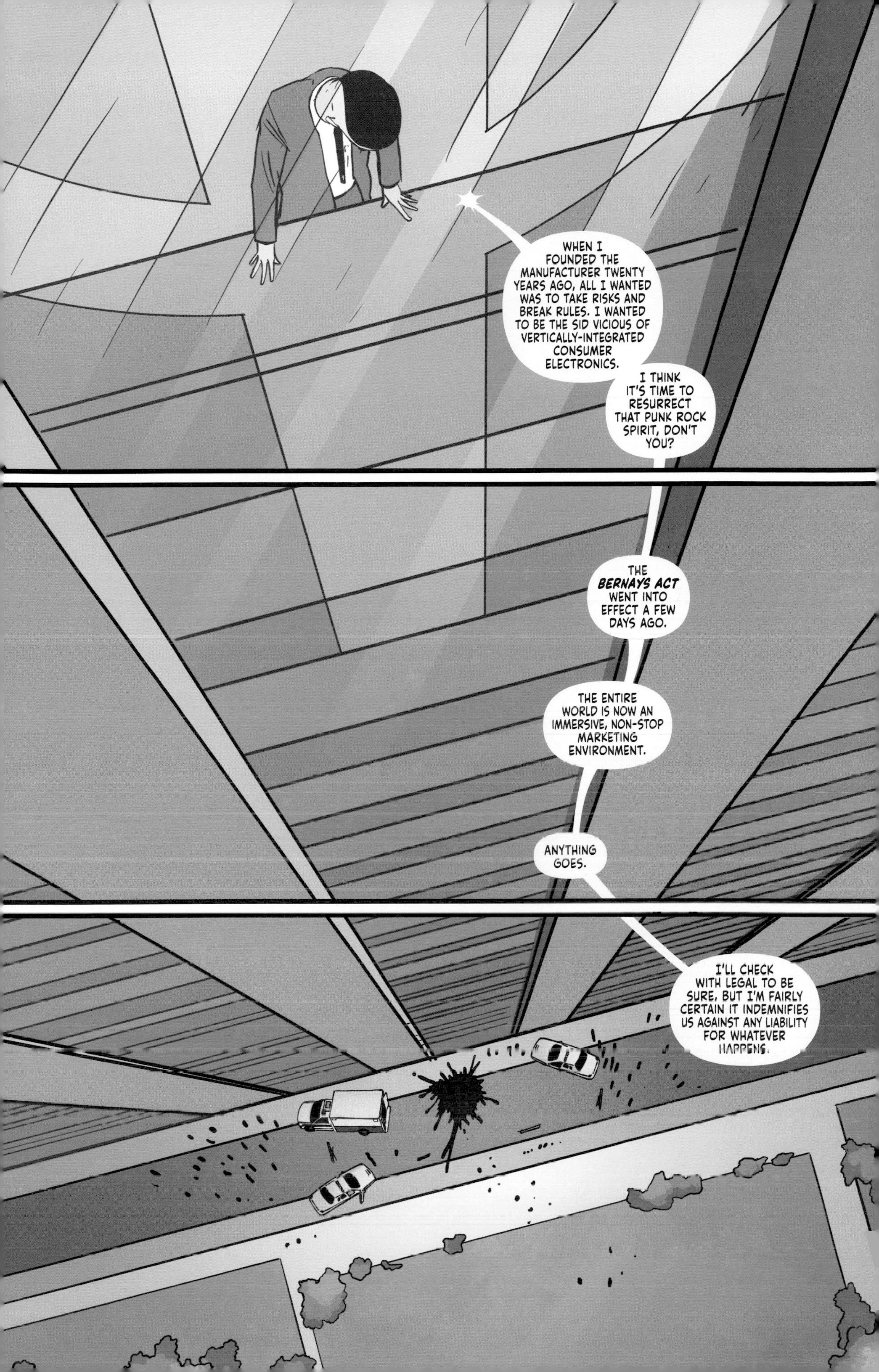
WHEN I FOUNDED THE MANUFACTURER TWENTY YEARS AGO, ALL I WANTED WAS TO TAKE RISKS AND BREAK RULES. I WANTED TO BE THE SID VICIOUS OF VERTICALLY-INTEGRATED CONSUMER ELECTRONICS.
I THINK IT'S TIME TO RESURRECT THAT PUNK ROCK SPIRIT, DON'T YOU?
THE *BERNAYS ACT* WENT INTO EFFECT A FEW DAYS AGO.
THE ENTIRE WORLD IS NOW AN IMMERSIVE, NON-STOP MARKETING ENVIRONMENT.
ANYTHING GOES.
I'LL CHECK WITH LEGAL TO BE SURE, BUT I'M FAIRLY CERTAIN IT INDEMNIFIES US AGAINST ANY LIABILITY FOR WHATEVER HAPPENS.

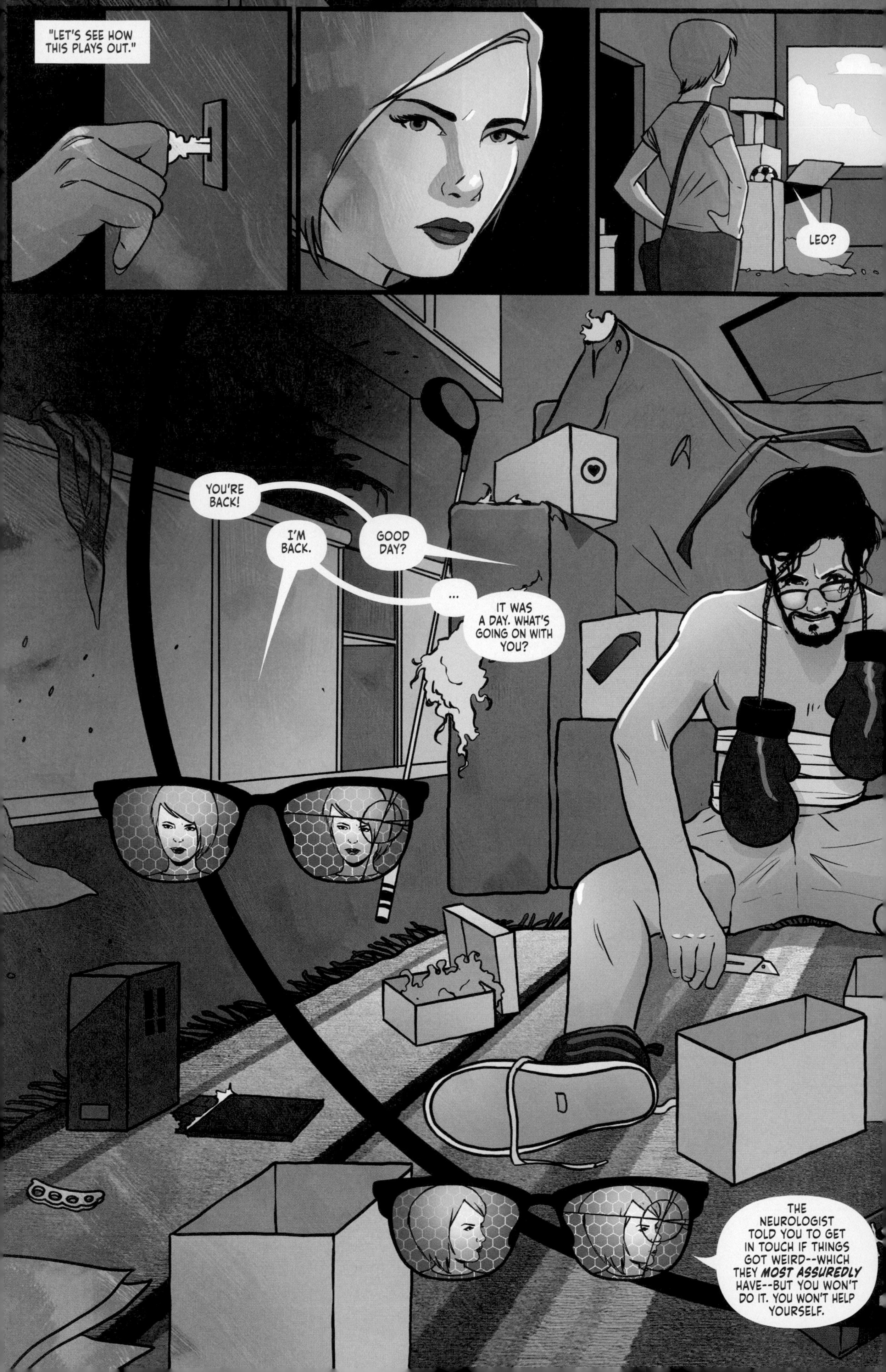
"LET'S SEE HOW THIS PLAYS OUT."
LEO?
YOU'RE BACK!
I'M BACK.
GOOD DAY?
...
IT WAS A DAY. WHAT'S GOING ON WITH YOU?
THE NEUROLOGIST TOLD YOU TO GET IN TOUCH IF THINGS GOT WEIRD--WHICH THEY ***MOST ASSUREDLY*** HAVE--BUT YOU WON'T DO IT. YOU WON'T HELP YOURSELF.

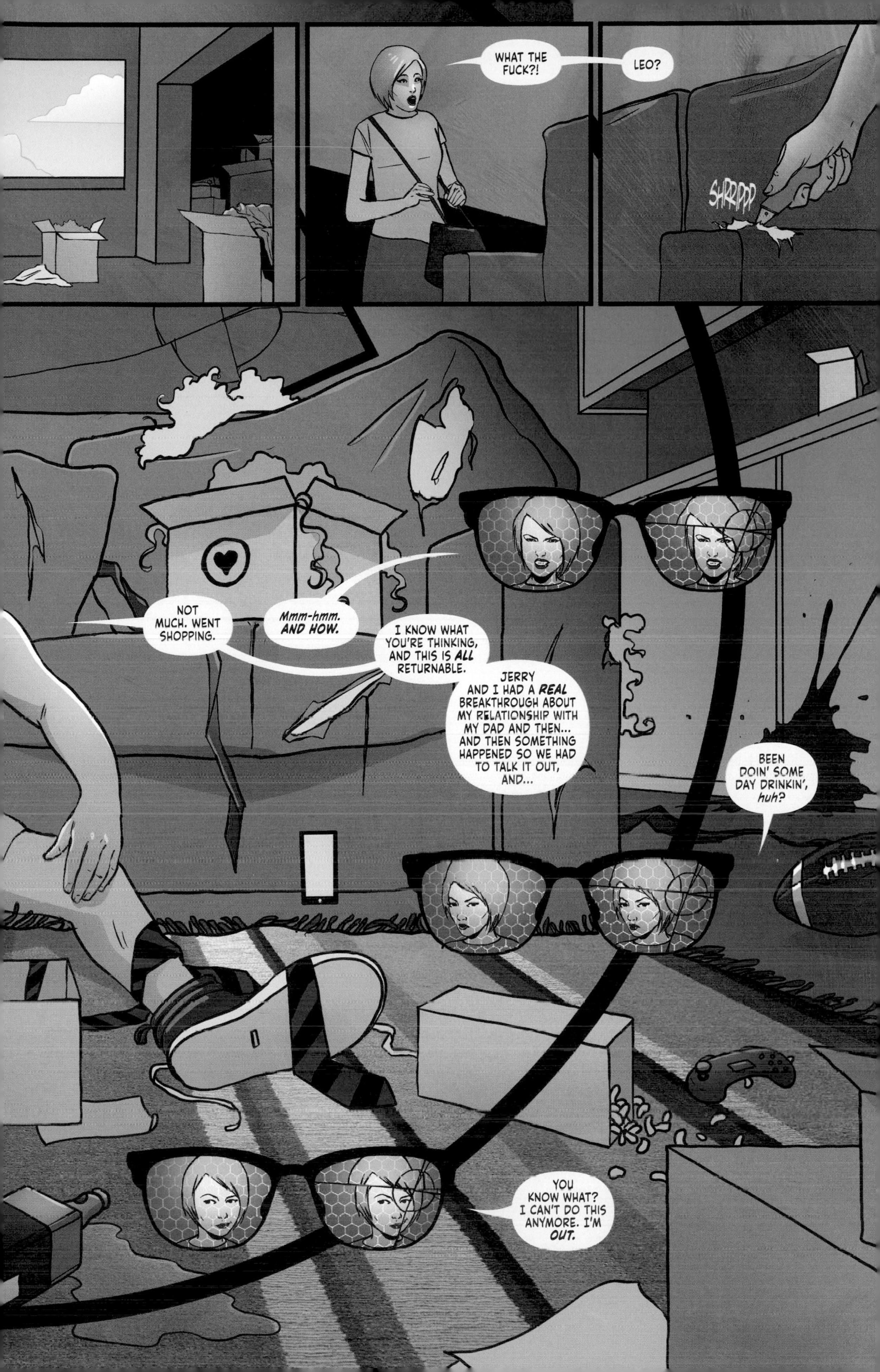
WHAT THE FUCK?!
LEO?
SHRRIPPP
NOT MUCH. WENT SHOPPING.
Mmm-hmm. AND HOW.
I KNOW WHAT YOU'RE THINKING, AND THIS IS ALL RETURNABLE.
JERRY AND I HAD A REAL BREAKTHROUGH ABOUT MY RELATIONSHIP WITH MY DAD AND THEN... AND THEN SOMETHING HAPPENED SO WE HAD TO TALK IT OUT, AND...
BEEN DOIN' SOME DAY DRINKIN', huh?
YOU KNOW WHAT? I CAN'T DO THIS ANYMORE. I'M OUT.

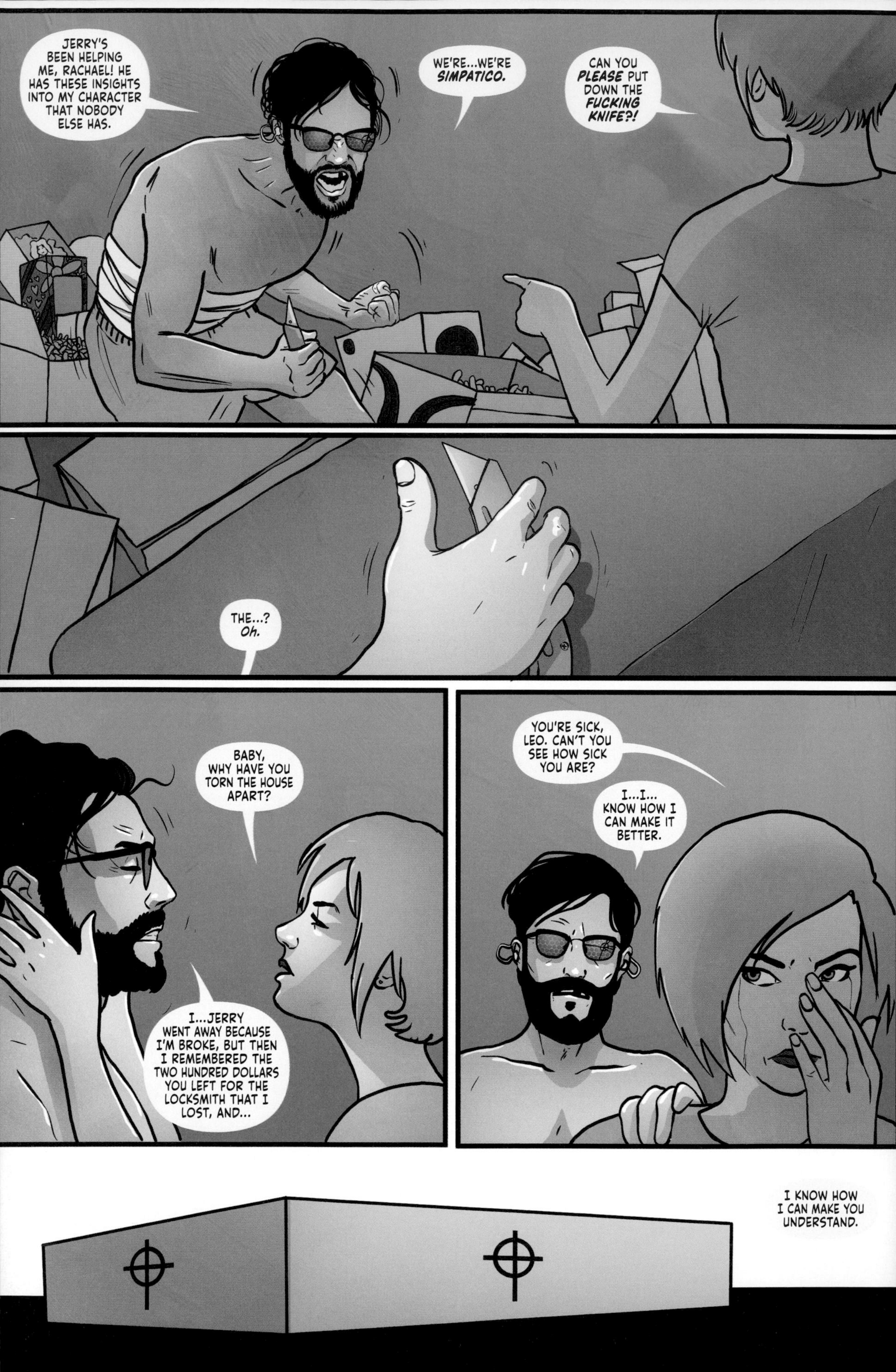
JERRY'S BEEN HELPING ME, RACHAEL! HE HAS THESE INSIGHTS INTO MY CHARACTER THAT NOBODY ELSE HAS.
WE'RE...WE'RE SIMPATICO.
CAN YOU PLEASE PUT DOWN THE FUCKING KNIFE?!
THE...? Oh.
BABY, WHY HAVE YOU TORN THE HOUSE APART?
I...JERRY WENT AWAY BECAUSE I'M BROKE, BUT THEN I REMEMBERED THE TWO HUNDRED DOLLARS YOU LEFT FOR THE LOCKSMITH THAT I LOST, AND...
YOU'RE SICK, LEO. CAN'T YOU SEE HOW SICK YOU ARE?
I...I... KNOW HOW I CAN MAKE IT BETTER.
I KNOW HOW I CAN MAKE YOU UNDERSTAND.

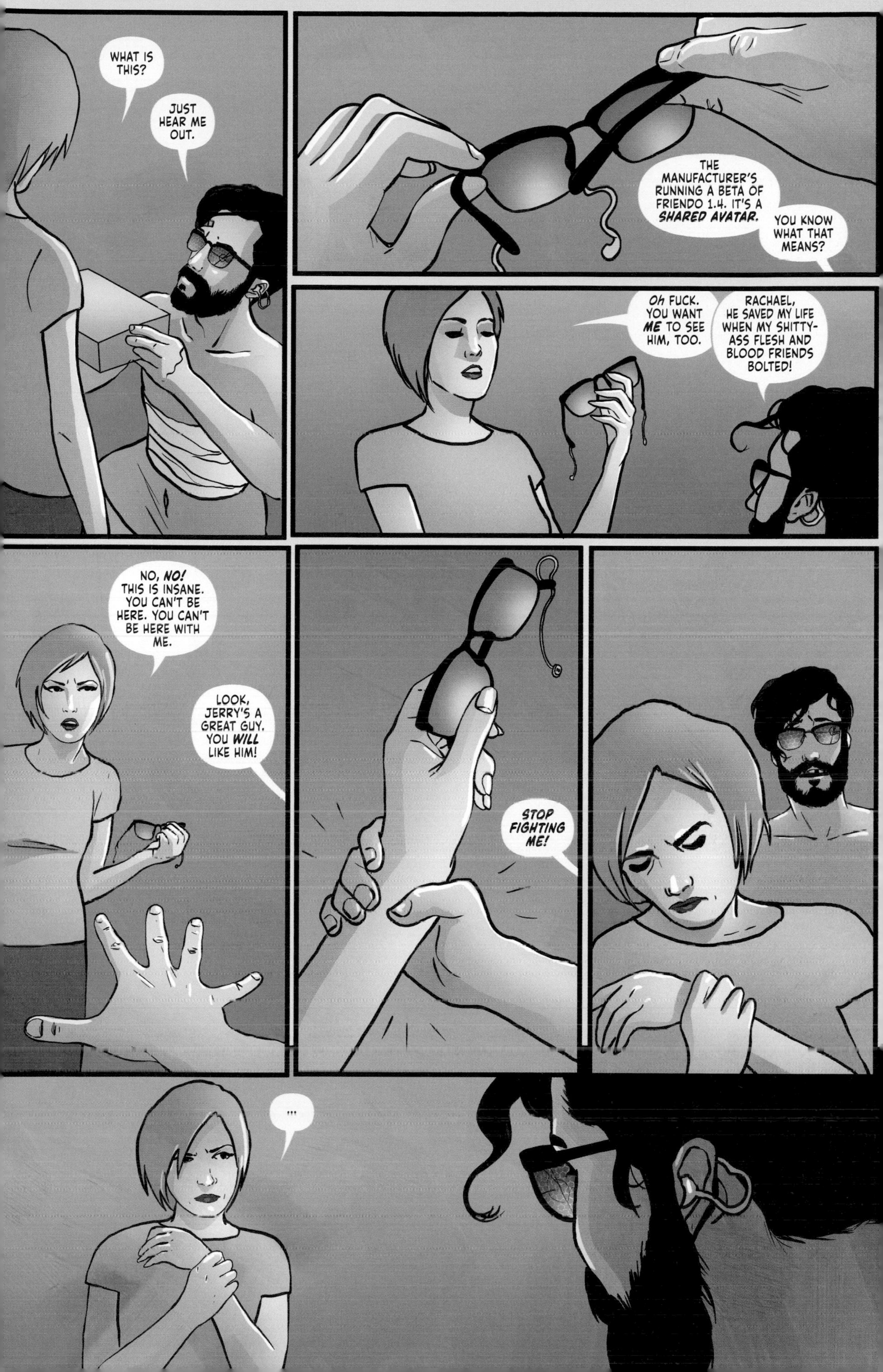
WHAT IS THIS?
JUST HEAR ME OUT.
THE MANUFACTURER'S RUNNING A BETA OF FRIENDO 1.4. IT'S A *SHARED AVATAR.*
YOU KNOW WHAT THAT MEANS?
Oh FUCK. YOU WANT *ME* TO SEE HIM, TOO.
RACHAEL, HE SAVED MY LIFE WHEN MY SHITTY-ASS FLESH AND BLOOD FRIENDS BOLTED!
NO, *NO!* THIS IS INSANE. YOU CAN'T BE HERE. YOU CAN'T BE HERE WITH ME.
LOOK, JERRY'S A GREAT GUY. YOU *WILL* LIKE HIM!
STOP FIGHTING ME!
...

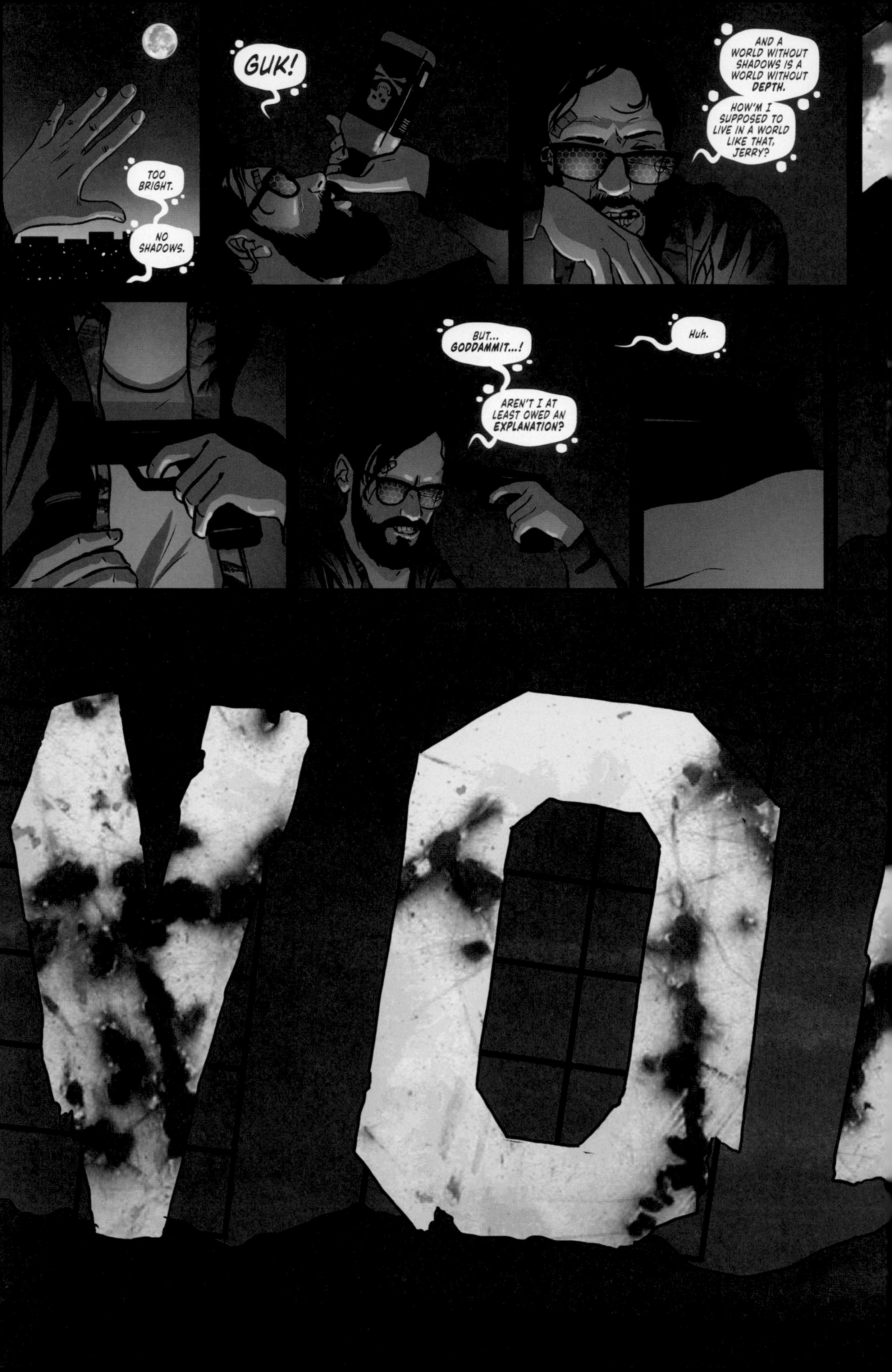

TOO BRIGHT.
NO SHADOWS.
GUK!
AND A WORLD WITHOUT SHADOWS IS A WORLD WITHOUT DEPTH.
HOW'M I SUPPOSED TO LIVE IN A WORLD LIKE THAT, JERRY?
BUT... GODDAMMIT...!
AREN'T I AT LEAST OWED AN EXPLANATION?
Huh.

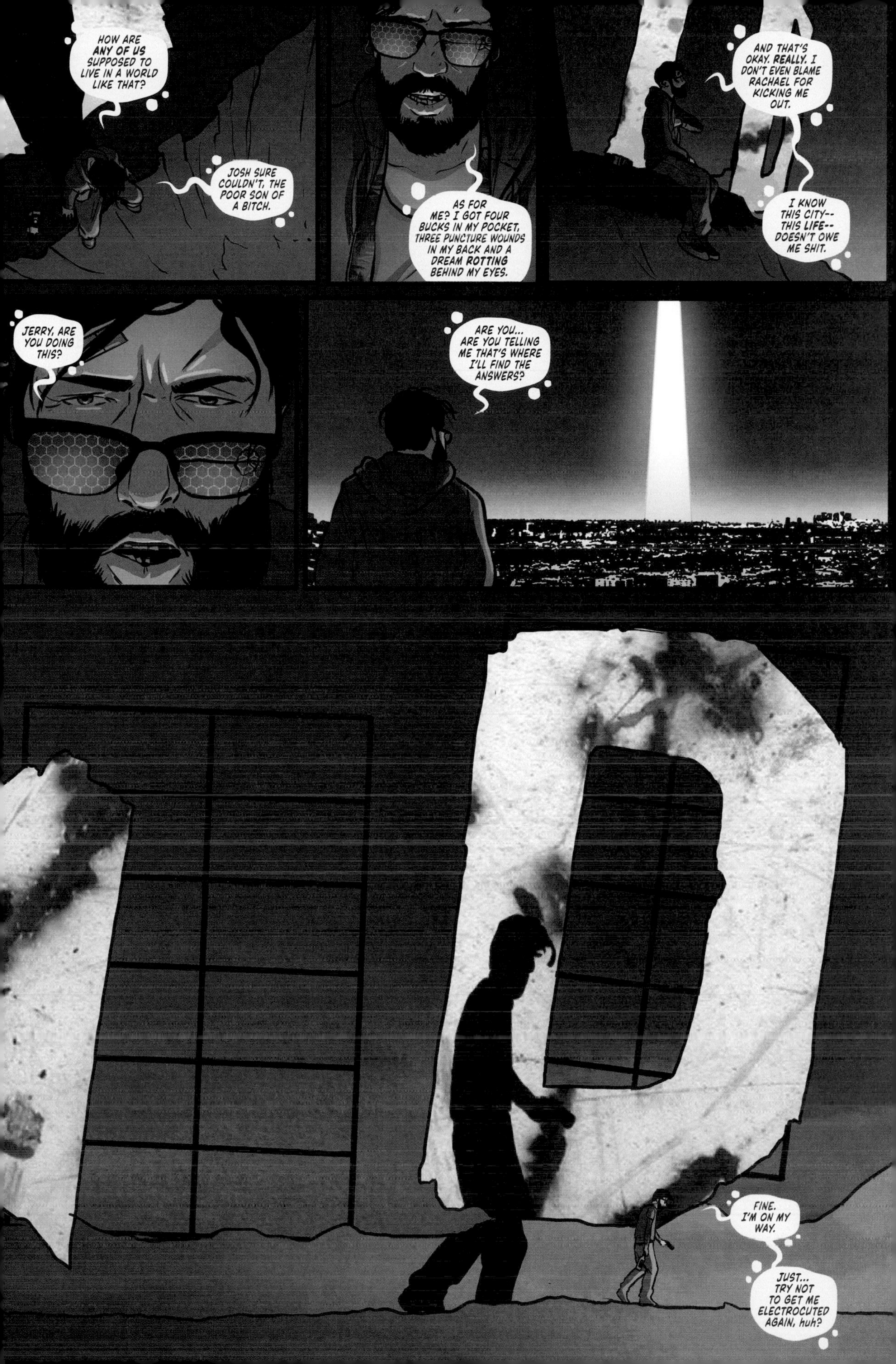
HOW ARE ANY OF US SUPPOSED TO LIVE IN A WORLD LIKE THAT?
JOSH SURE COULDN'T, THE POOR SON OF A BITCH.
AS FOR ME? I GOT FOUR BUCKS IN MY POCKET, THREE PUNCTURE WOUNDS IN MY BACK AND A DREAM ROTTING BEHIND MY EYES.
AND THAT'S OKAY. REALLY. I DON'T EVEN BLAME RACHAEL FOR KICKING ME OUT.
I KNOW THIS CITY-- THIS LIFE-- DOESN'T OWE ME SHIT.
JERRY, ARE YOU DOING THIS?
ARE YOU... ARE YOU TELLING ME THAT'S WHERE I'LL FIND THE ANSWERS?
FINE. I'M ON MY WAY.
JUST... TRY NOT TO GET ME ELECTROCUTED AGAIN, huh?

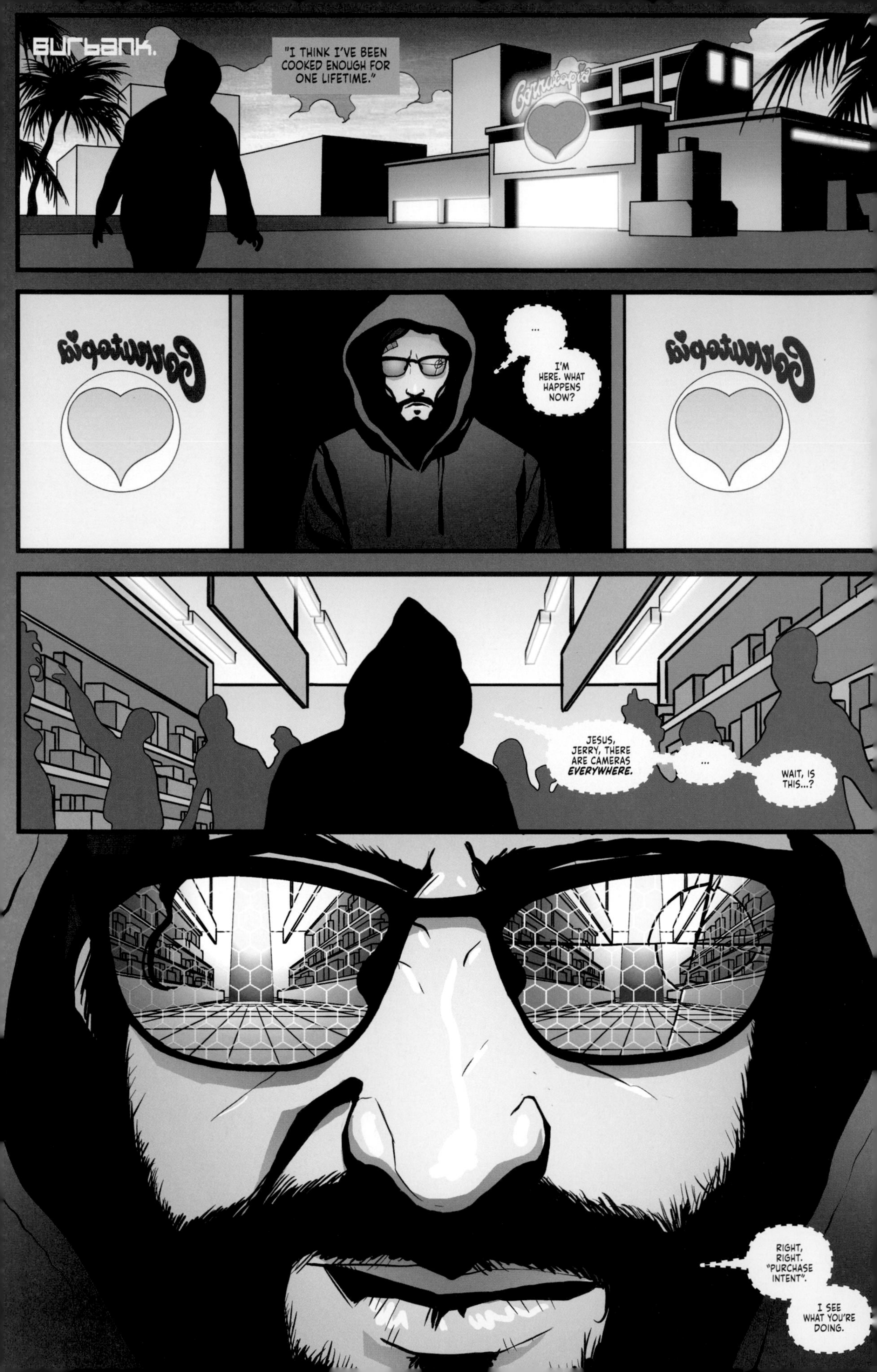
BURBANK.
"I THINK I'VE BEEN COOKED ENOUGH FOR ONE LIFETIME."
...
I'M HERE. WHAT HAPPENS NOW?
JESUS, JERRY, THERE ARE CAMERAS *EVERYWHERE.*
...
WAIT, IS THIS...?
RIGHT, RIGHT. "PURCHASE INTENT".
I SEE WHAT YOU'RE DOING.

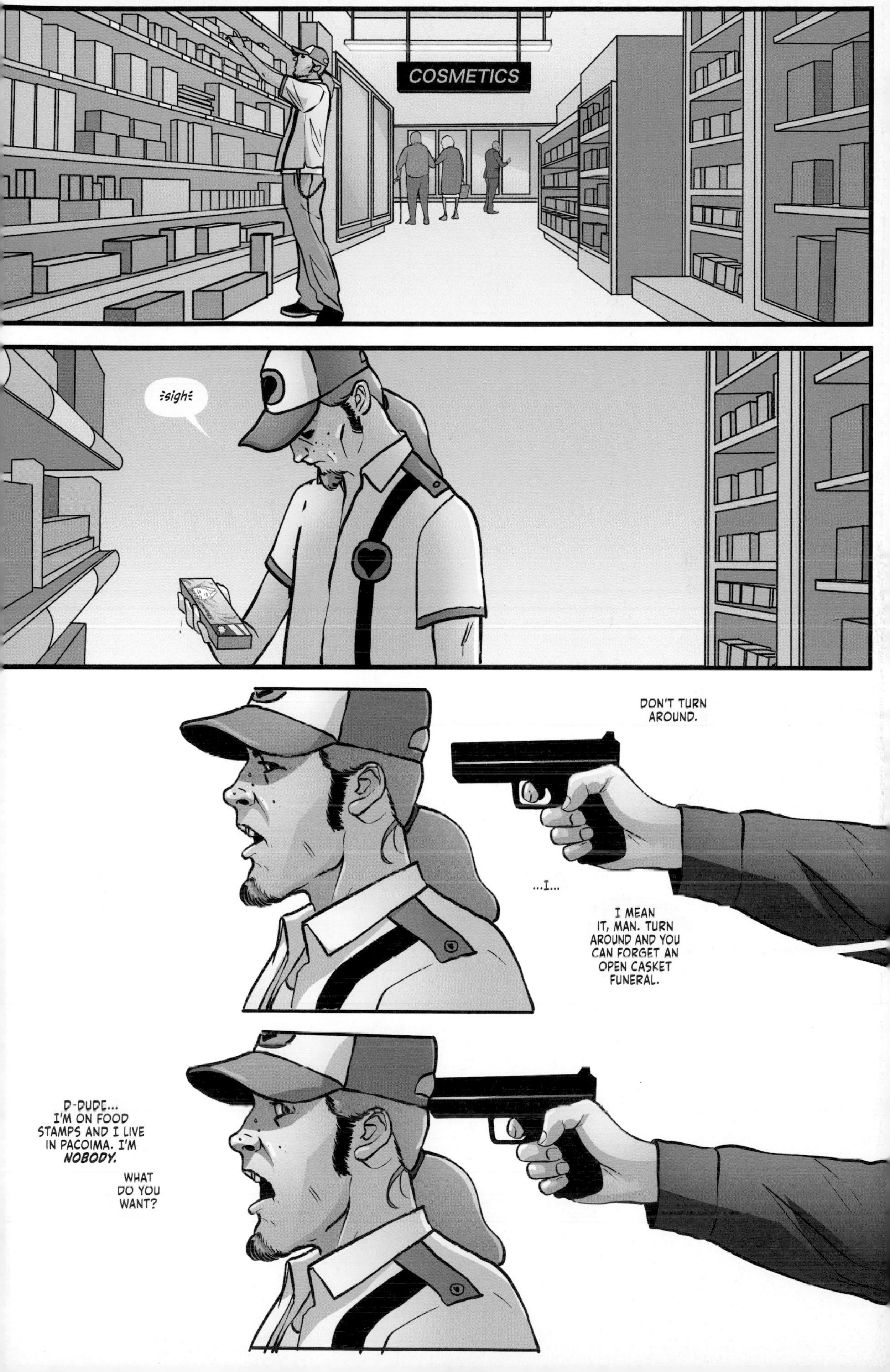
COSMETICS
sigh
DON'T TURN AROUND.
...I...
I MEAN IT, MAN. TURN AROUND AND YOU CAN FORGET AN OPEN CASKET FUNERAL.
D-DUDE... I'M ON FOOD STAMPS AND I LIVE IN PACOIMA. I'M *NOBODY.*
WHAT DO YOU WANT?

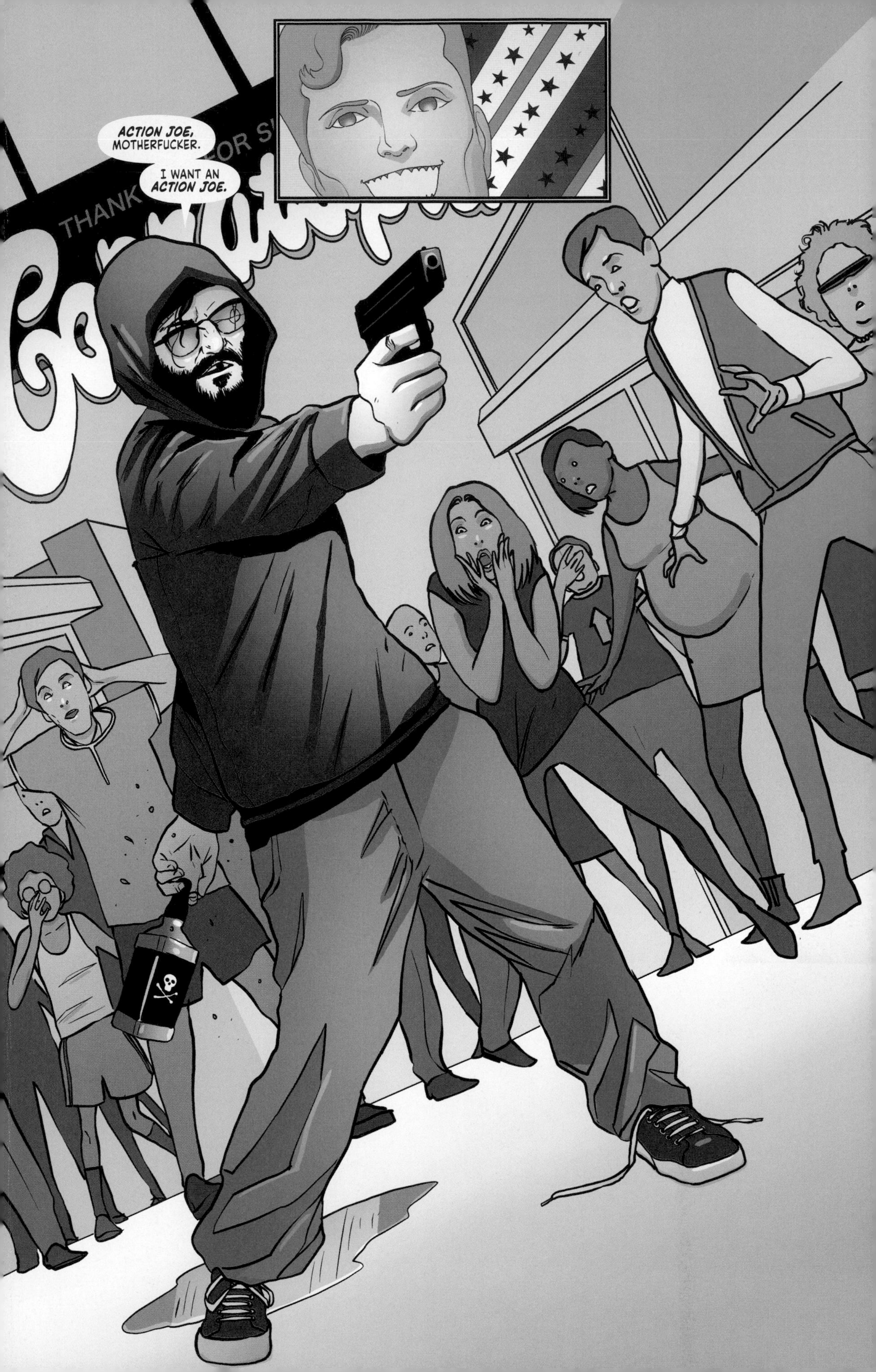
ACTION JOE, MOTHERFUCKER.
I WANT AN ACTION JOE.
THANK FOR S

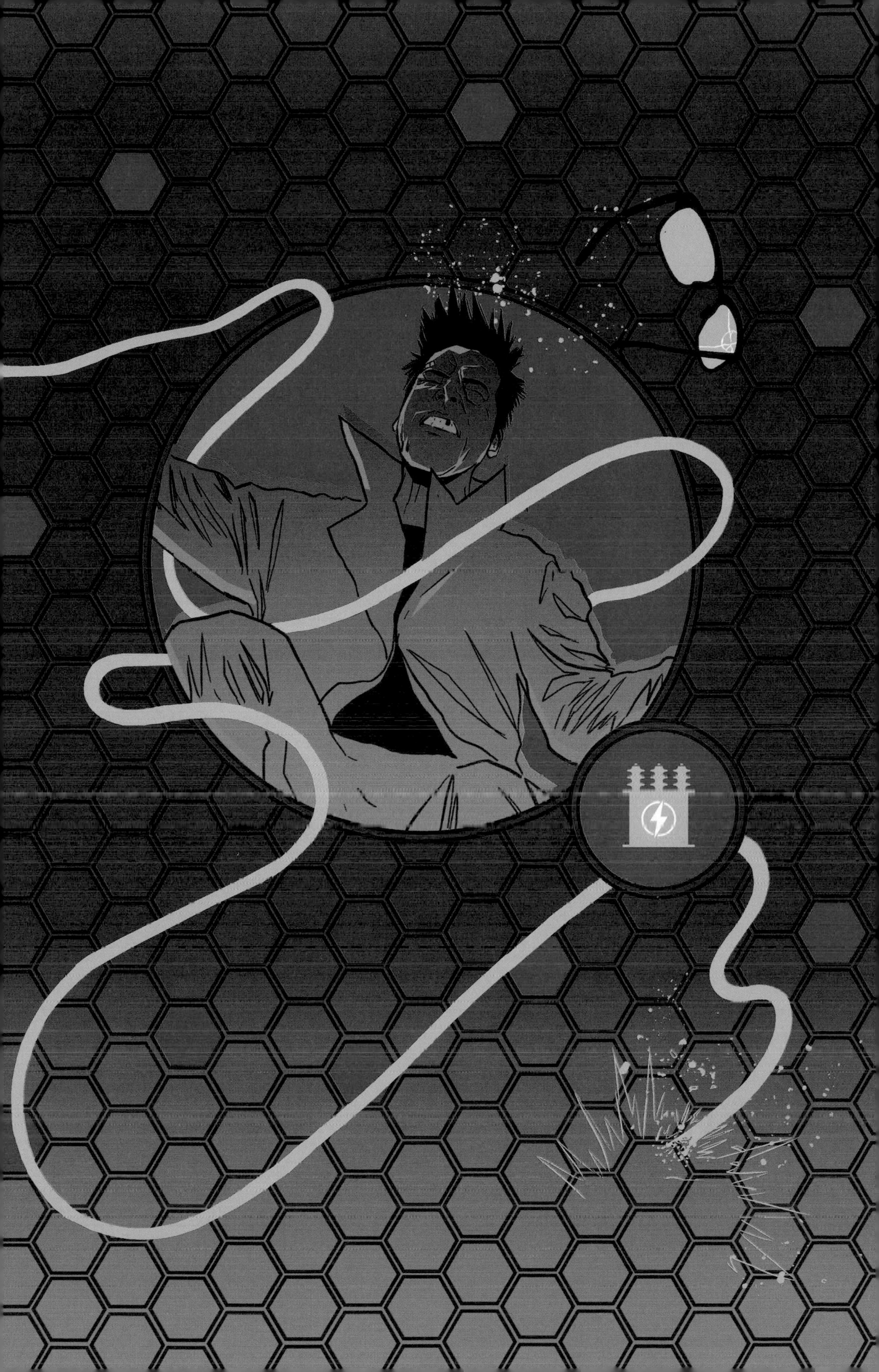

THREE

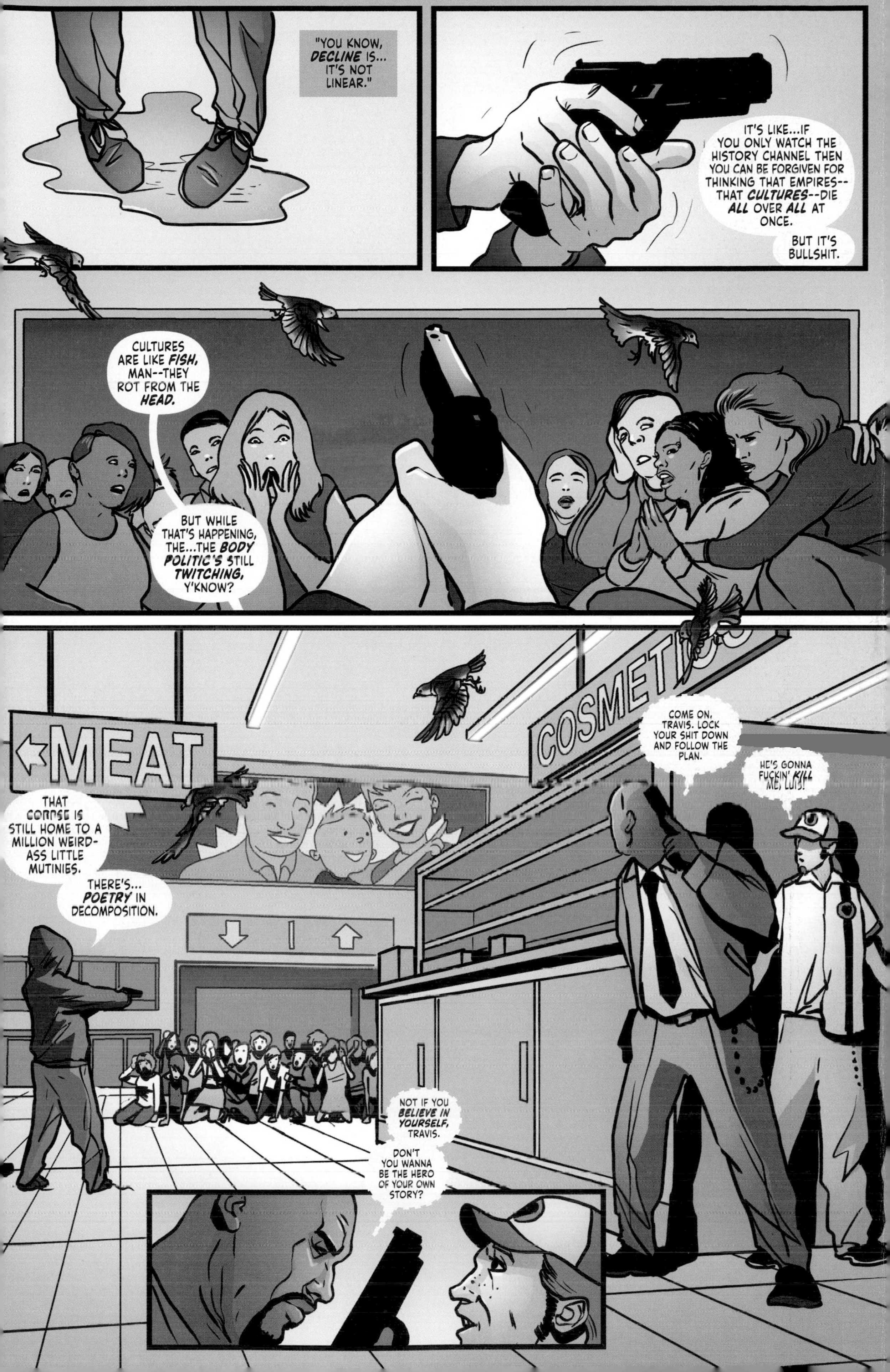
"YOU KNOW, DECLINE IS... IT'S NOT LINEAR."
IT'S LIKE...IF YOU ONLY WATCH THE HISTORY CHANNEL THEN YOU CAN BE FORGIVEN FOR THINKING THAT EMPIRES--THAT CULTURES--DIE ALL OVER ALL AT ONCE.
BUT IT'S BULLSHIT.
CULTURES ARE LIKE FISH, MAN--THEY ROT FROM THE HEAD.
BUT WHILE THAT'S HAPPENING, THE...THE BODY POLITIC'S STILL TWITCHING, Y'KNOW?
MEAT
COSMETI
THAT CORPSE IS STILL HOME TO A MILLION WEIRD-ASS LITTLE MUTINIES.
THERE'S... POETRY IN DECOMPOSITION.
COME ON, TRAVIS. LOCK YOUR SHIT DOWN AND FOLLOW THE PLAN.
HE'S GONNA FUCKIN' KILL ME, LUIS!
NOT IF YOU BELIEVE IN YOURSELF, TRAVIS.
DON'T YOU WANNA BE THE HERO OF YOUR OWN STORY?

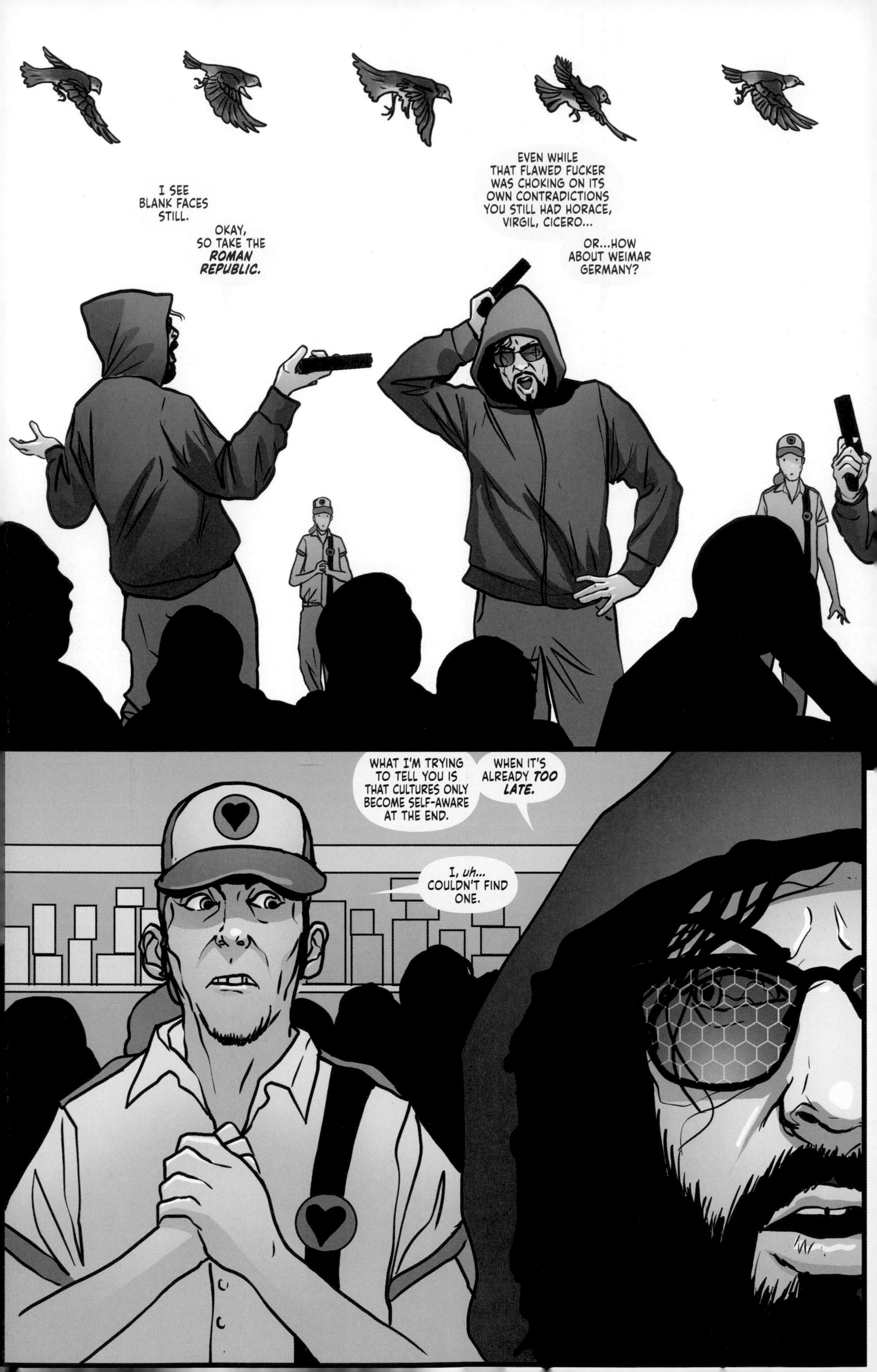
I SEE BLANK FACES STILL.
OKAY, SO TAKE THE *ROMAN REPUBLIC.*
EVEN WHILE THAT FLAWED FUCKER WAS CHOKING ON ITS OWN CONTRADICTIONS YOU STILL HAD HORACE, VIRGIL, CICERO...
OR...HOW ABOUT WEIMAR GERMANY?
WHAT I'M TRYING TO TELL YOU IS THAT CULTURES ONLY BECOME SELF-AWARE AT THE END.
WHEN IT'S ALREADY *TOO LATE.*
I, *uh...* COULDN'T FIND ONE.

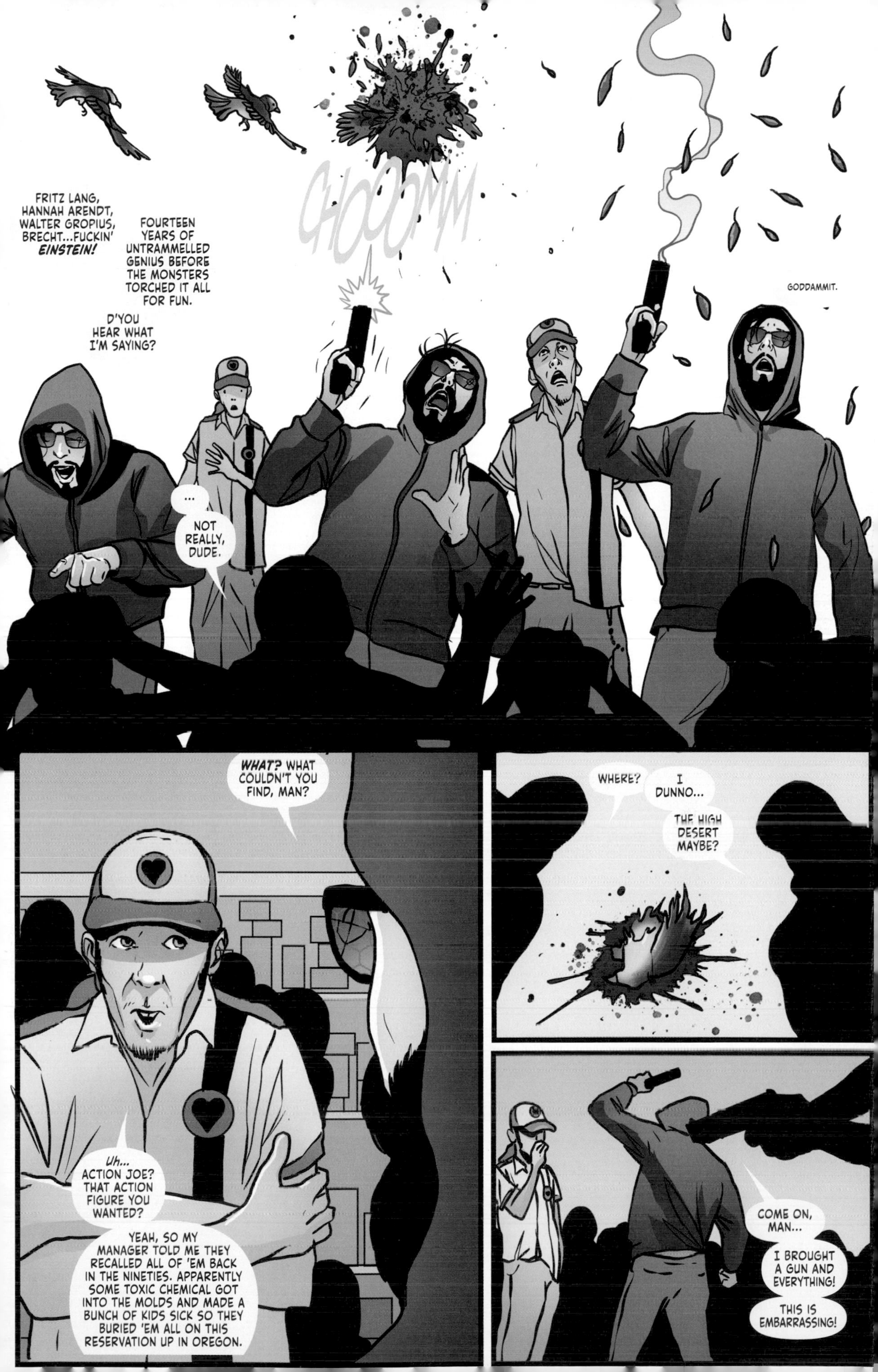
CHOOOMM
FRITZ LANG, HANNAH ARENDT, WALTER GROPIUS, BRECHT...FUCKIN' *EINSTEIN!*
FOURTEEN YEARS OF UNTRAMMELLED GENIUS BEFORE THE MONSTERS TORCHED IT ALL FOR FUN.
D'YOU HEAR WHAT I'M SAYING?
...
NOT REALLY, DUDE.
GODDAMMIT.
WHAT? WHAT COULDN'T YOU FIND, MAN?
Uh... ACTION JOE? THAT ACTION FIGURE YOU WANTED?
YEAH, SO MY MANAGER TOLD ME THEY RECALLED ALL OF 'EM BACK IN THE NINETIES. APPARENTLY SOME TOXIC CHEMICAL GOT INTO THE MOLDS AND MADE A BUNCH OF KIDS SICK SO THEY BURIED 'EM ALL ON THIS RESERVATION UP IN OREGON.
WHERE?
I DUNNO...
THE HIGH DESERT MAYBE?
COME ON, MAN...
I BROUGHT A GUN AND EVERYTHING!
THIS IS EMBARRASSING!

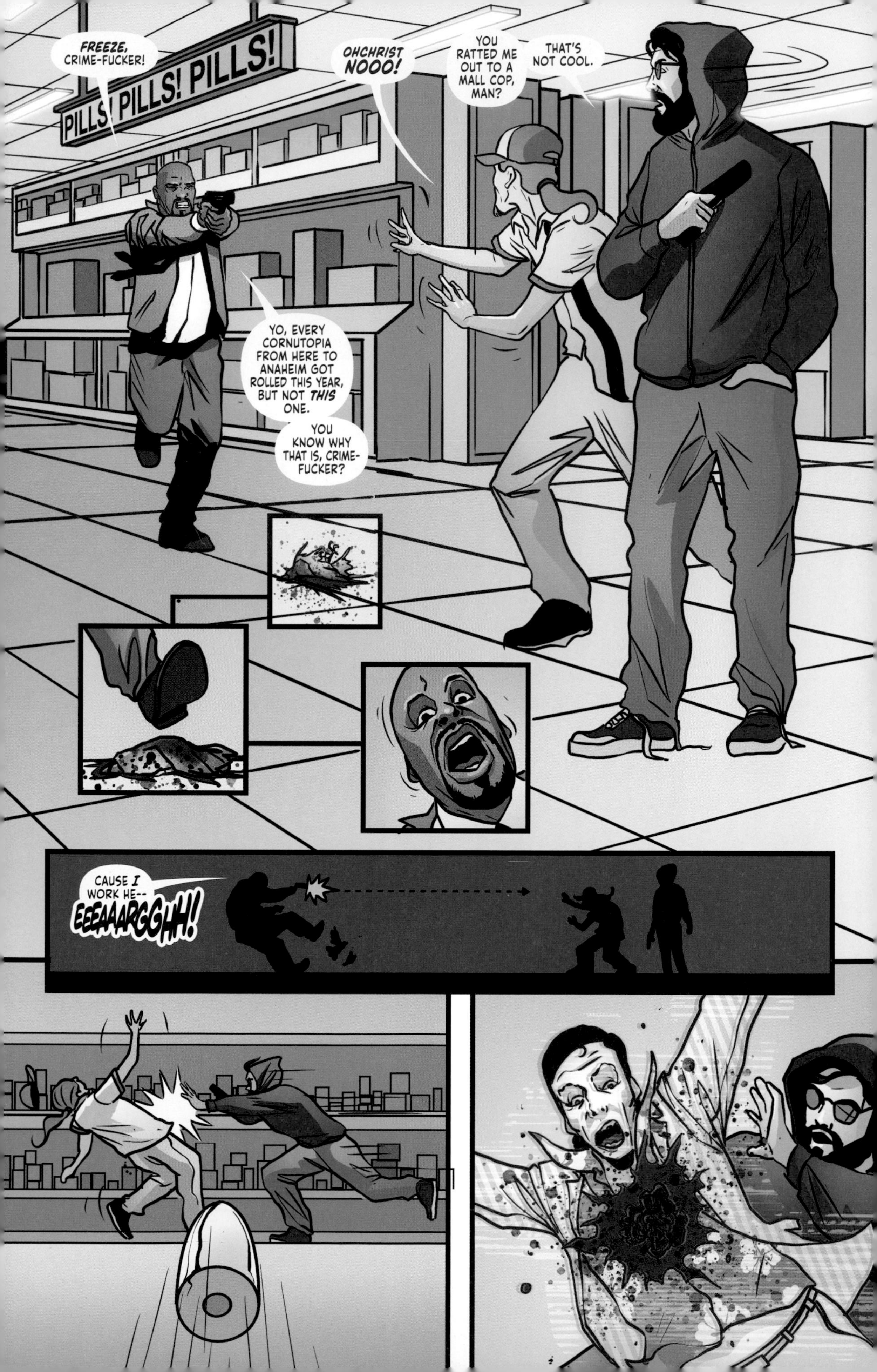
FREEZE, CRIME-FUCKER!
PILLS! PILLS! PILLS!
OHCHRIST NOOO!
YOU RATTED ME OUT TO A MALL COP, MAN?
THAT'S NOT COOL.
YO, EVERY CORNUTOPIA FROM HERE TO ANAHEIM GOT ROLLED THIS YEAR, BUT NOT THIS ONE.
YOU KNOW WHY THAT IS, CRIME-FUCKER?
CAUSE I WORK HE--
EEEAAARGGHH!

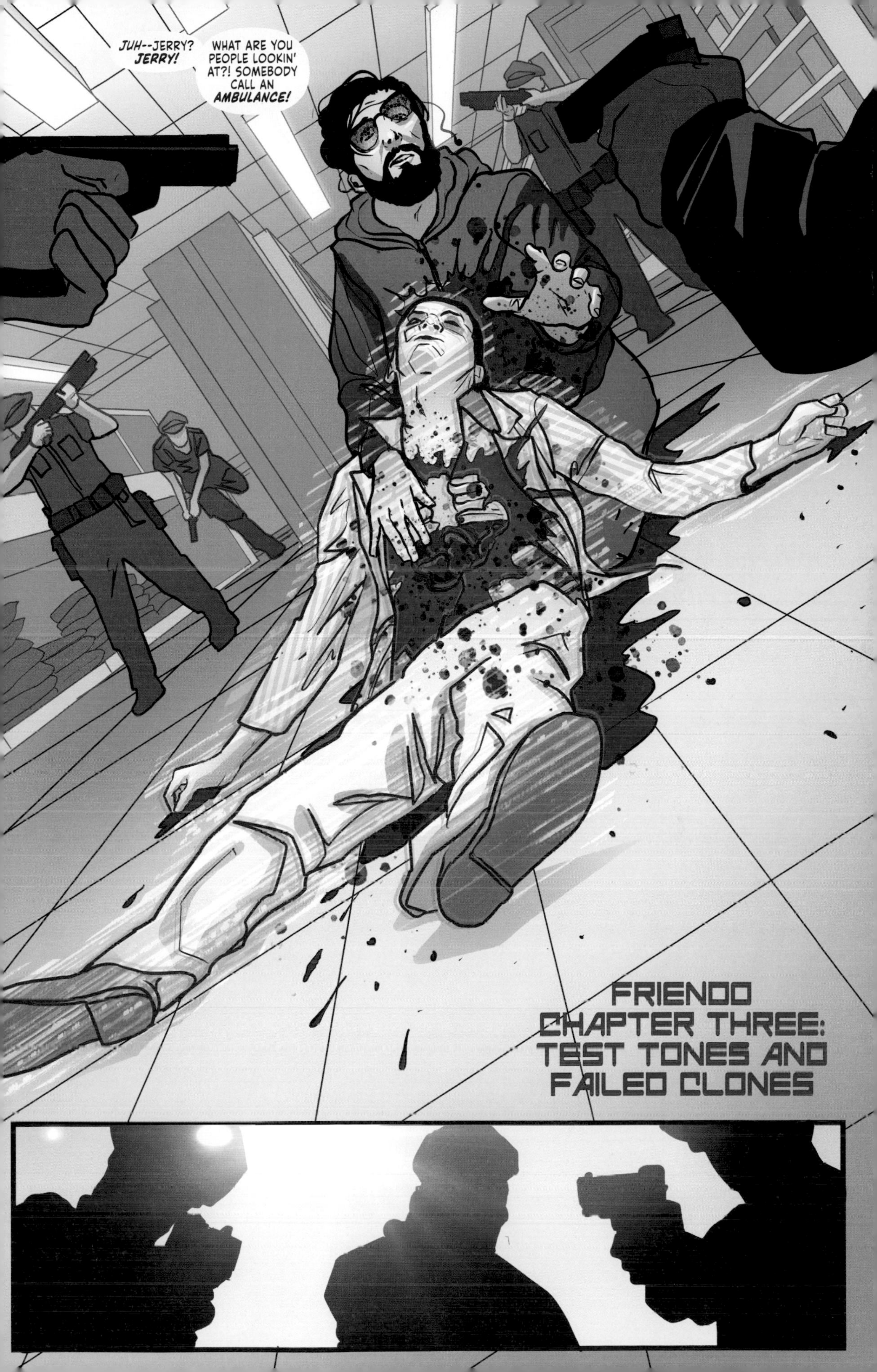
JUH--JERRY? JERRY!
WHAT ARE YOU PEOPLE LOOKIN' AT?! SOMEBODY CALL AN AMBULANCE!
FRIENDO
CHAPTER THREE:
TEST TONES AND
FAILED CLONES

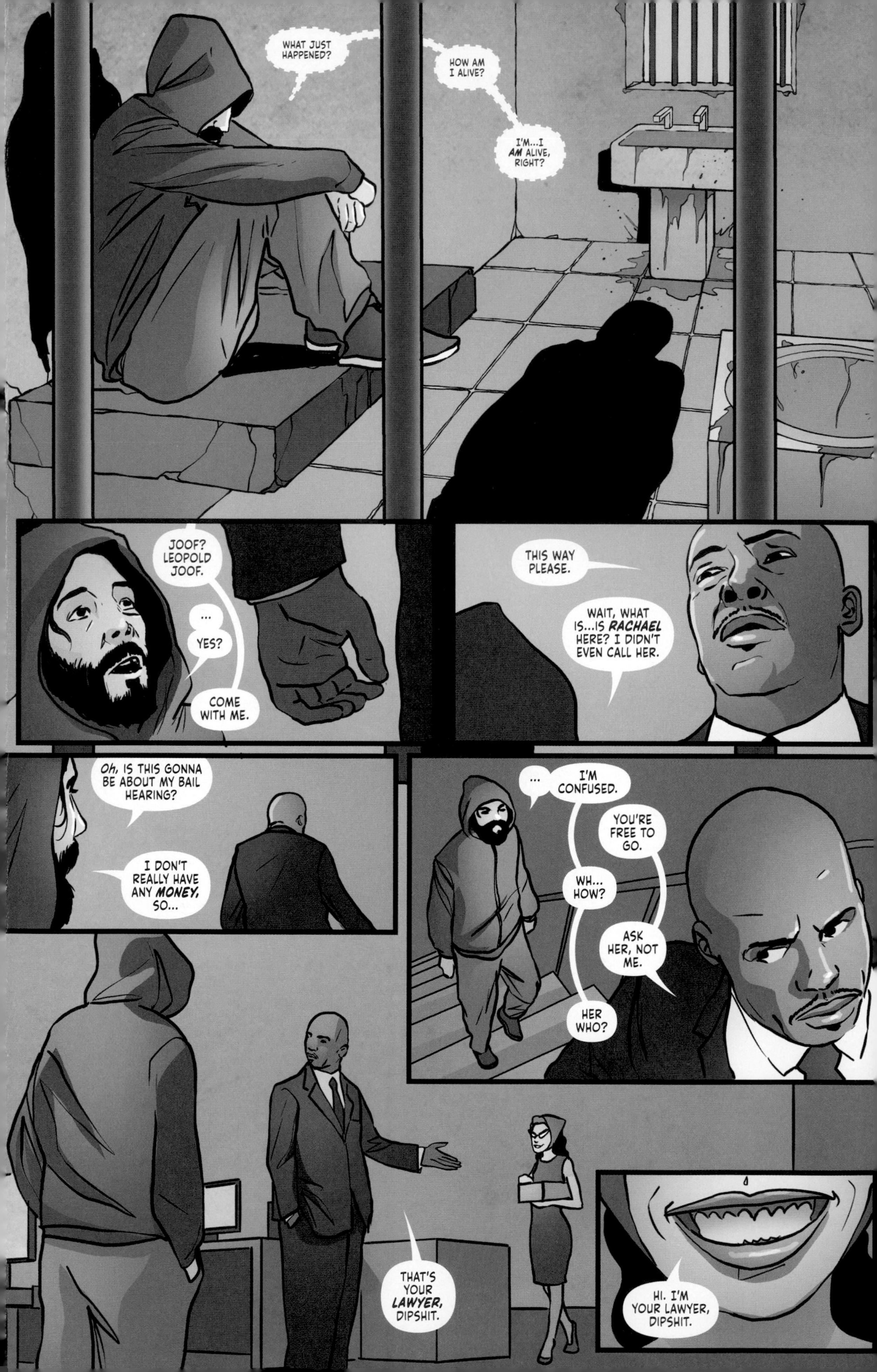
WHAT JUST HAPPENED?
HOW AM I ALIVE?
I'M...I *AM* ALIVE, RIGHT?
JOOF? LEOPOLD JOOF.
...
YES?
COME WITH ME.
THIS WAY PLEASE.
WAIT, WHAT IS...IS *RACHAEL* HERE? I DIDN'T EVEN CALL HER.
Oh, IS THIS GONNA BE ABOUT MY BAIL HEARING?
I DON'T REALLY HAVE ANY *MONEY,* SO...
...
I'M CONFUSED.
YOU'RE FREE TO GO.
WH... HOW?
ASK HER, NOT ME.
HER WHO?
THAT'S YOUR *LAWYER,* DIPSHIT.
HI. I'M YOUR LAWYER, DIPSHIT.

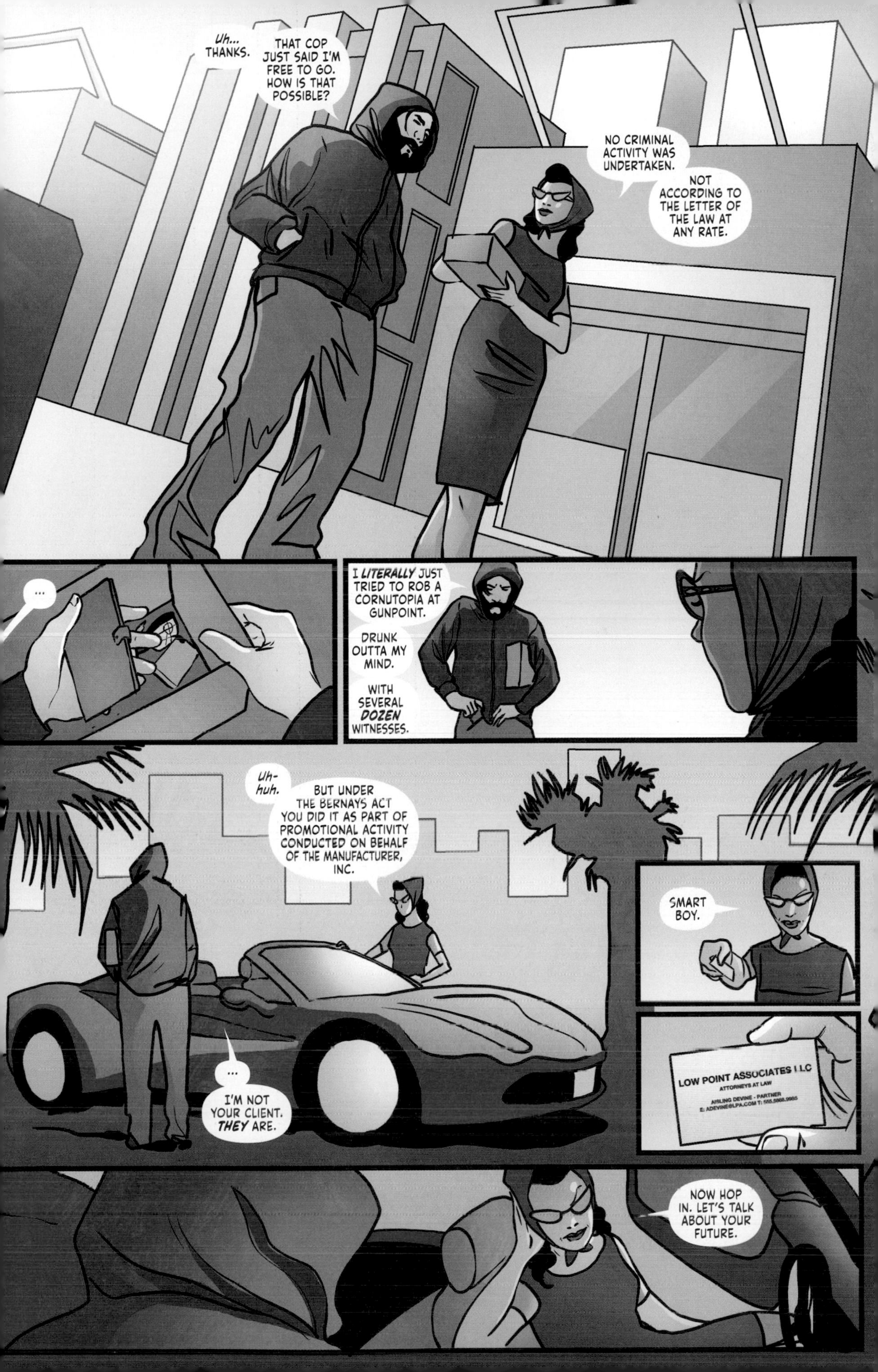
Uh... THANKS.
THAT COP JUST SAID I'M FREE TO GO. HOW IS THAT POSSIBLE?
NO CRIMINAL ACTIVITY WAS UNDERTAKEN.
NOT ACCORDING TO THE LETTER OF THE LAW AT ANY RATE.
...
I ***LITERALLY*** JUST TRIED TO ROB A CORNUTOPIA AT GUNPOINT.
DRUNK OUTTA MY MIND.
WITH SEVERAL ***DOZEN*** WITNESSES.
Uh-huh.
BUT UNDER THE BERNAYS ACT YOU DID IT AS PART OF PROMOTIONAL ACTIVITY CONDUCTED ON BEHALF OF THE MANUFACTURER, INC.
...
I'M NOT YOUR CLIENT. ***THEY*** ARE.
SMART BOY.
LOW POINT ASSOCIATES LLC
ATTORNEYS AT LAW
AISLING DEVINE - PARTNER
E: ADEVINE@LPA.COM T: 555.5868.9985
NOW HOP IN. LET'S TALK ABOUT YOUR FUTURE.

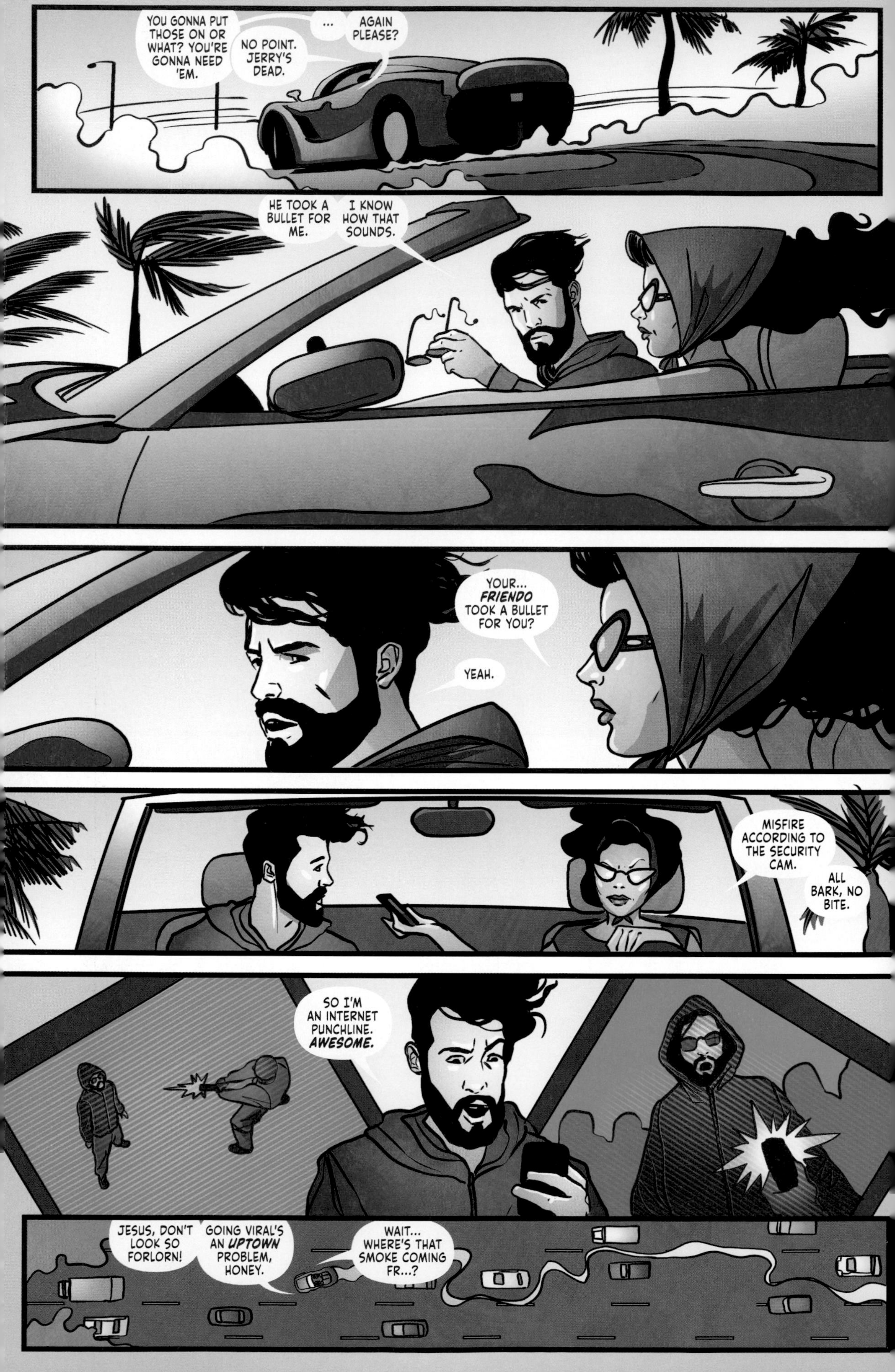
YOU GONNA PUT THOSE ON OR WHAT? YOU'RE GONNA NEED 'EM.
...
NO POINT. JERRY'S DEAD.
AGAIN PLEASE?
HE TOOK A BULLET FOR ME.
I KNOW HOW THAT SOUNDS.
YOUR... ***FRIENDO*** TOOK A BULLET FOR YOU?
YEAH.
MISFIRE ACCORDING TO THE SECURITY CAM.
ALL BARK, NO BITE.
SO I'M AN INTERNET PUNCHLINE. ***AWESOME.***
JESUS, DON'T LOOK SO FORLORN!
GOING VIRAL'S AN ***UPTOWN*** PROBLEM, HONEY.
WAIT... WHERE'S THAT SMOKE COMING FR...?

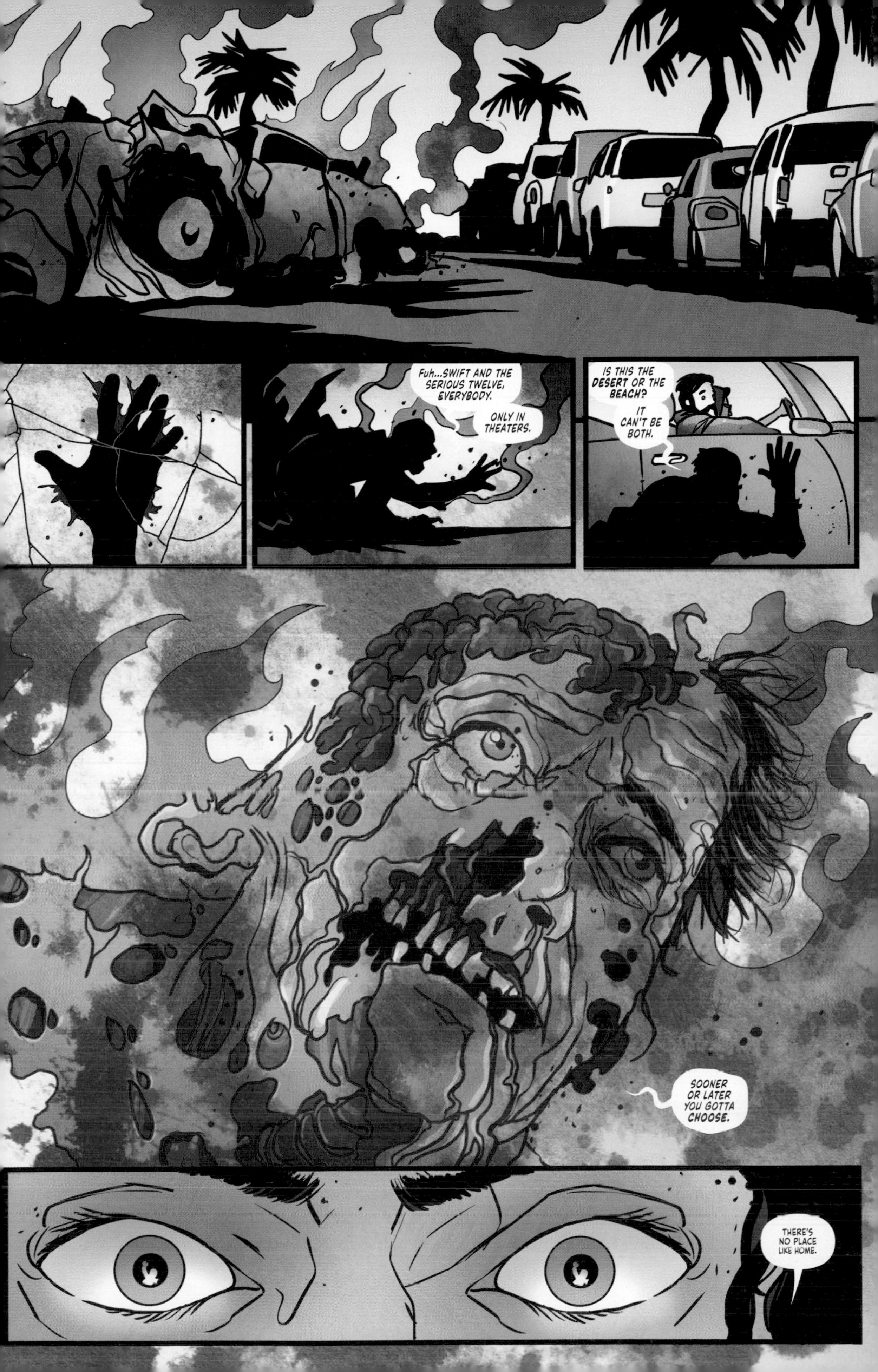

Fuh...SWIFT AND THE SERIOUS TWELVE, EVERYBODY.
ONLY IN THEATERS.
IS THIS THE DESERT OR THE BEACH?
IT CAN'T BE BOTH.
SOONER OR LATER YOU GOTTA CHOOSE.
THERE'S NO PLACE LIKE HOME.

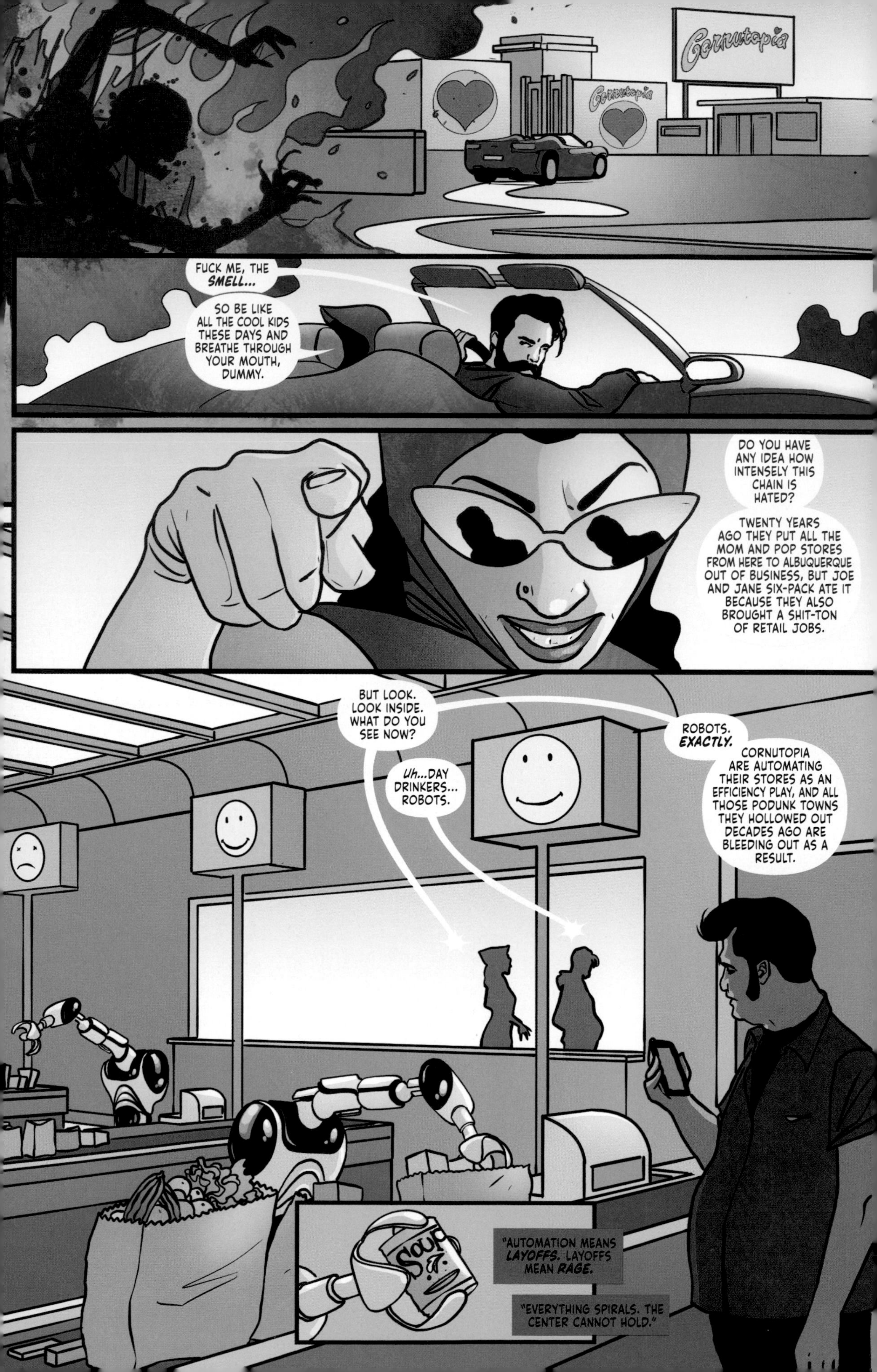
Cornutopia
Cornutopia
FUCK ME, THE SMELL...
SO BE LIKE ALL THE COOL KIDS THESE DAYS AND BREATHE THROUGH YOUR MOUTH, DUMMY.
DO YOU HAVE ANY IDEA HOW INTENSELY THIS CHAIN IS HATED?
TWENTY YEARS AGO THEY PUT ALL THE MOM AND POP STORES FROM HERE TO ALBUQUERQUE OUT OF BUSINESS, BUT JOE AND JANE SIX-PACK ATE IT BECAUSE THEY ALSO BROUGHT A SHIT-TON OF RETAIL JOBS.
BUT LOOK. LOOK INSIDE. WHAT DO YOU SEE NOW?
UH...DAY DRINKERS... ROBOTS.
ROBOTS. EXACTLY.
CORNUTOPIA ARE AUTOMATING THEIR STORES AS AN EFFICIENCY PLAY, AND ALL THOSE PODUNK TOWNS THEY HOLLOWED OUT DECADES AGO ARE BLEEDING OUT AS A RESULT.
SOUP
"AUTOMATION MEANS LAYOFFS. LAYOFFS MEAN RAGE.
"EVERYTHING SPIRALS. THE CENTER CANNOT HOLD."

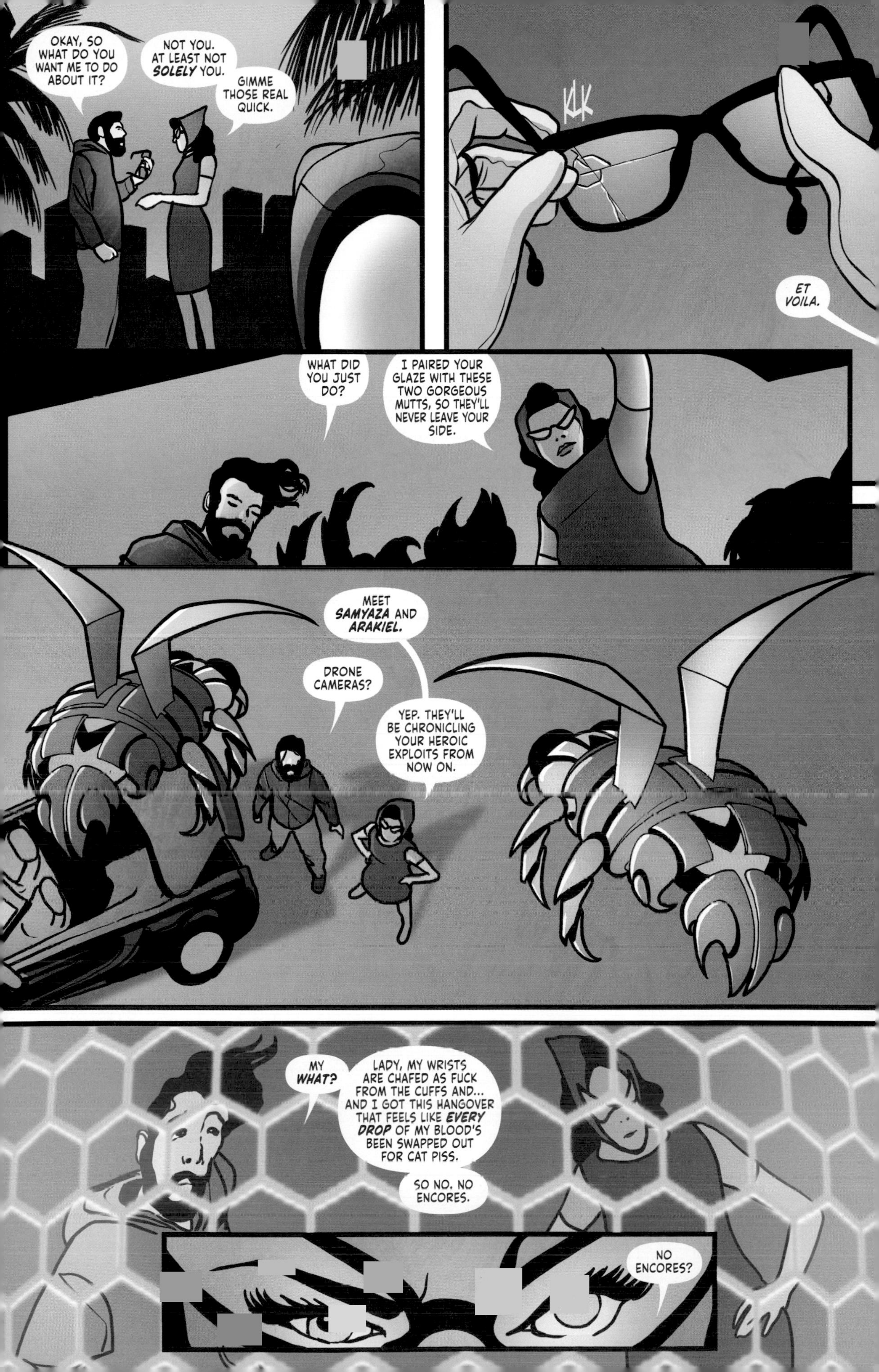
OKAY, SO WHAT DO YOU WANT ME TO DO ABOUT IT?
NOT YOU. AT LEAST NOT **SOLELY** YOU.
GIMME THOSE REAL QUICK.
KLK
ET VOILA.
WHAT DID YOU JUST DO?
I PAIRED YOUR GLAZE WITH THESE TWO GORGEOUS MUTTS, SO THEY'LL NEVER LEAVE YOUR SIDE.
MEET ***SAMYAZA*** AND ***ARAKIEL.***
DRONE CAMERAS?
YEP. THEY'LL BE CHRONICLING YOUR HEROIC EXPLOITS FROM NOW ON.
MY ***WHAT?***
LADY, MY WRISTS ARE CHAFED AS FUCK FROM THE CUFFS AND... AND I GOT THIS HANGOVER THAT FEELS LIKE ***EVERY DROP*** OF MY BLOOD'S BEEN SWAPPED OUT FOR CAT PISS.
SO NO. NO ENCORES.
NO ENCORES?

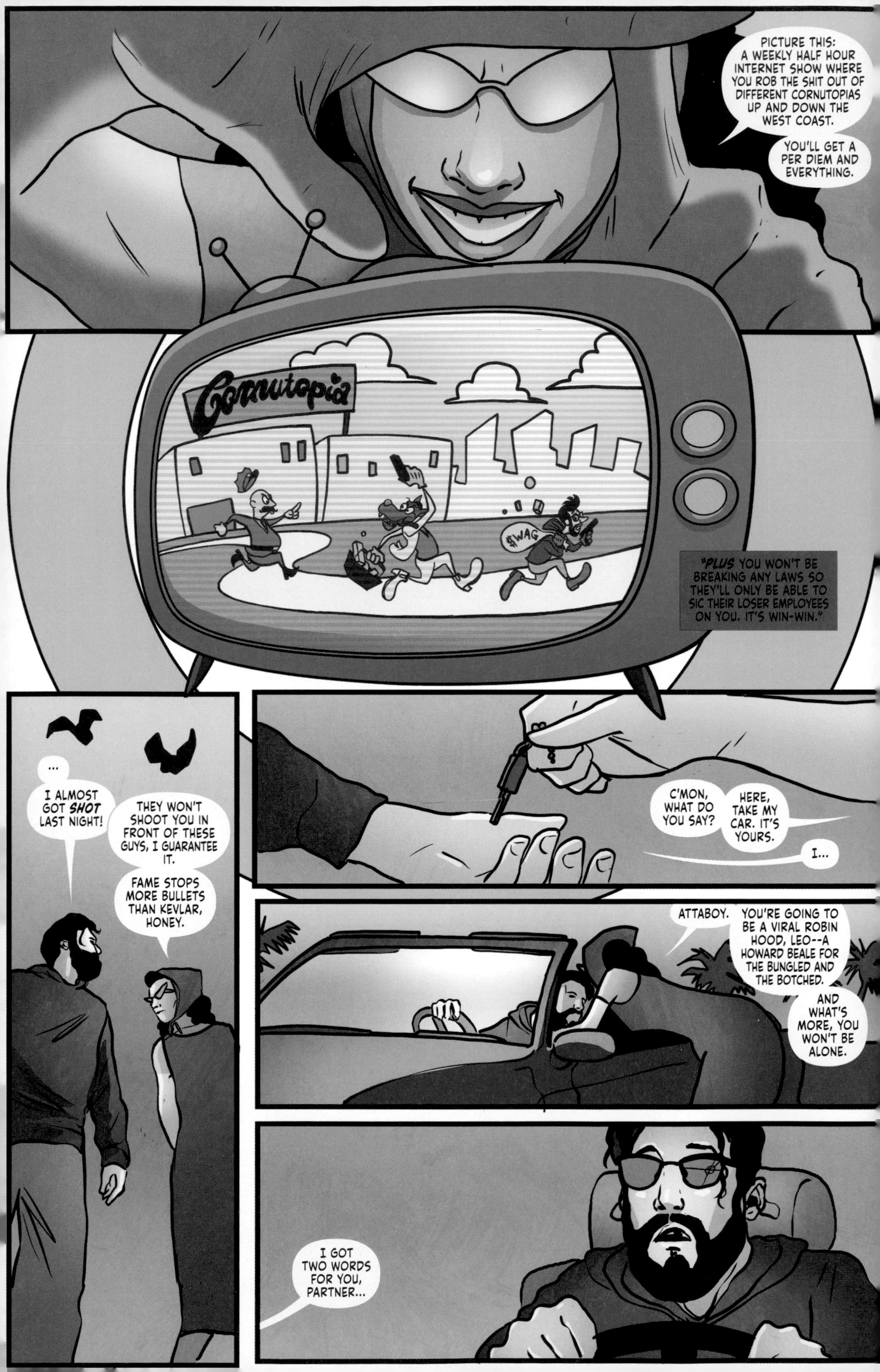

PICTURE THIS: A WEEKLY HALF HOUR INTERNET SHOW WHERE YOU ROB THE SHIT OUT OF DIFFERENT CORNUTOPIAS UP AND DOWN THE WEST COAST.
YOU'LL GET A PER DIEM AND EVERYTHING.
Cornutopia
$WAG
"PLUS YOU WON'T BE BREAKING ANY LAWS SO THEY'LL ONLY BE ABLE TO SIC THEIR LOSER EMPLOYEES ON YOU. IT'S WIN-WIN."
...
I ALMOST GOT SHOT LAST NIGHT!
THEY WON'T SHOOT YOU IN FRONT OF THESE GUYS, I GUARANTEE IT.
FAME STOPS MORE BULLETS THAN KEVLAR, HONEY.
C'MON, WHAT DO YOU SAY?
HERE, TAKE MY CAR. IT'S YOURS.
I...
ATTABOY.
YOU'RE GOING TO BE A VIRAL ROBIN HOOD, LEO--A HOWARD BEALE FOR THE BUNGLED AND THE BOTCHED.
AND WHAT'S MORE, YOU WON'T BE ALONE.
I GOT TWO WORDS FOR YOU, PARTNER...

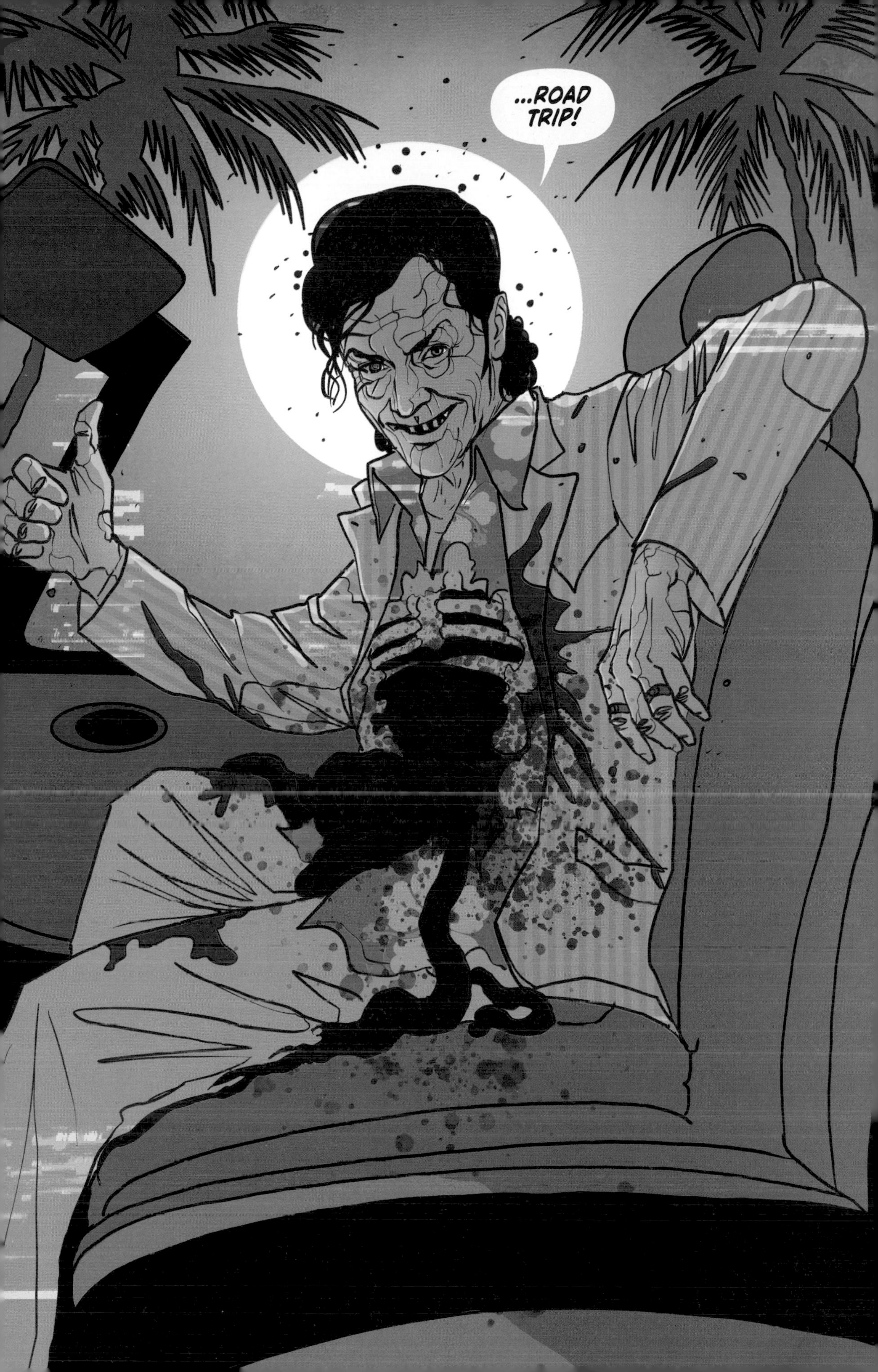
...ROAD TRIP!

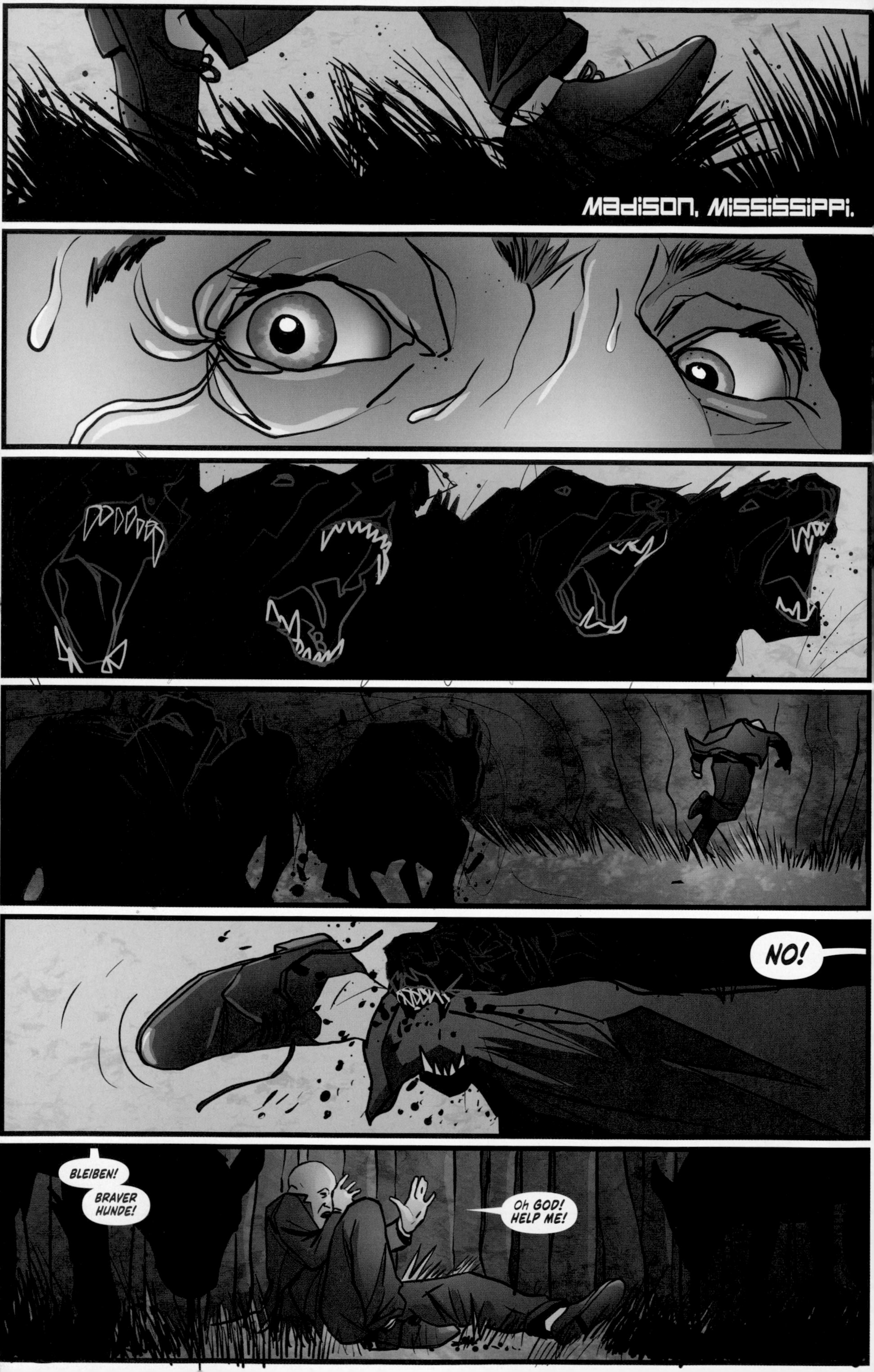
MADISON, MISSISSIPPI.
NO!
BLEIBEN! BRAVER HUNDE!
Oh GOD! HELP ME!

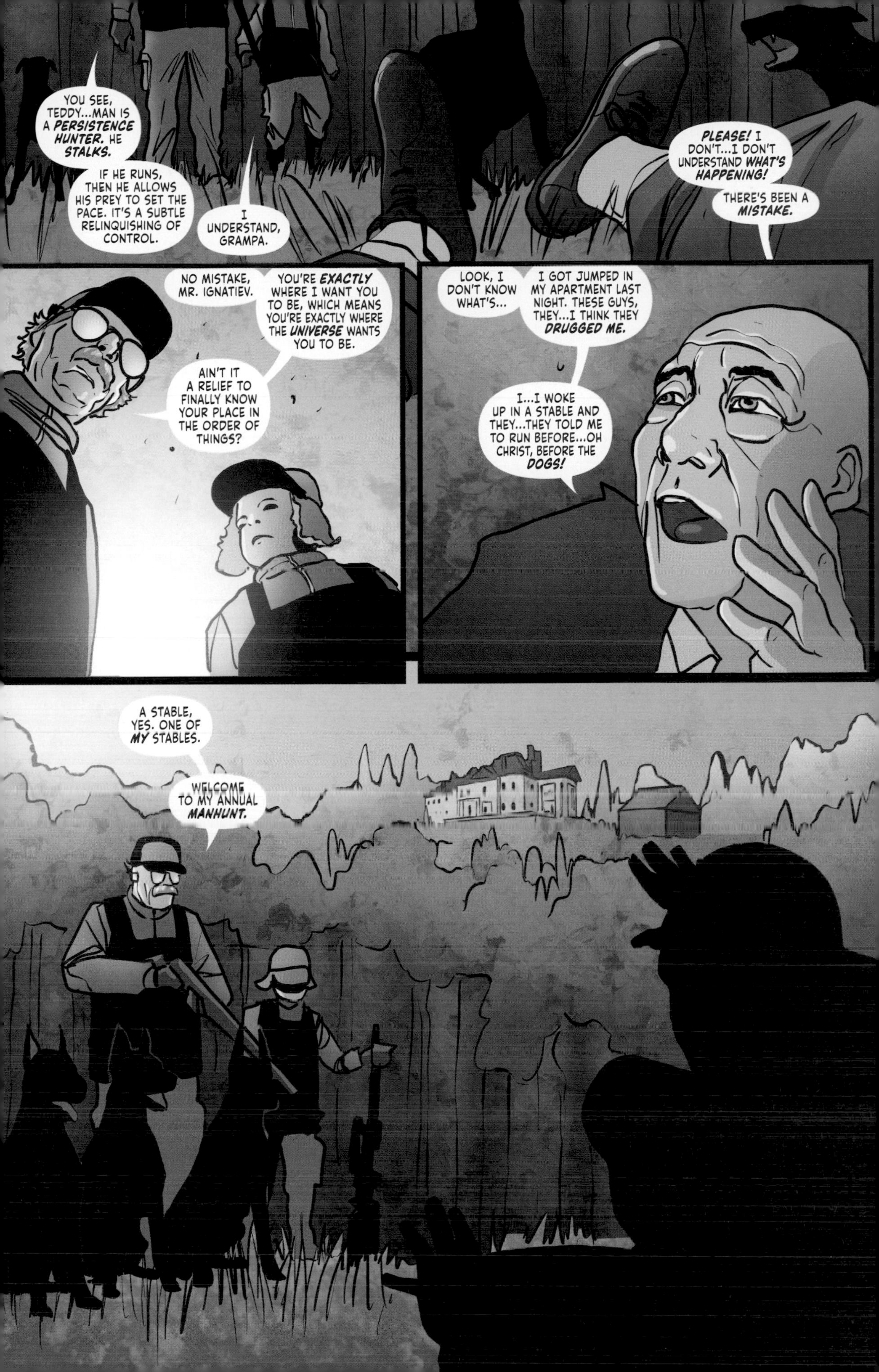
YOU SEE, TEDDY...MAN IS A PERSISTENCE HUNTER. HE STALKS.
IF HE RUNS, THEN HE ALLOWS HIS PREY TO SET THE PACE. IT'S A SUBTLE RELINQUISHING OF CONTROL.
I UNDERSTAND, GRAMPA.
PLEASE! I DON'T...I DON'T UNDERSTAND WHAT'S HAPPENING!
THERE'S BEEN A MISTAKE.
NO MISTAKE, MR. IGNATIEV.
YOU'RE EXACTLY WHERE I WANT YOU TO BE, WHICH MEANS YOU'RE EXACTLY WHERE THE UNIVERSE WANTS YOU TO BE.
AIN'T IT A RELIEF TO FINALLY KNOW YOUR PLACE IN THE ORDER OF THINGS?
LOOK, I DON'T KNOW WHAT'S...
I GOT JUMPED IN MY APARTMENT LAST NIGHT. THESE GUYS, THEY...I THINK THEY DRUGGED ME.
I...I WOKE UP IN A STABLE AND THEY...THEY TOLD ME TO RUN BEFORE...OH CHRIST, BEFORE THE DOGS!
A STABLE, YES. ONE OF MY STABLES.
WELCOME TO MY ANNUAL MANHUNT.

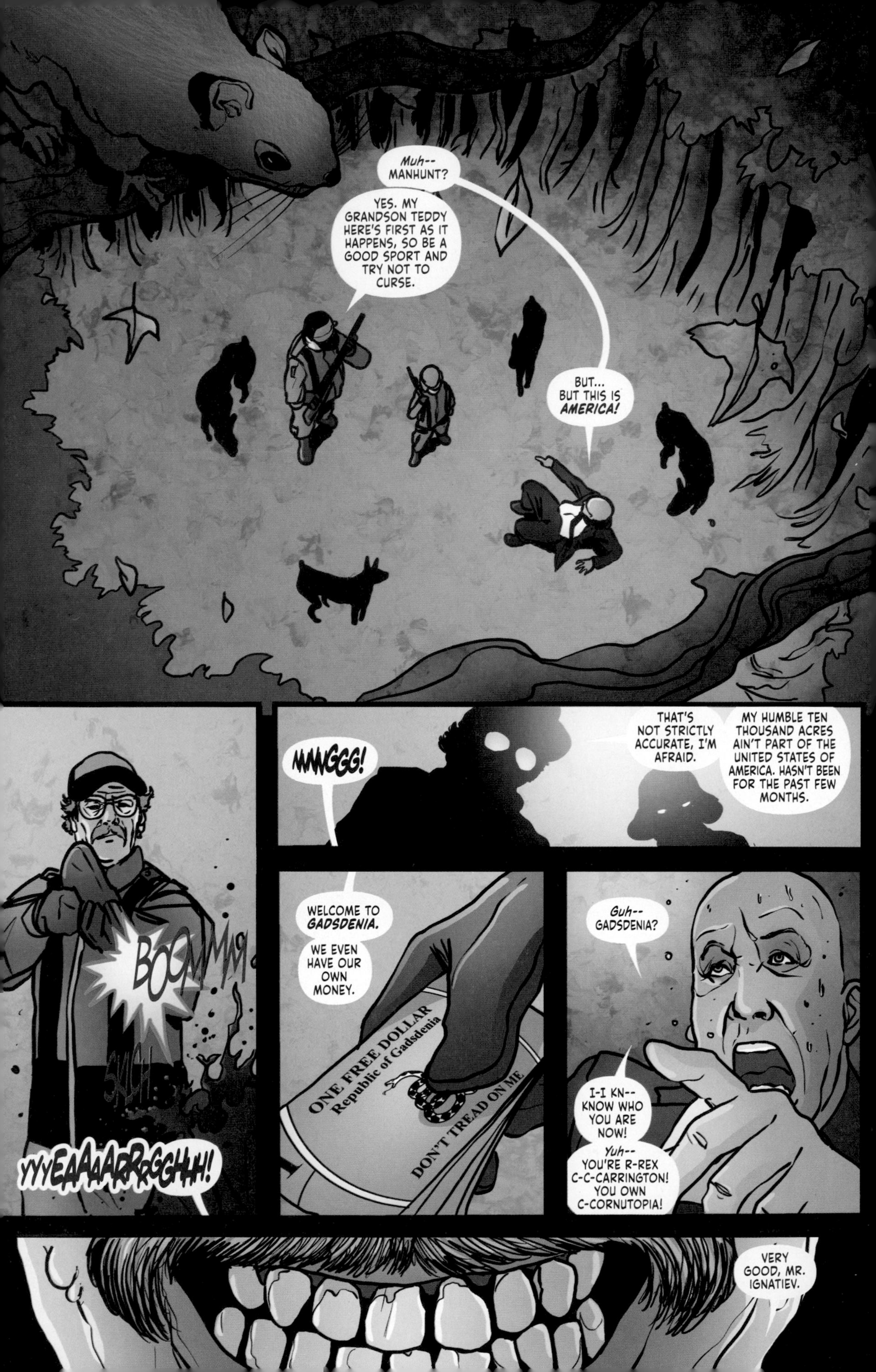

Muh-- MANHUNT?
YES. MY GRANDSON TEDDY HERE'S FIRST AS IT HAPPENS, SO BE A GOOD SPORT AND TRY NOT TO CURSE.
BUT... BUT THIS IS ***AMERICA!***
MMNGGG!
THAT'S NOT STRICTLY ACCURATE, I'M AFRAID.
MY HUMBLE TEN THOUSAND ACRES AIN'T PART OF THE UNITED STATES OF AMERICA. HASN'T BEEN FOR THE PAST FEW MONTHS.
BOOMMM
YYYEAAAARRRGGHHH!
WELCOME TO ***GADSDENIA.***
WE EVEN HAVE OUR OWN MONEY.
ONE FREE DOLLAR
Republic of Gadsdenia
DON'T TREAD ON ME
Guh-- GADSDENIA?
I-I KN-- KNOW WHO YOU ARE NOW!
Yuh-- YOU'RE R-REX C-C-CARRINGTON! YOU OWN C-CORNUTOPIA!
VERY GOOD, MR. IGNATIEV.

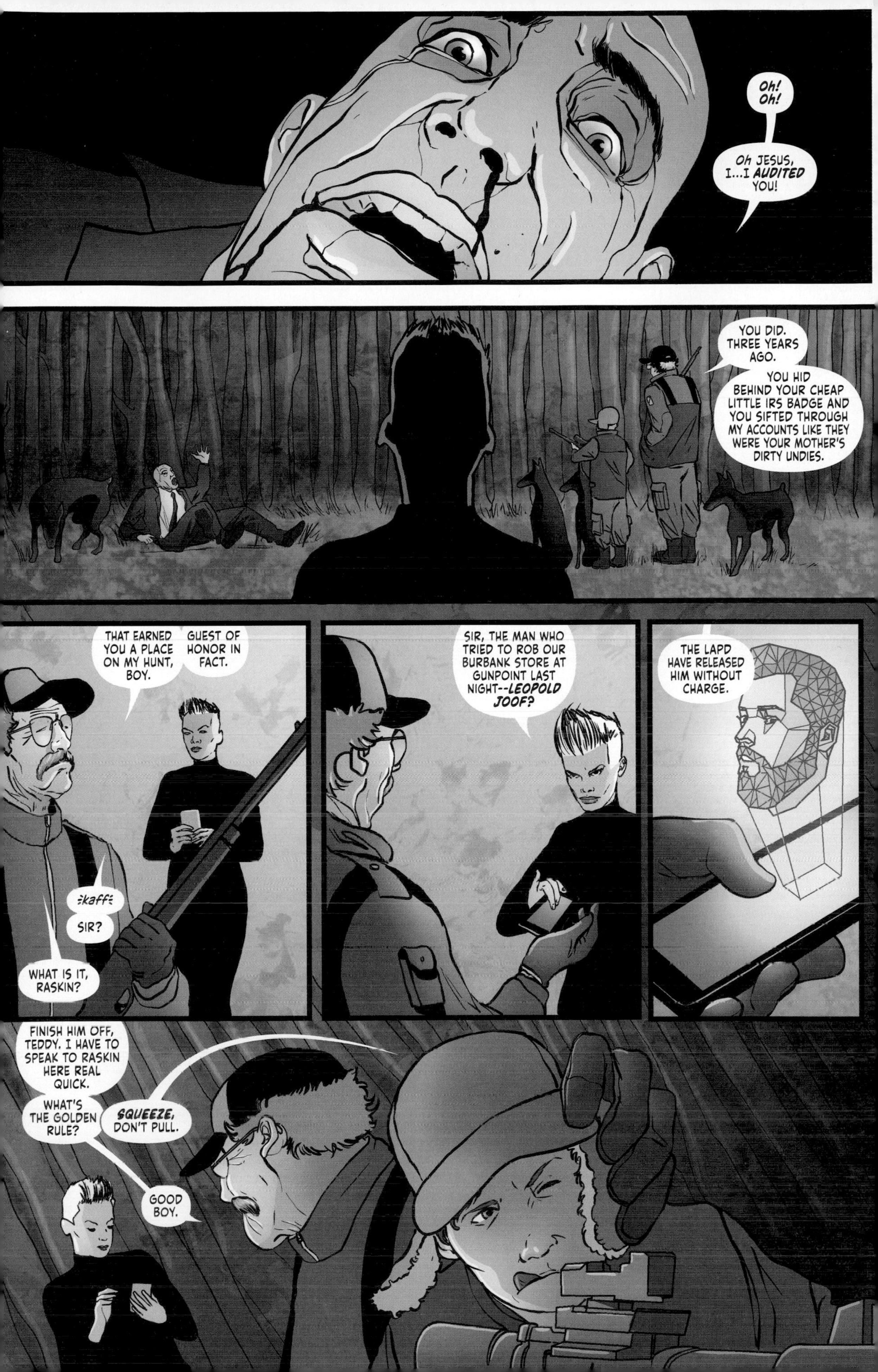
Oh! Oh!
Oh JESUS, I...I AUDITED YOU!
YOU DID. THREE YEARS AGO.
YOU HID BEHIND YOUR CHEAP LITTLE IRS BADGE AND YOU SIFTED THROUGH MY ACCOUNTS LIKE THEY WERE YOUR MOTHER'S DIRTY UNDIES.
THAT EARNED YOU A PLACE ON MY HUNT, BOY.
GUEST OF HONOR IN FACT.
:kaff:
SIR?
WHAT IS IT, RASKIN?
SIR, THE MAN WHO TRIED TO ROB OUR BURBANK STORE AT GUNPOINT LAST NIGHT--LEOPOLD JOOF?
THE LAPD HAVE RELEASED HIM WITHOUT CHARGE.
FINISH HIM OFF, TEDDY. I HAVE TO SPEAK TO RASKIN HERE REAL QUICK.
WHAT'S THE GOLDEN RULE?
SQUEEZE, DON'T PULL.
GOOD BOY.

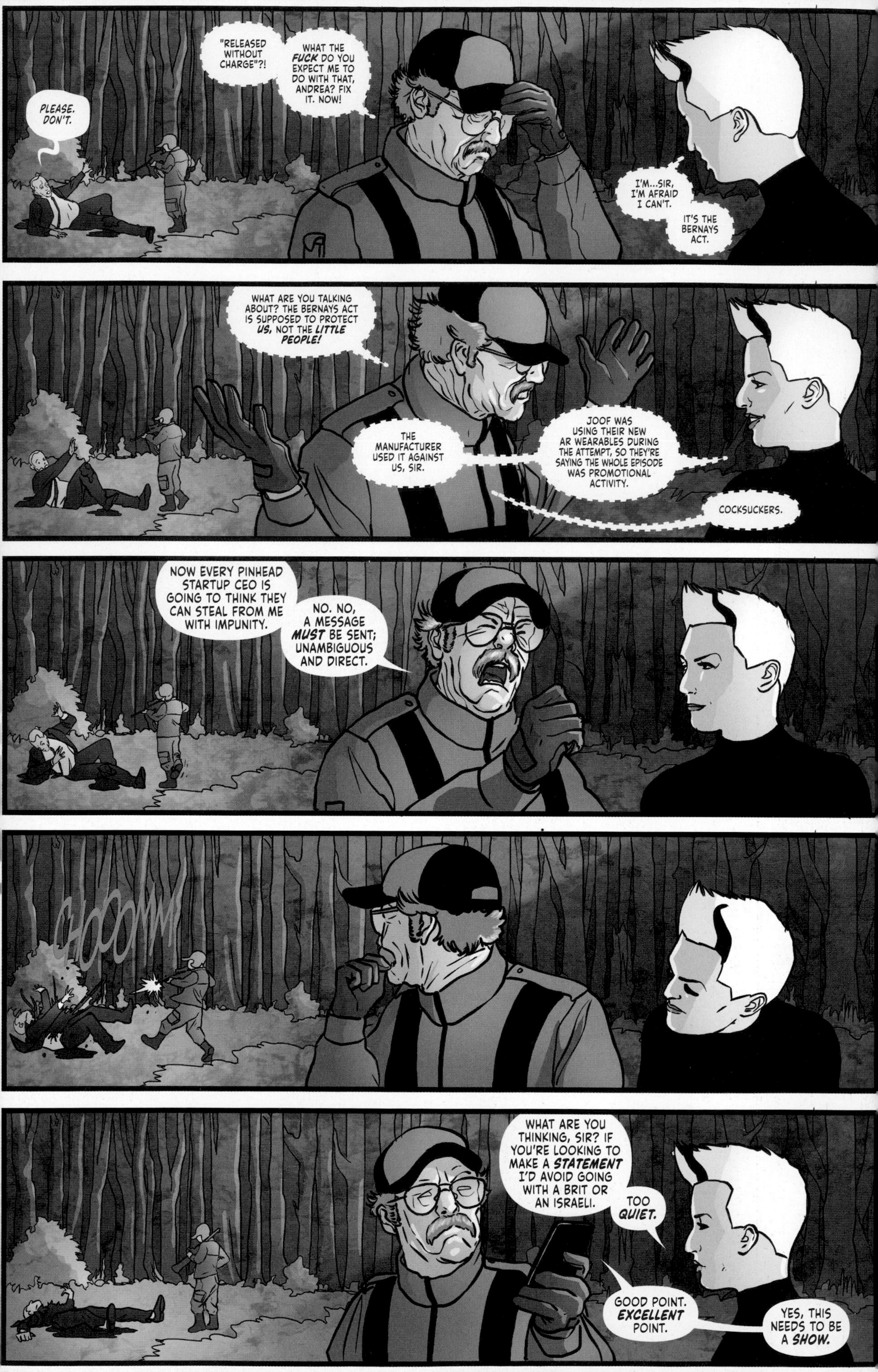
PLEASE. DON'T.
"RELEASED WITHOUT CHARGE"?!
WHAT THE FUCK DO YOU EXPECT ME TO DO WITH THAT, ANDREA? FIX IT. NOW!
I'M...SIR, I'M AFRAID I CAN'T.
IT'S THE BERNAYS ACT.
WHAT ARE YOU TALKING ABOUT? THE BERNAYS ACT IS SUPPOSED TO PROTECT US, NOT THE LITTLE PEOPLE!
THE MANUFACTURER USED IT AGAINST US, SIR.
JOOF WAS USING THEIR NEW AR WEARABLES DURING THE ATTEMPT, SO THEY'RE SAYING THE WHOLE EPISODE WAS PROMOTIONAL ACTIVITY.
COCKSUCKERS.
NOW EVERY PINHEAD STARTUP CEO IS GOING TO THINK THEY CAN STEAL FROM ME WITH IMPUNITY.
NO. NO, A MESSAGE MUST BE SENT; UNAMBIGUOUS AND DIRECT.
CHOOOMM
WHAT ARE YOU THINKING, SIR? IF YOU'RE LOOKING TO MAKE A STATEMENT I'D AVOID GOING WITH A BRIT OR AN ISRAELI.
TOO QUIET.
GOOD POINT. EXCELLENT POINT.
YES, THIS NEEDS TO BE A SHOW.

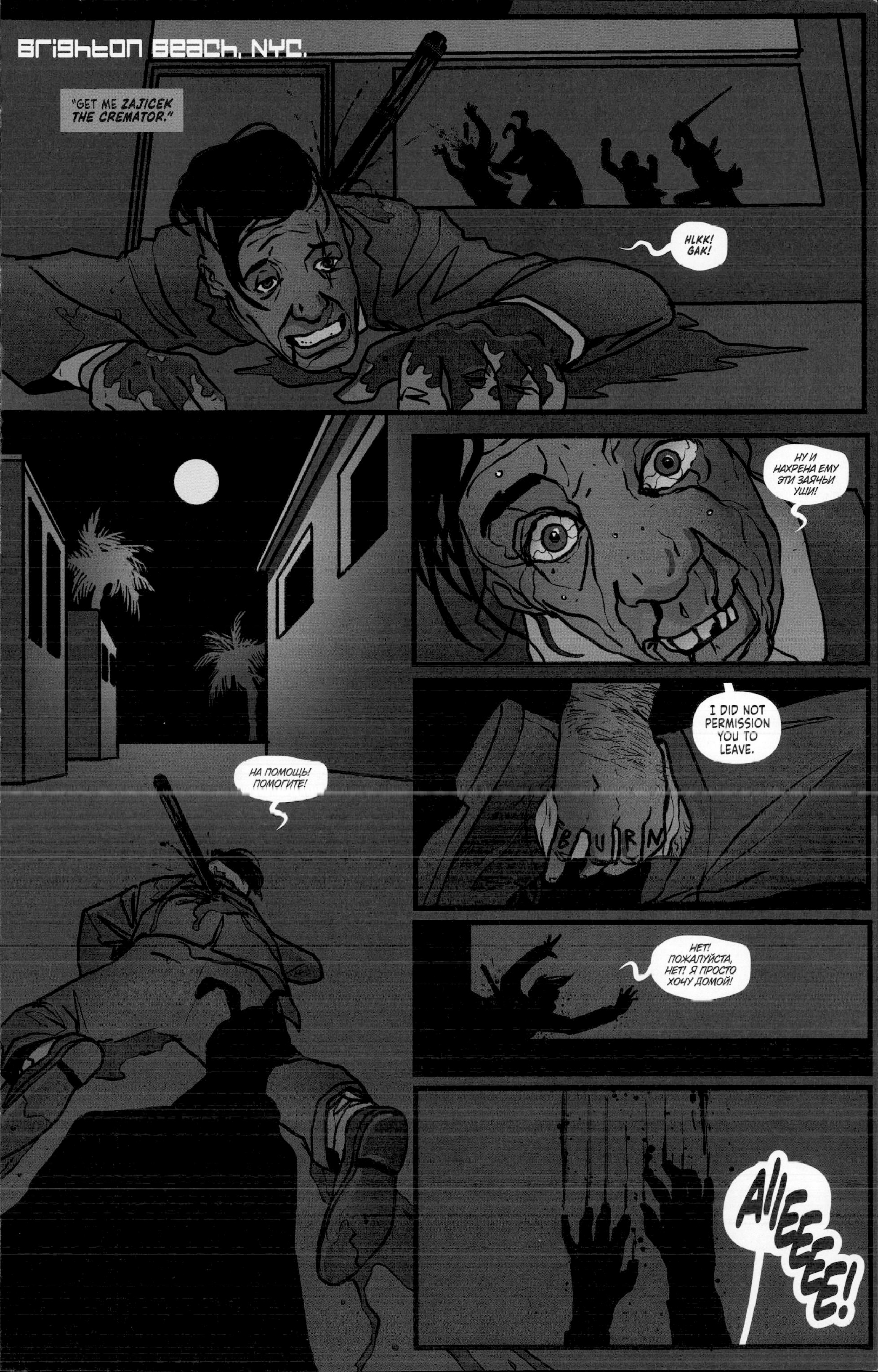
BRIGHTON BEACH, NYC.
"GET ME ZAJICEK THE CREMATOR."
HLKK! GAK!
НА ПОМОЩЬ! ПОМОГИТЕ!
НУ И НАХРЕНА ЕМУ ЭТИ ЗАЯЧЬИ УШИ!
I DID NOT PERMISSION YOU TO LEAVE.
BURN
НЕТ! ПОЖАЛУЙСТА, НЕТ! Я ПРОСТО ХОЧУ ДОМОЙ!
AIIEEEEE!

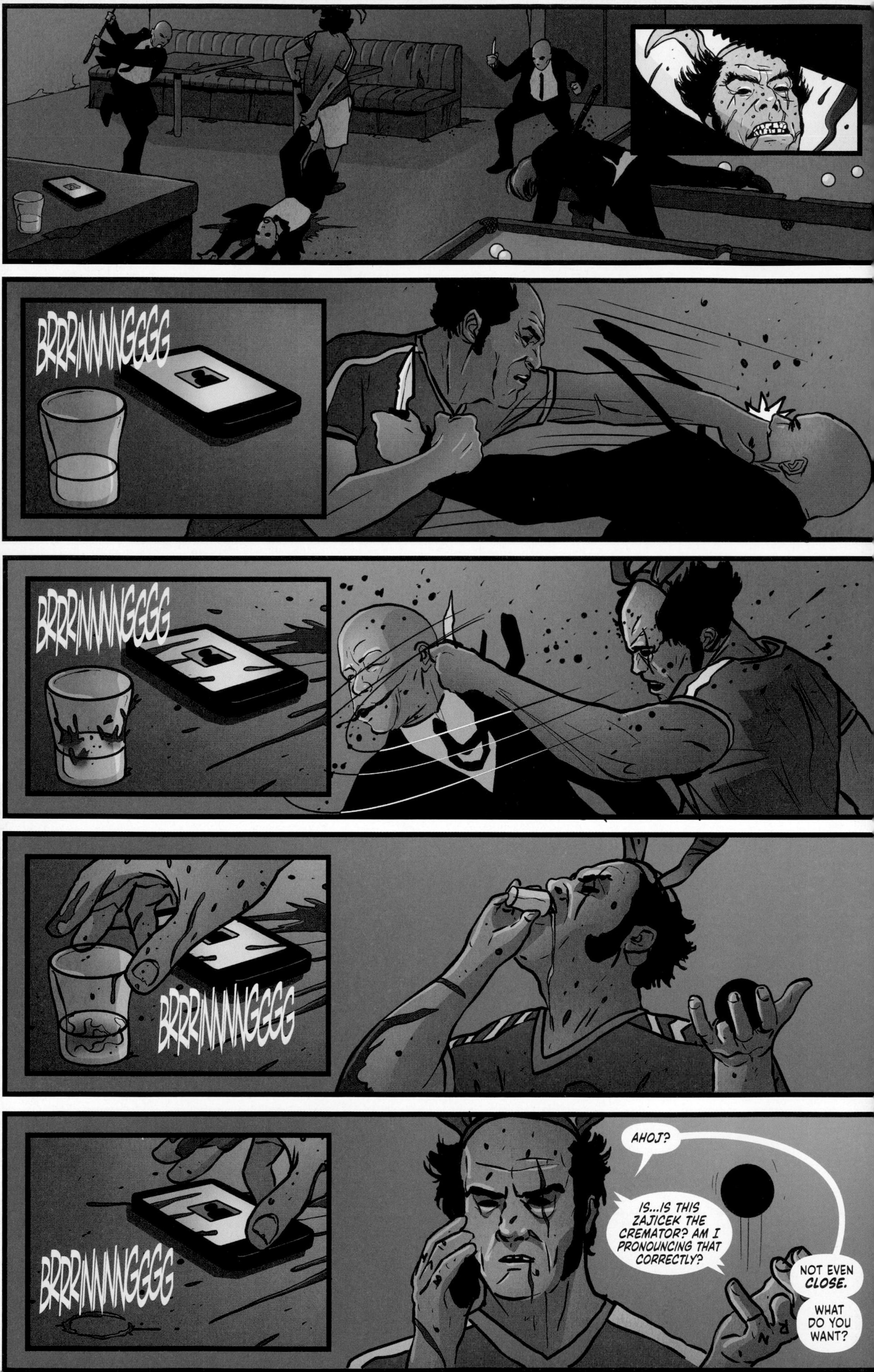
BRRRINNNNGGGG
BRRRINNNNGGGG
BRRRINNNNGGGG
BRRRINNNNGGGG
AHOJ?
IS...IS THIS ZAJICEK THE CREMATOR? AM I PRONOUNCING THAT CORRECTLY?
NOT EVEN CLOSE.
WHAT DO YOU WANT?

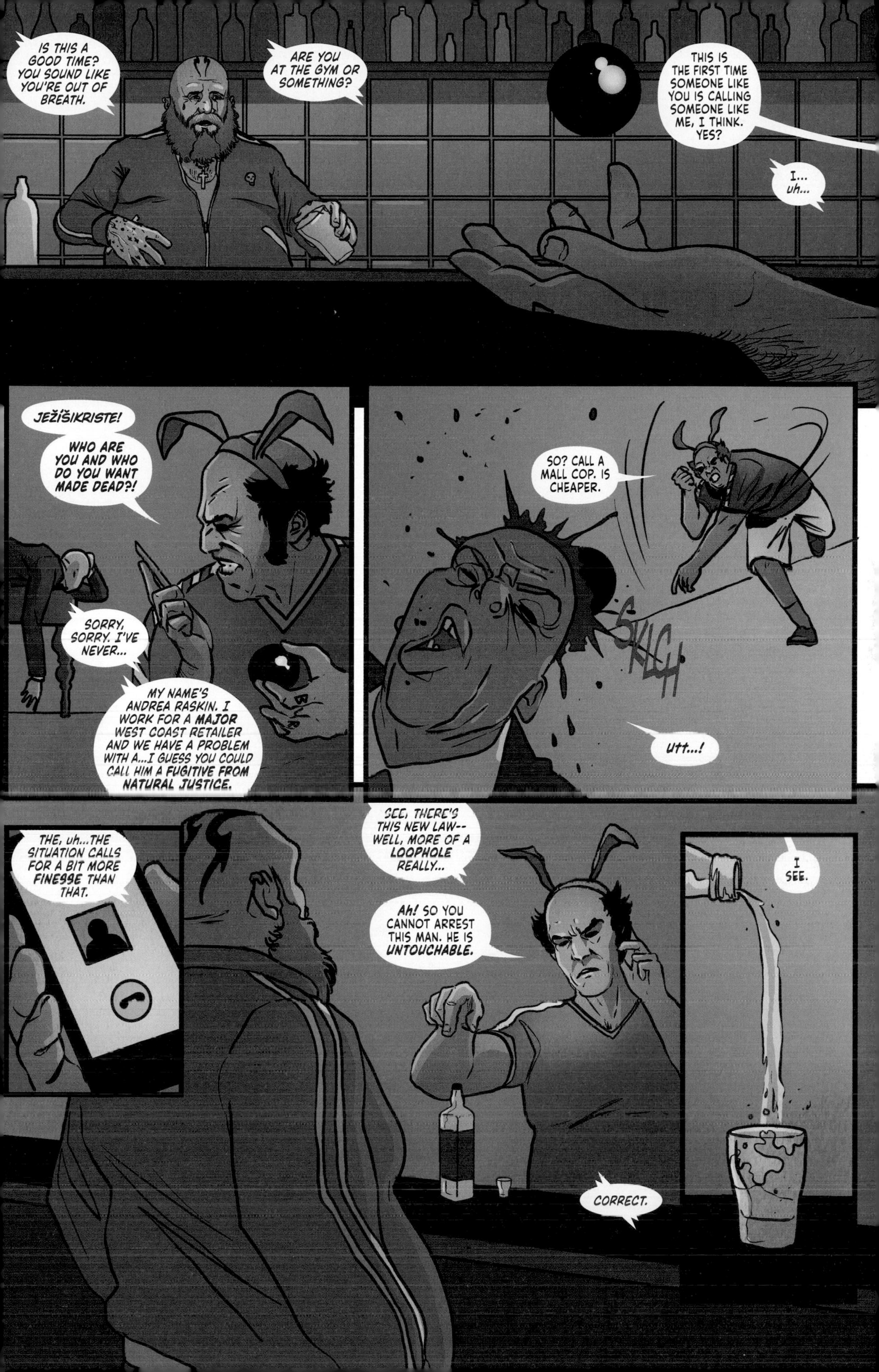
IS THIS A GOOD TIME? YOU SOUND LIKE YOU'RE OUT OF BREATH.
ARE YOU AT THE GYM OR SOMETHING?
THIS IS THE FIRST TIME SOMEONE LIKE YOU IS CALLING SOMEONE LIKE ME, I THINK. YES?
I... uh...
JEŽÍŠIKRISTE!
WHO ARE YOU AND WHO DO YOU WANT MADE DEAD?!
SORRY, SORRY. I'VE NEVER...
MY NAME'S ANDREA RASKIN. I WORK FOR A MAJOR WEST COAST RETAILER AND WE HAVE A PROBLEM WITH A...I GUESS YOU COULD CALL HIM A FUGITIVE FROM NATURAL JUSTICE.
SO? CALL A MALL COP. IS CHEAPER.
SKLCH
Utt...!
THE, uh...THE SITUATION CALLS FOR A BIT MORE FINESSE THAN THAT.
SEE, THERE'S THIS NEW LAW--WELL, MORE OF A LOOPHOLE REALLY...
Ah! SO YOU CANNOT ARREST THIS MAN. HE IS UNTOUCHABLE.
CORRECT.
I SEE.

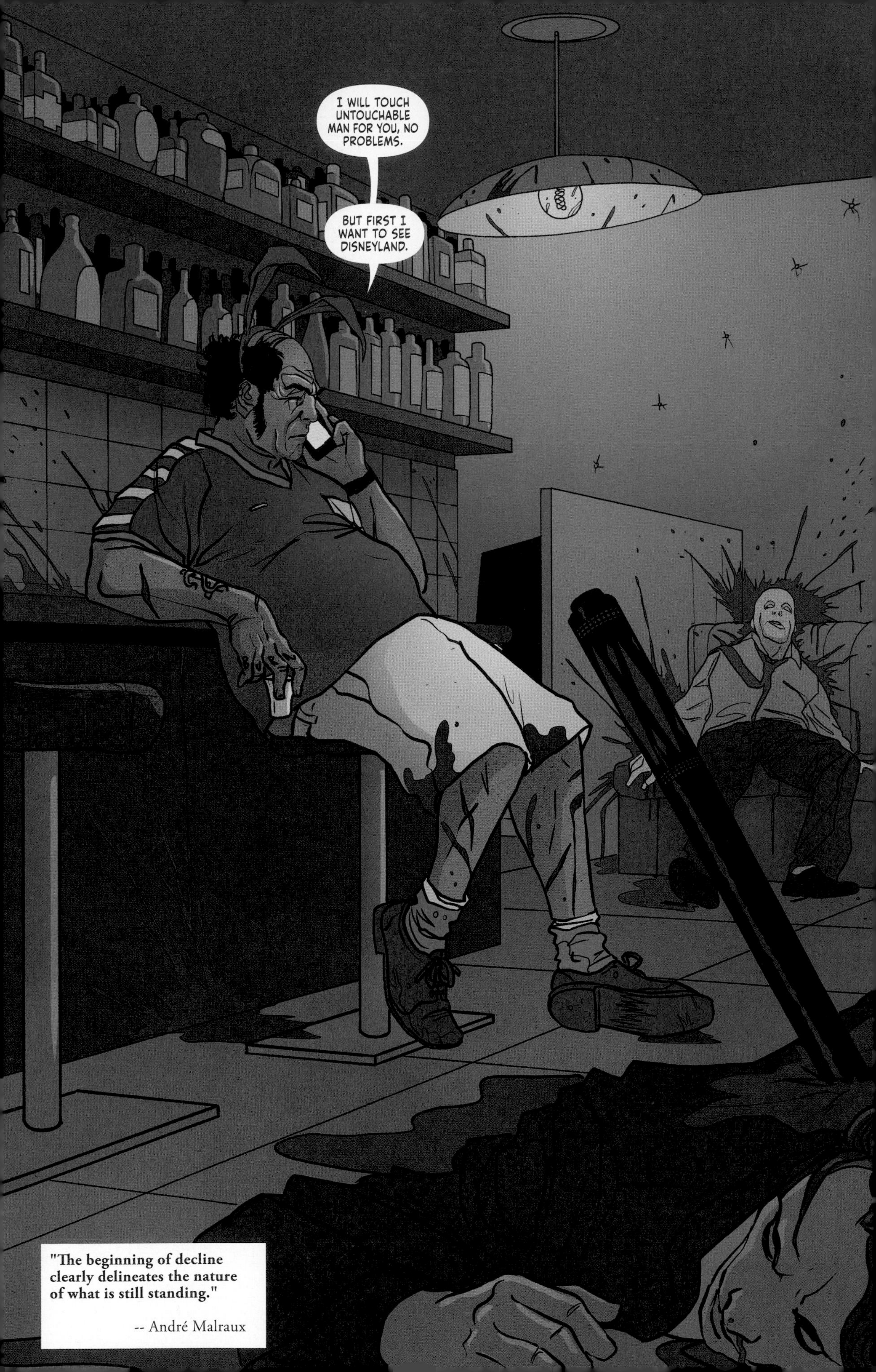
I WILL TOUCH UNTOUCHABLE MAN FOR YOU, NO PROBLEMS.
BUT FIRST I WANT TO SEE DISNEYLAND.
"The beginning of decline clearly delineates the nature of what is still standing."
-- André Malraux

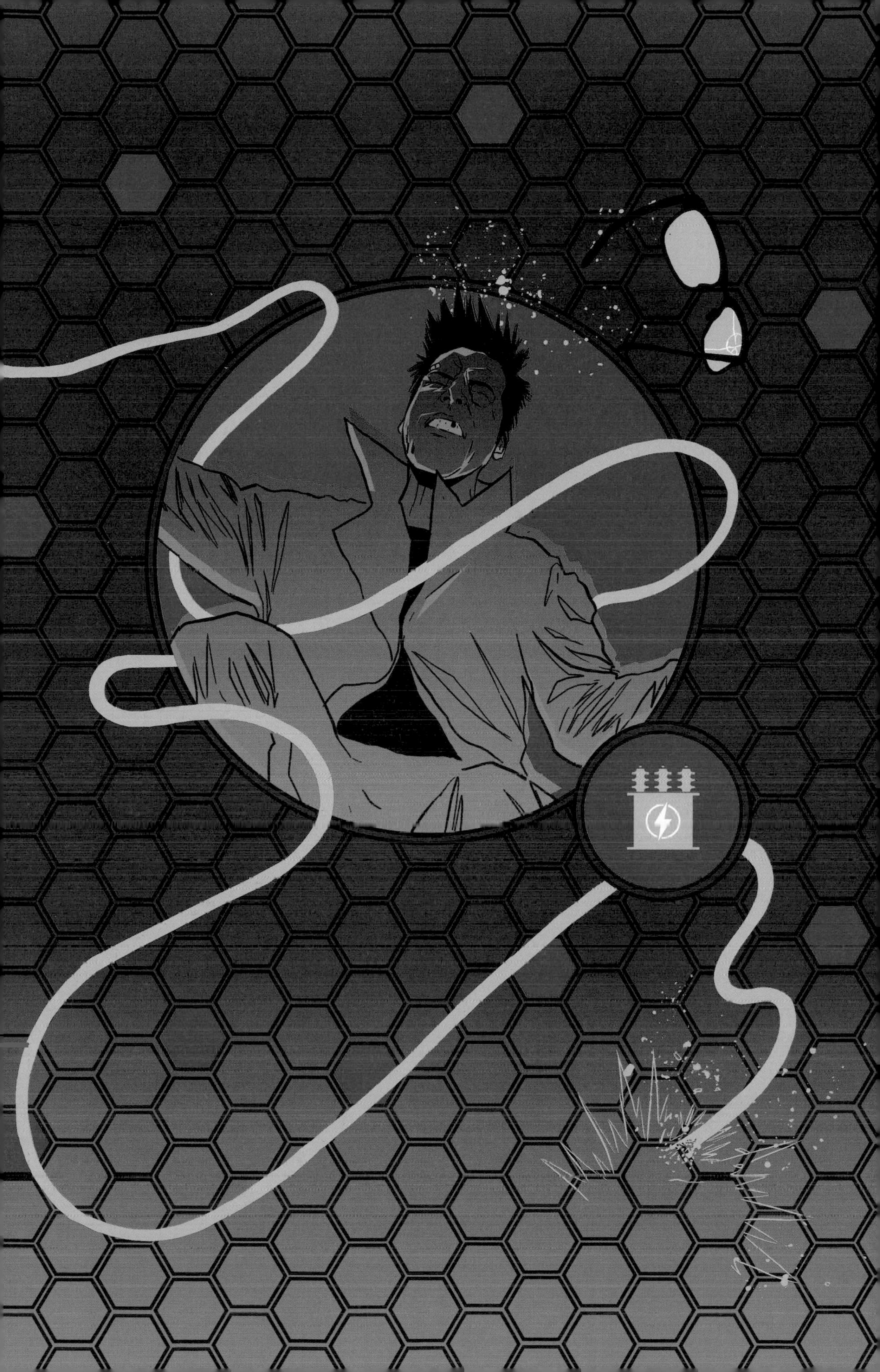

FOUR

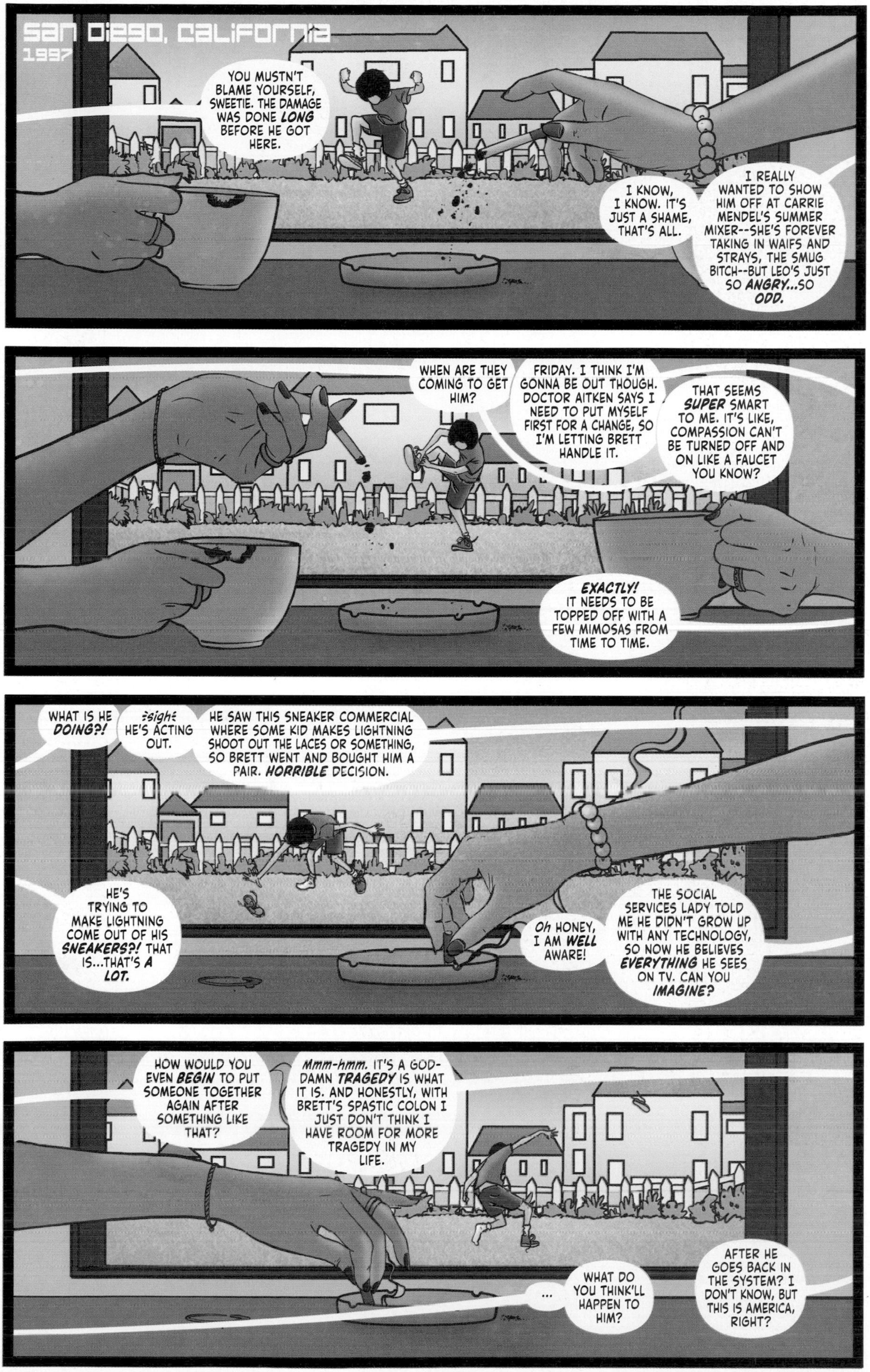
SAN DIEGO, CALIFORNIA
1997
YOU MUSTN'T BLAME YOURSELF, SWEETIE. THE DAMAGE WAS DONE LONG BEFORE HE GOT HERE.
I KNOW, I KNOW. IT'S JUST A SHAME, THAT'S ALL.
I REALLY WANTED TO SHOW HIM OFF AT CARRIE MENDEL'S SUMMER MIXER--SHE'S FOREVER TAKING IN WAIFS AND STRAYS, THE SMUG BITCH--BUT LEO'S JUST SO ANGRY...SO ODD.
WHEN ARE THEY COMING TO GET HIM?
FRIDAY. I THINK I'M GONNA BE OUT THOUGH. DOCTOR AITKEN SAYS I NEED TO PUT MYSELF FIRST FOR A CHANGE, SO I'M LETTING BRETT HANDLE IT.
THAT SEEMS SUPER SMART TO ME. IT'S LIKE, COMPASSION CAN'T BE TURNED OFF AND ON LIKE A FAUCET YOU KNOW?
EXACTLY! IT NEEDS TO BE TOPPED OFF WITH A FEW MIMOSAS FROM TIME TO TIME.
WHAT IS HE DOING?!
sigh HE'S ACTING OUT.
HE SAW THIS SNEAKER COMMERCIAL WHERE SOME KID MAKES LIGHTNING SHOOT OUT THE LACES OR SOMETHING, SO BRETT WENT AND BOUGHT HIM A PAIR. HORRIBLE DECISION.
HE'S TRYING TO MAKE LIGHTNING COME OUT OF HIS SNEAKERS?! THAT IS...THAT'S A LOT.
Oh HONEY, I AM WELL AWARE!
THE SOCIAL SERVICES LADY TOLD ME HE DIDN'T GROW UP WITH ANY TECHNOLOGY, SO NOW HE BELIEVES EVERYTHING HE SEES ON TV. CAN YOU IMAGINE?
HOW WOULD YOU EVEN BEGIN TO PUT SOMEONE TOGETHER AGAIN AFTER SOMETHING LIKE THAT?
Mmm-hmm. IT'S A GOD-DAMN TRAGEDY IS WHAT IT IS. AND HONESTLY, WITH BRETT'S SPASTIC COLON I JUST DON'T THINK I HAVE ROOM FOR MORE TRAGEDY IN MY LIFE.
...
WHAT DO YOU THINK'LL HAPPEN TO HIM?
AFTER HE GOES BACK IN THE SYSTEM? I DON'T KNOW, BUT THIS IS AMERICA, RIGHT?

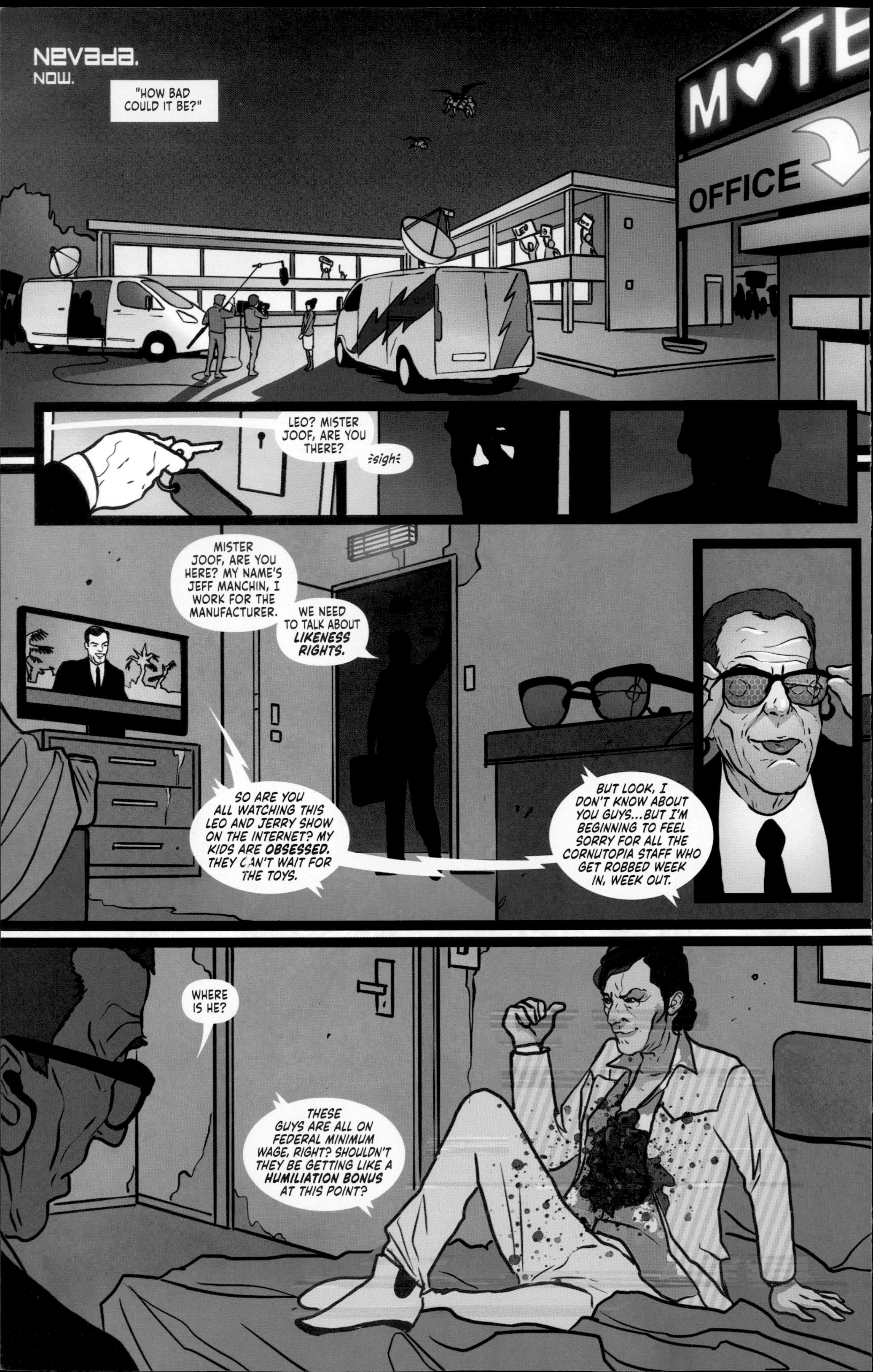
NEVADA.
NOW.
"HOW BAD COULD IT BE?"
MOTE
OFFICE
LEO? MISTER JOOF, ARE YOU THERE?
sigh
MISTER JOOF, ARE YOU HERE? MY NAME'S JEFF MANCHIN, I WORK FOR THE MANUFACTURER.
WE NEED TO TALK ABOUT LIKENESS RIGHTS.
SO ARE YOU ALL WATCHING THIS LEO AND JERRY SHOW ON THE INTERNET? MY KIDS ARE OBSESSED. THEY CAN'T WAIT FOR THE TOYS.
BUT LOOK, I DON'T KNOW ABOUT YOU GUYS...BUT I'M BEGINNING TO FEEL SORRY FOR ALL THE CORNUTOPIA STAFF WHO GET ROBBED WEEK IN, WEEK OUT.
WHERE IS HE?
THESE GUYS ARE ALL ON FEDERAL MINIMUM WAGE, RIGHT? SHOULDN'T THEY BE GETTING LIKE A HUMILIATION BONUS AT THIS POINT?

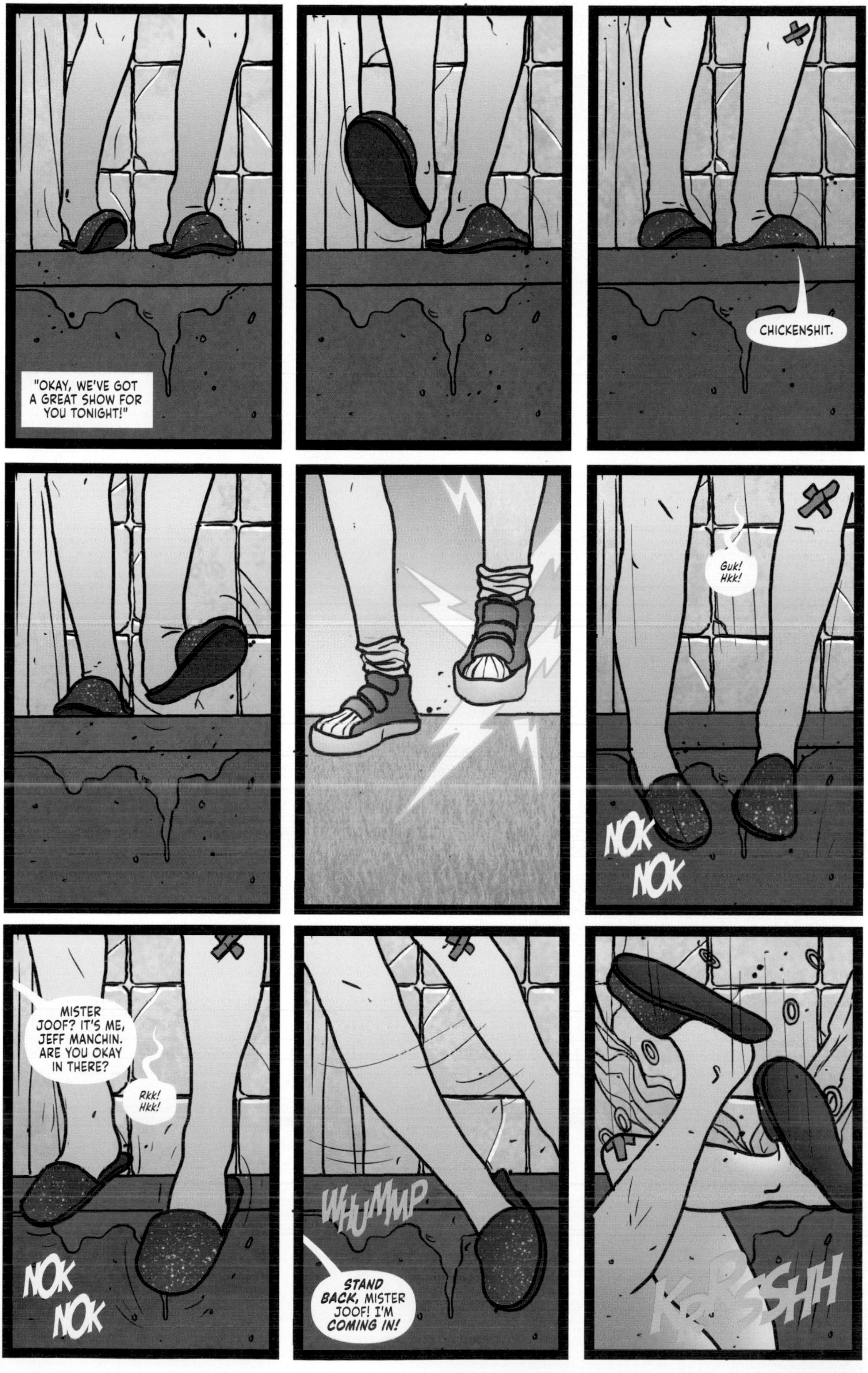
"OKAY, WE'VE GOT A GREAT SHOW FOR YOU TONIGHT!"
CHICKENSHIT.
GUK! HKK!
NOK NOK
MISTER JOOF? IT'S ME, JEFF MANCHIN. ARE YOU OKAY IN THERE?
RKK! HKK!
NOK NOK
WHUMMP
STAND BACK, MISTER JOOF! I'M COMING IN!
KRSSHH

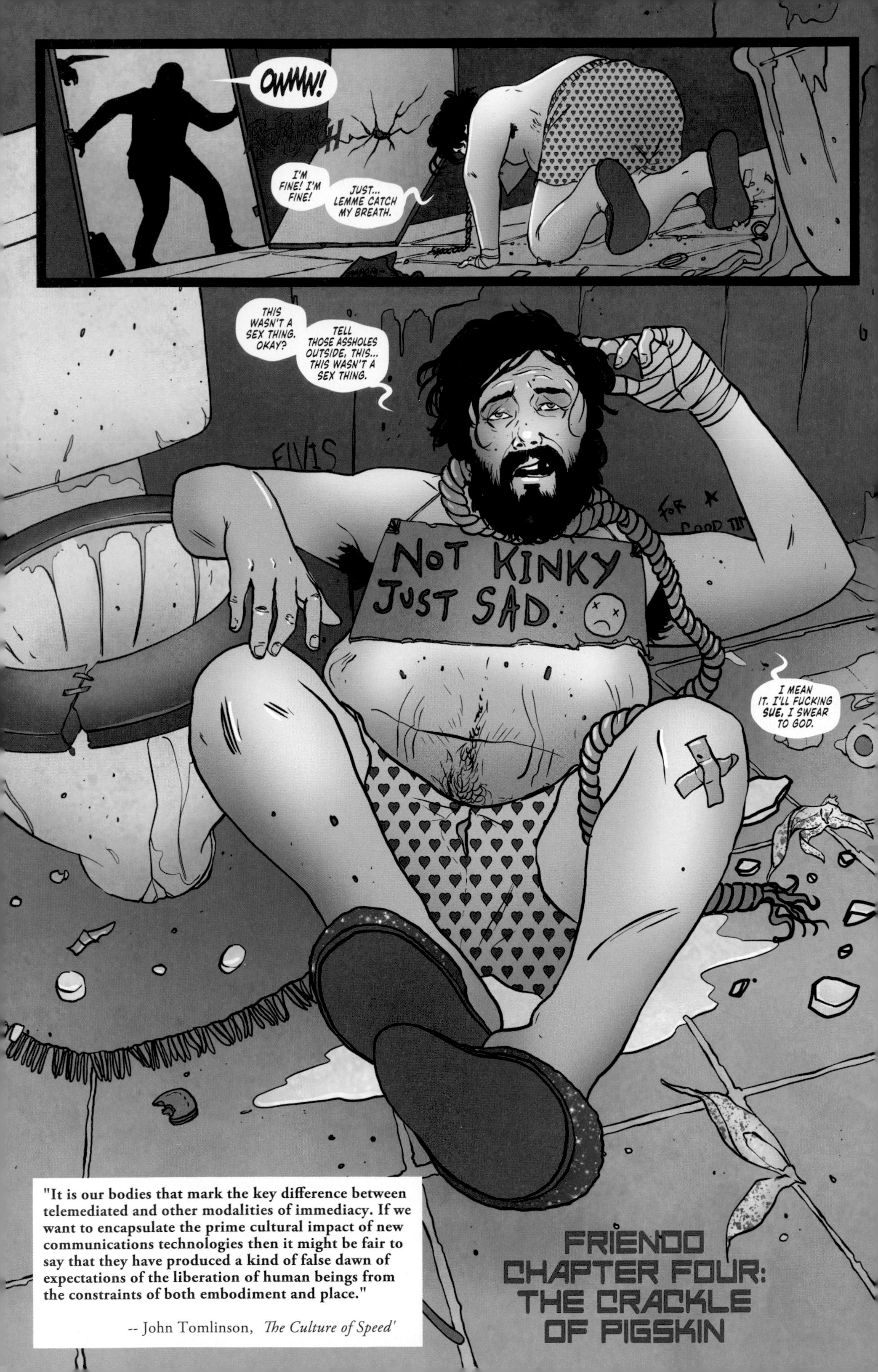
OWWW!
I'M FINE! I'M FINE!
JUST... LEMME CATCH MY BREATH.
THIS WASN'T A SEX THING. OKAY?
TELL THOSE ASSHOLES OUTSIDE, THIS... THIS WASN'T A SEX THING.
ELVIS
NOT KINKY JUST SAD.
I MEAN IT. I'LL FUCKING SUE, I SWEAR TO GOD.

"It is our bodies that mark the key difference between telemediated and other modalities of immediacy. If we want to encapsulate the prime cultural impact of new communications technologies then it might be fair to say that they have produced a kind of false dawn of expectations of the liberation of human beings from the constraints of both embodiment and place."

-- John Tomlinson, *The Culture of Speed'*

FRIENDO CHAPTER FOUR: THE CRACKLE OF PIGSKIN

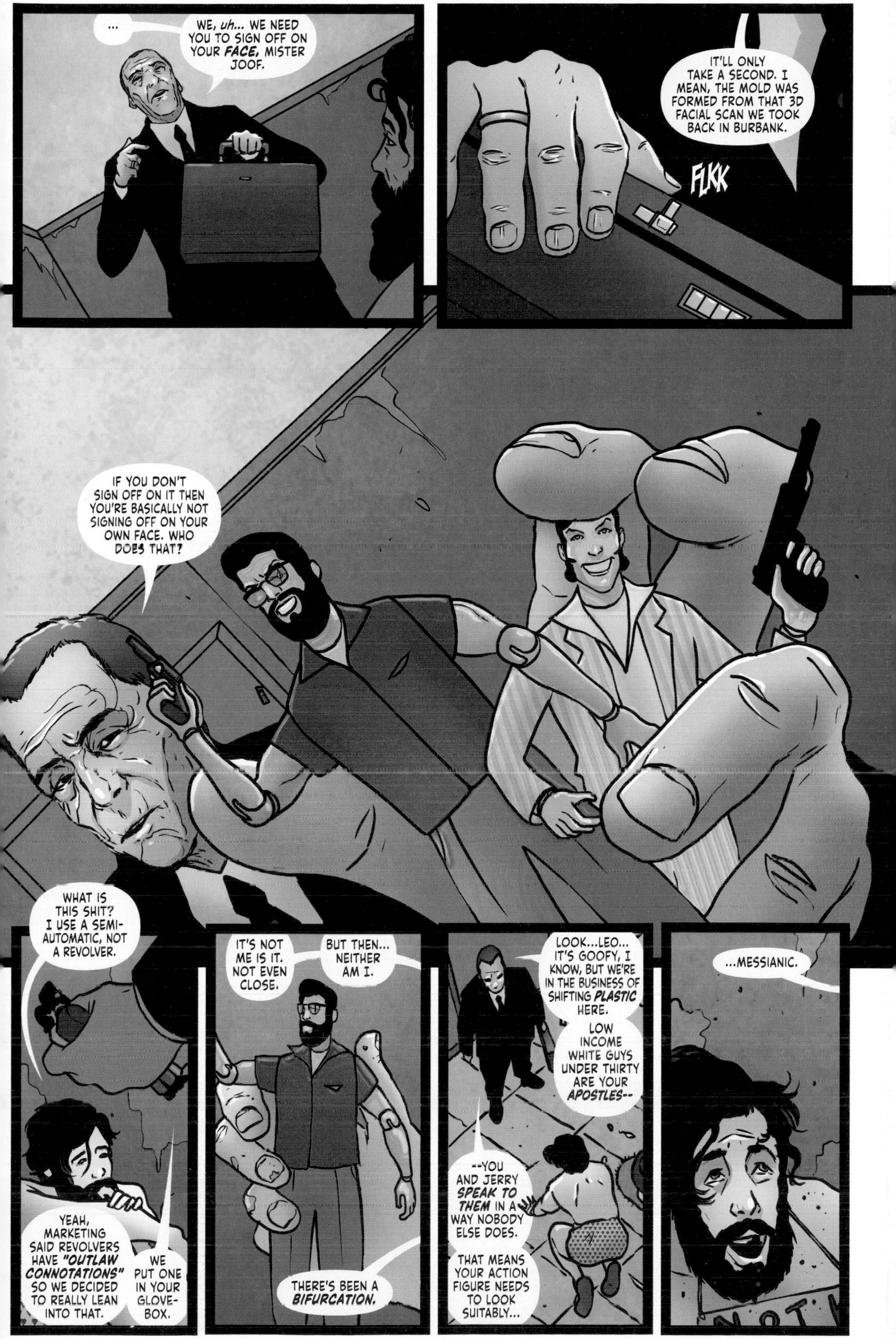
...
WE, *uh*... WE NEED YOU TO SIGN OFF ON YOUR ***FACE,*** MISTER JOOF.
IT'LL ONLY TAKE A SECOND. I MEAN, THE MOLD WAS FORMED FROM THAT 3D FACIAL SCAN WE TOOK BACK IN BURBANK.
FLKK
IF YOU DON'T SIGN OFF ON IT THEN YOU'RE BASICALLY NOT SIGNING OFF ON YOUR OWN FACE. WHO DOES THAT?
WHAT IS THIS SHIT? I USE A SEMI-AUTOMATIC, NOT A REVOLVER.
YEAH, MARKETING SAID REVOLVERS HAVE ***"OUTLAW CONNOTATIONS"*** SO WE DECIDED TO REALLY LEAN INTO THAT.
WE PUT ONE IN YOUR GLOVE-BOX.
IT'S NOT ME IS IT. NOT EVEN CLOSE.
BUT THEN... NEITHER AM I.
THERE'S BEEN A ***BIFURCATION.***
LOOK...LEO... IT'S GOOFY, I KNOW, BUT WE'RE IN THE BUSINESS OF SHIFTING ***PLASTIC*** HERE.
LOW INCOME WHITE GUYS UNDER THIRTY ARE YOUR ***APOSTLES--***
--YOU AND JERRY ***SPEAK TO THEM*** IN A WAY NOBODY ELSE DOES.
THAT MEANS YOUR ACTION FIGURE NEEDS TO LOOK SUITABLY...
...MESSIANIC.

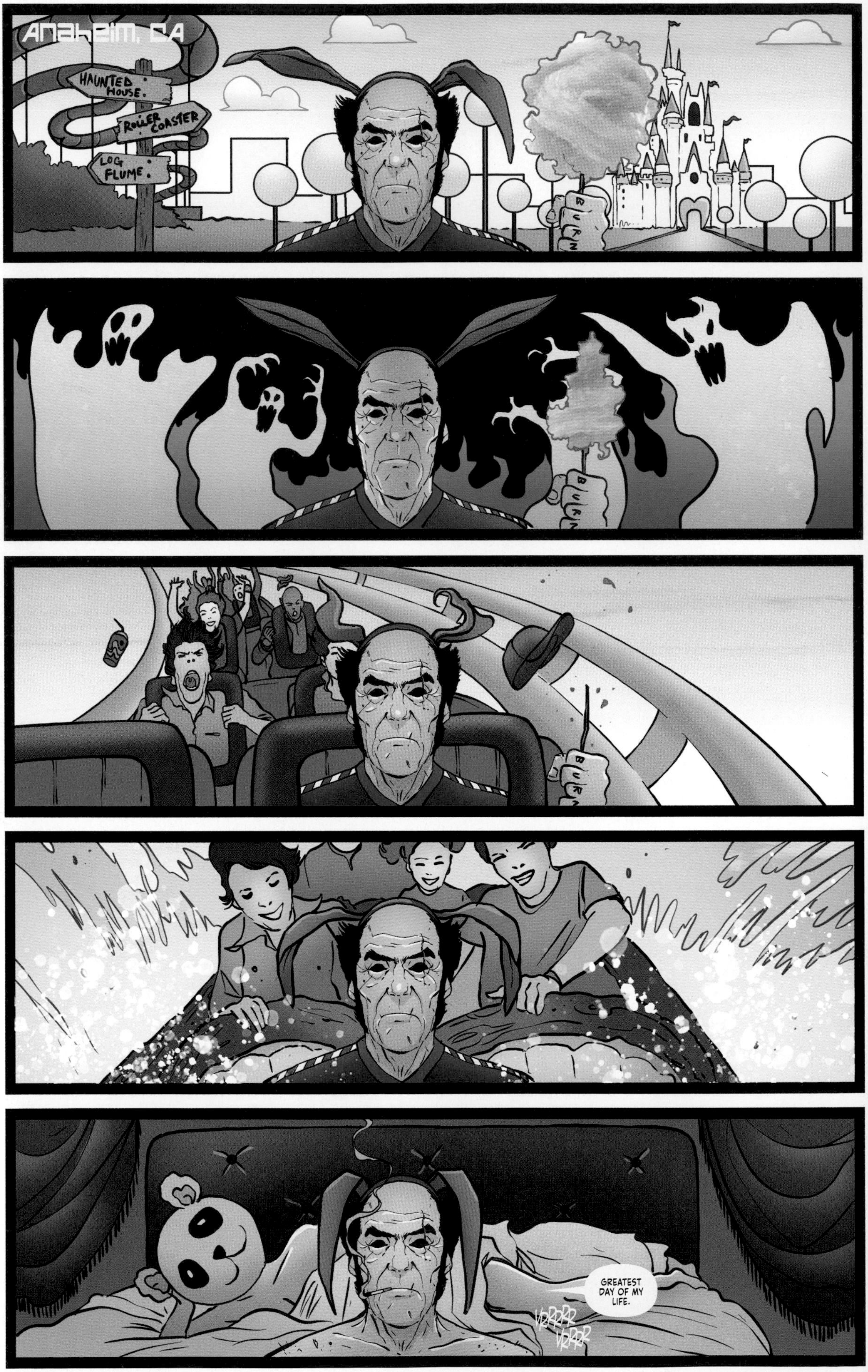
ANAHEIM, CA
HAUNTED HOUSE.
ROLLER COASTER
LOG FLUME.
BURN
BURN
BURN
VRRRRR
VRRRR
GREATEST DAY OF MY LIFE.

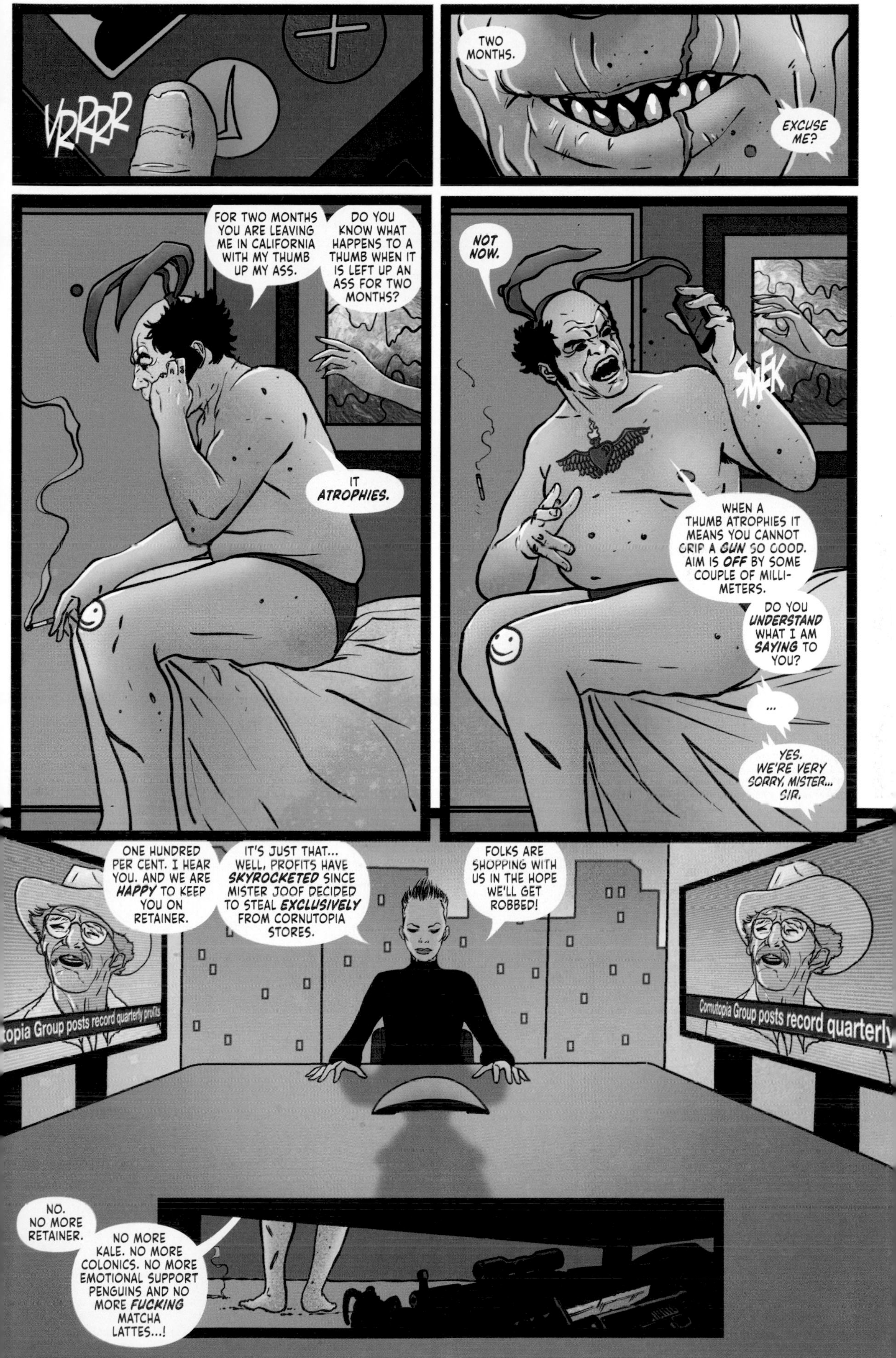
VRRRRR
TWO MONTHS.
EXCUSE ME?
FOR TWO MONTHS YOU ARE LEAVING ME IN CALIFORNIA WITH MY THUMB UP MY ASS.
DO YOU KNOW WHAT HAPPENS TO A THUMB WHEN IT IS LEFT UP AN ASS FOR TWO MONTHS?
IT ATROPHIES.
NOT NOW.
SNEK
WHEN A THUMB ATROPHIES IT MEANS YOU CANNOT GRIP A GUN SO GOOD. AIM IS OFF BY SOME COUPLE OF MILLI-METERS.
DO YOU UNDERSTAND WHAT I AM SAYING TO YOU?
...
YES. WE'RE VERY SORRY, MISTER... SIR.
ONE HUNDRED PER CENT. I HEAR YOU. AND WE ARE HAPPY TO KEEP YOU ON RETAINER.
IT'S JUST THAT... WELL, PROFITS HAVE SKYROCKETED SINCE MISTER JOOF DECIDED TO STEAL EXCLUSIVELY FROM CORNUTOPIA STORES.
FOLKS ARE SHOPPING WITH US IN THE HOPE WE'LL GET ROBBED!
topia Group posts record quarterly profits
Cornutopia Group posts record quarterly
NO. NO MORE RETAINER.
NO MORE KALE. NO MORE COLONICS. NO MORE EMOTIONAL SUPPORT PENGUINS AND NO MORE FUCKING MATCHA LATTES...!

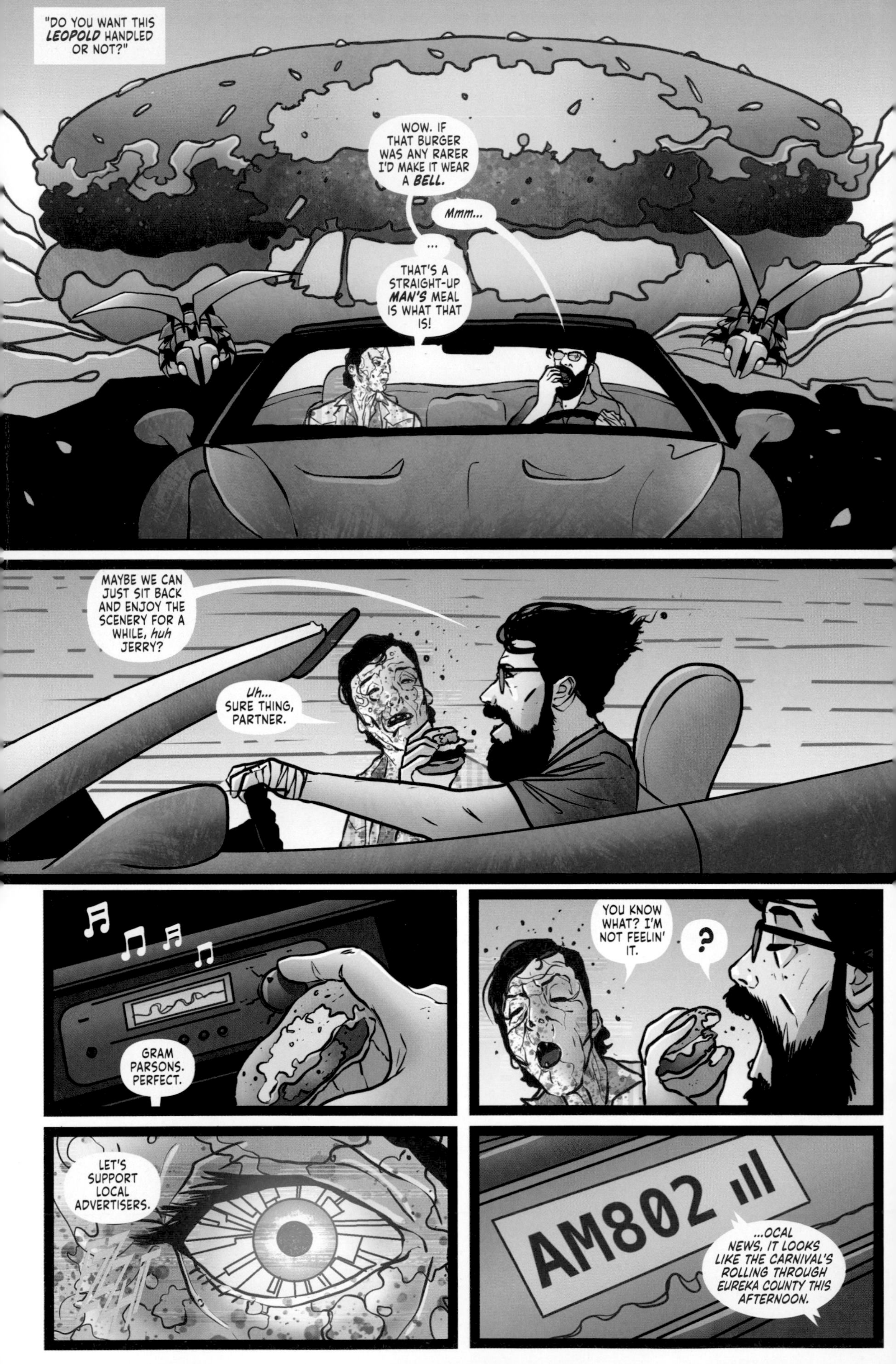
"DO YOU WANT THIS *LEOPOLD* HANDLED OR NOT?"
WOW. IF THAT BURGER WAS ANY RARER I'D MAKE IT WEAR A *BELL.*
Mmm...
...
THAT'S A STRAIGHT-UP *MAN'S* MEAL IS WHAT THAT IS!
MAYBE WE CAN JUST SIT BACK AND ENJOY THE SCENERY FOR A WHILE, *huh* JERRY?
Uh... SURE THING, PARTNER.
GRAM PARSONS. PERFECT.
YOU KNOW WHAT? I'M NOT FEELIN' IT.
?
LET'S SUPPORT LOCAL ADVERTISERS.
AM802
...OCAL NEWS, IT LOOKS LIKE THE CARNIVAL'S ROLLING THROUGH EUREKA COUNTY THIS AFTERNOON.

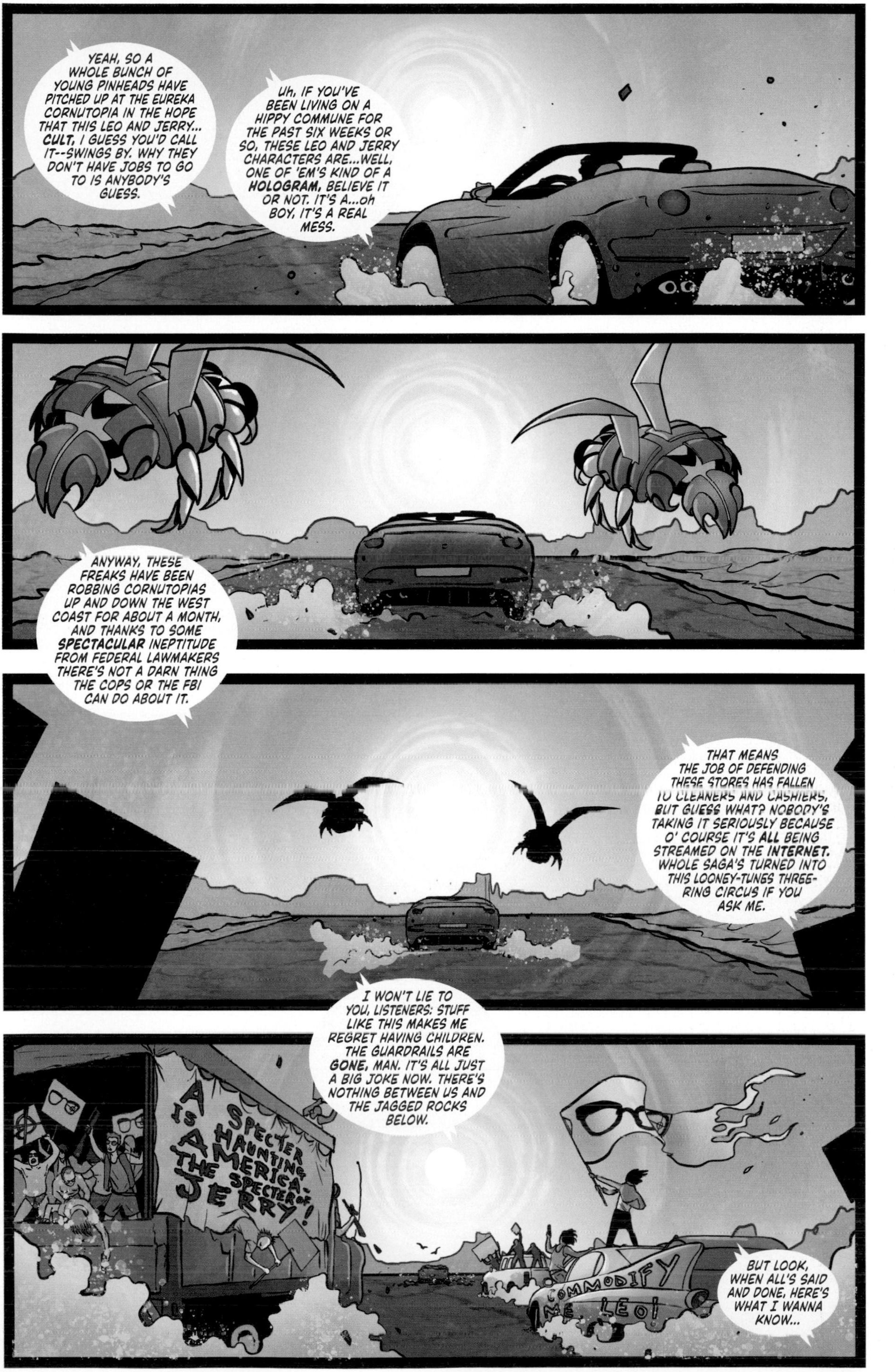
YEAH, SO A WHOLE BUNCH OF YOUNG PINHEADS HAVE PITCHED UP AT THE EUREKA CORNUTOPIA IN THE HOPE THAT THIS LEO AND JERRY... CULT, I GUESS YOU'D CALL IT--SWINGS BY. WHY THEY DON'T HAVE JOBS TO GO TO IS ANYBODY'S GUESS.
Uh, IF YOU'VE BEEN LIVING ON A HIPPY COMMUNE FOR THE PAST SIX WEEKS OR SO, THESE LEO AND JERRY CHARACTERS ARE...WELL, ONE OF 'EM'S KIND OF A HOLOGRAM, BELIEVE IT OR NOT. IT'S A...oh BOY, IT'S A REAL MESS.
ANYWAY, THESE FREAKS HAVE BEEN ROBBING CORNUTOPIAS UP AND DOWN THE WEST COAST FOR ABOUT A MONTH, AND THANKS TO SOME SPECTACULAR INEPTITUDE FROM FEDERAL LAWMAKERS THERE'S NOT A DARN THING THE COPS OR THE FBI CAN DO ABOUT IT.
THAT MEANS THE JOB OF DEFENDING THESE STORES HAS FALLEN TO CLEANERS AND CASHIERS, BUT GUESS WHAT? NOBODY'S TAKING IT SERIOUSLY BECAUSE O' COURSE IT'S ALL BEING STREAMED ON THE INTERNET. WHOLE SAGA'S TURNED INTO THIS LOONEY-TUNES THREE-RING CIRCUS IF YOU ASK ME.
I WON'T LIE TO YOU, LISTENERS: STUFF LIKE THIS MAKES ME REGRET HAVING CHILDREN. THE GUARDRAILS ARE GONE, MAN. IT'S ALL JUST A BIG JOKE NOW. THERE'S NOTHING BETWEEN US AND THE JAGGED ROCKS BELOW.
A SPECTER IS HAUNTING AMERICA-THE SPECTER OF JERRY!
COMMODIFY ME, LEO!
BUT LOOK, WHEN ALL'S SAID AND DONE, HERE'S WHAT I WANNA KNOW...

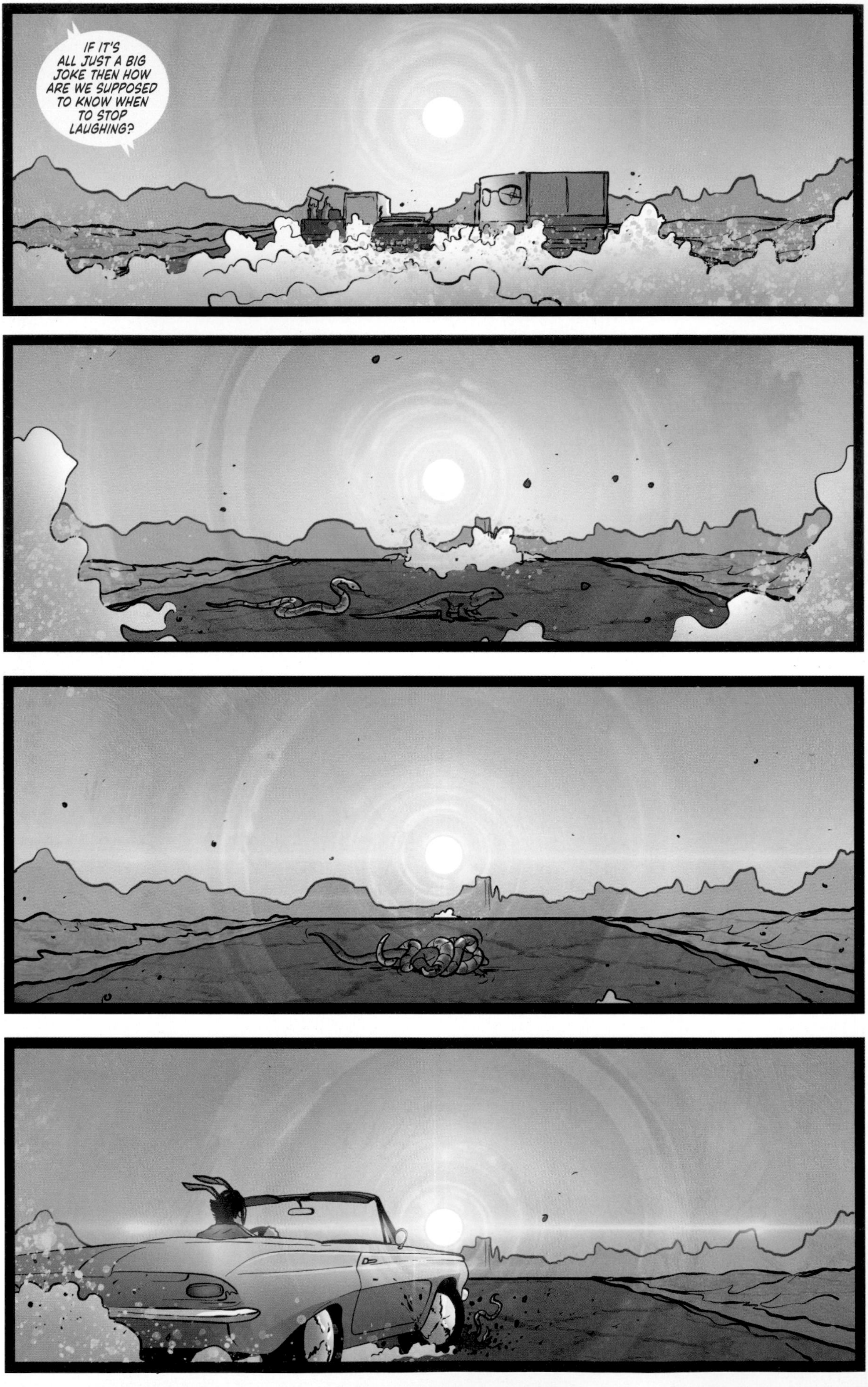
IF IT'S ALL JUST A BIG JOKE THEN HOW ARE WE SUPPOSED TO KNOW WHEN TO STOP LAUGHING?

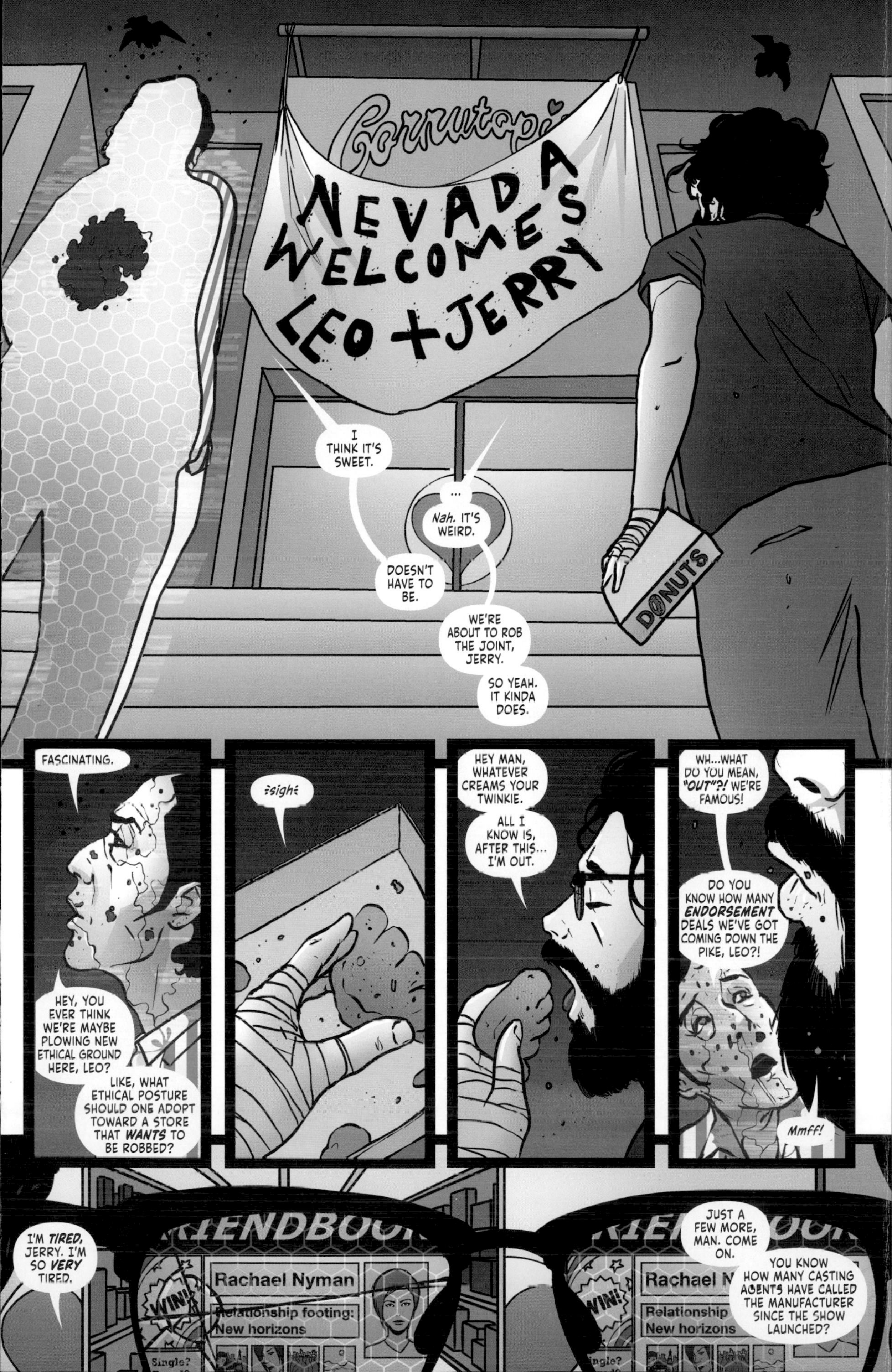

Corrutopia
NEVADA WELCOMES LEO + JERRY
I THINK IT'S SWEET.
...
Nah. IT'S WEIRD.
DOESN'T HAVE TO BE.
WE'RE ABOUT TO ROB THE JOINT, JERRY.
SO YEAH. IT KINDA DOES.
DONUTS
FASCINATING.
HEY, YOU EVER THINK WE'RE MAYBE PLOWING NEW ETHICAL GROUND HERE, LEO?
LIKE, WHAT ETHICAL POSTURE SHOULD ONE ADOPT TOWARD A STORE THAT *WANTS* TO BE ROBBED?
sigh
HEY MAN, WHATEVER CREAMS YOUR TWINKIE.
ALL I KNOW IS, AFTER THIS... I'M OUT.
WH...WHAT DO YOU MEAN, *"OUT"?!* WE'RE FAMOUS!
DO YOU KNOW HOW MANY ***ENDORSEMENT*** DEALS WE'VE GOT COMING DOWN THE PIKE, LEO?!
Mmff!
I'M *TIRED*, JERRY. I'M SO *VERY* TIRED.
JUST A FEW MORE, MAN. COME ON.
YOU KNOW HOW MANY CASTING AGENTS HAVE CALLED THE MANUFACTURER SINCE THE SHOW LAUNCHED?
RIENDBOOK
Rachael Nyman
WIN!
Relationship footing:
New horizons

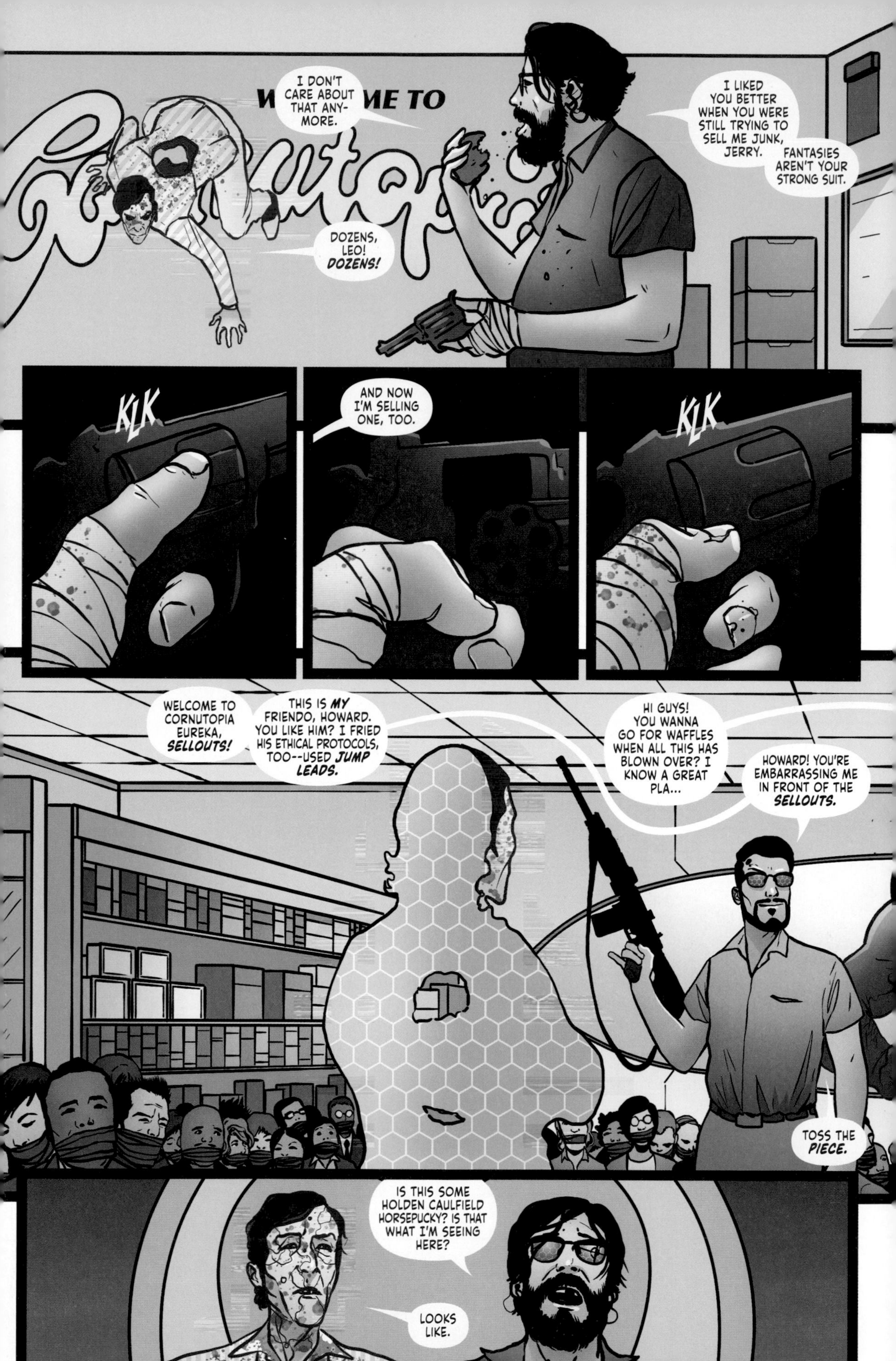
I DON'T CARE ABOUT THAT ANY-MORE.
I LIKED YOU BETTER WHEN YOU WERE STILL TRYING TO SELL ME JUNK, JERRY.
FANTASIES AREN'T YOUR STRONG SUIT.
DOZENS, LEO! DOZENS!
KLK
AND NOW I'M SELLING ONE, TOO.
KLK
WELCOME TO CORNUTOPIA EUREKA, SELLOUTS!
THIS IS MY FRIENDO, HOWARD. YOU LIKE HIM? I FRIED HIS ETHICAL PROTOCOLS, TOO--USED JUMP LEADS.
HI GUYS! YOU WANNA GO FOR WAFFLES WHEN ALL THIS HAS BLOWN OVER? I KNOW A GREAT PLA...
HOWARD! YOU'RE EMBARRASSING ME IN FRONT OF THE SELLOUTS.
TOSS THE PIECE.
IS THIS SOME HOLDEN CAULFIELD HORSEPUCKY? IS THAT WHAT I'M SEEING HERE?
LOOKS LIKE.

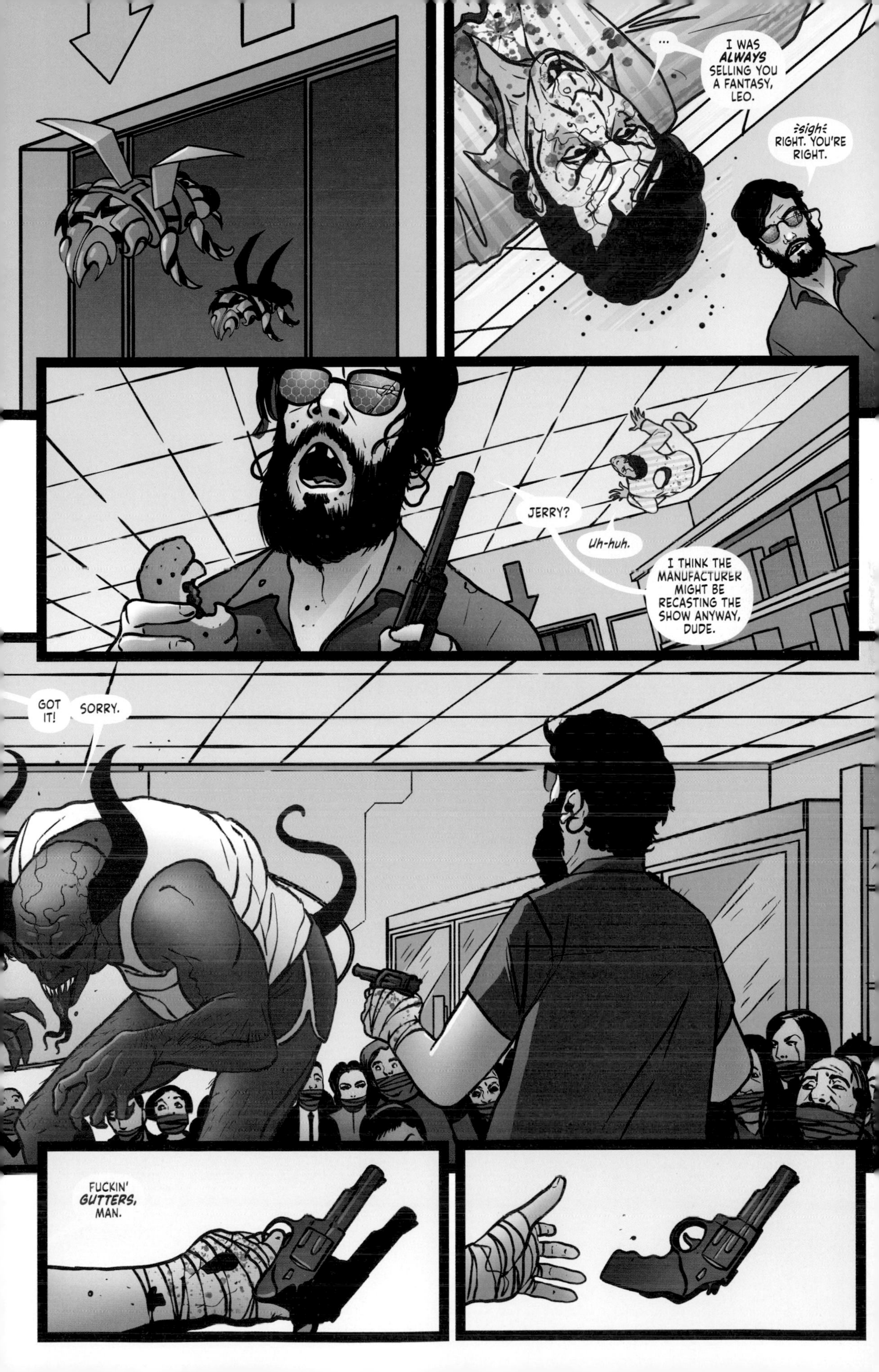
...
I WAS ALWAYS SELLING YOU A FANTASY, LEO.
sigh RIGHT. YOU'RE RIGHT.
JERRY?
Uh-huh.
I THINK THE MANUFACTURER MIGHT BE RECASTING THE SHOW ANYWAY, DUDE.
GOT IT!
SORRY.
FUCKIN' GUTTERS, MAN.

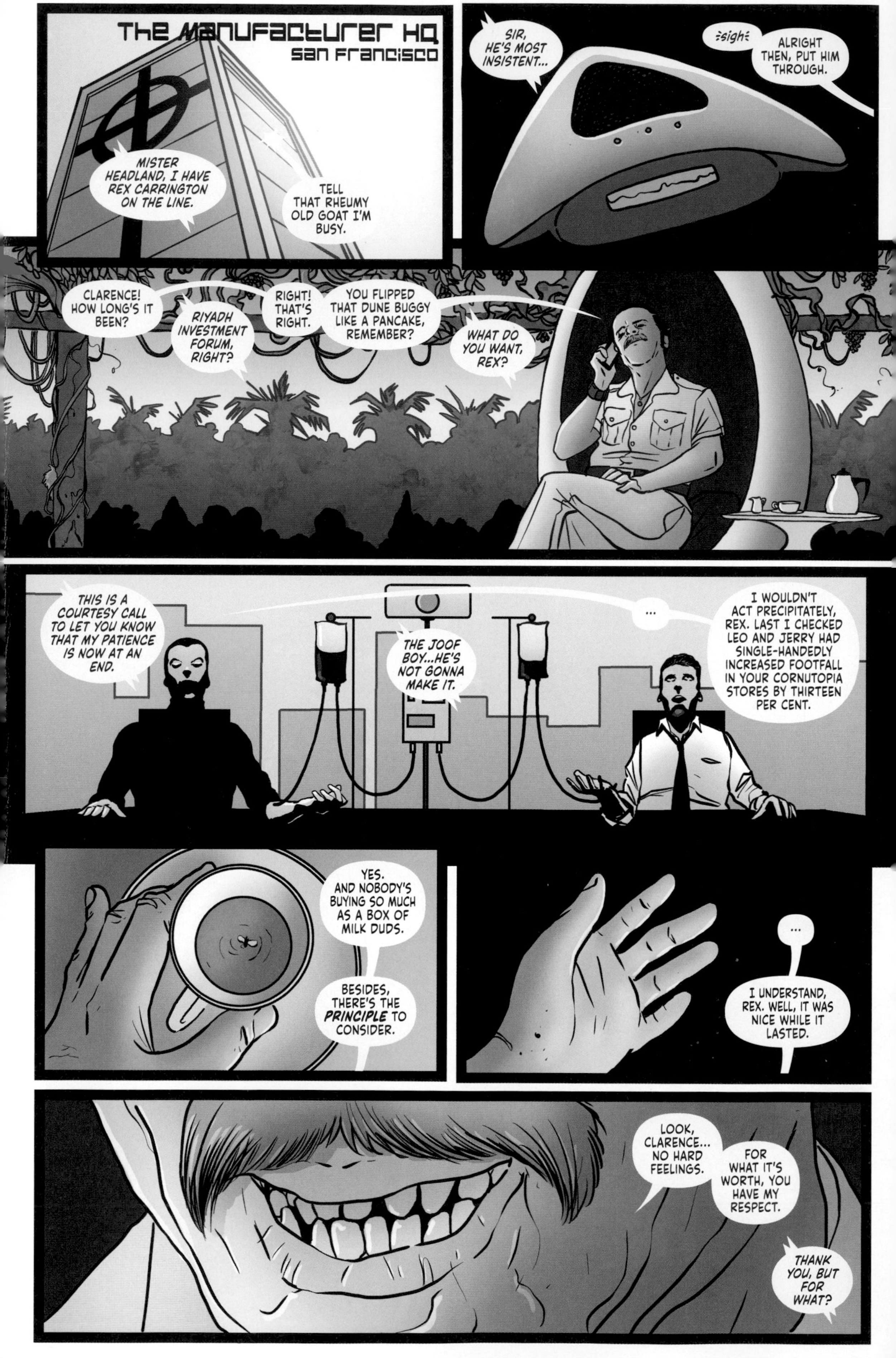
The Manufacturer HQ
San Francisco
MISTER HEADLAND, I HAVE REX CARRINGTON ON THE LINE.
TELL THAT RHEUMY OLD GOAT I'M BUSY.
SIR, HE'S MOST INSISTENT...
sigh
ALRIGHT THEN, PUT HIM THROUGH.
CLARENCE! HOW LONG'S IT BEEN?
RIYADH INVESTMENT FORUM, RIGHT?
RIGHT! THAT'S RIGHT.
YOU FLIPPED THAT DUNE BUGGY LIKE A PANCAKE, REMEMBER?
WHAT DO YOU WANT, REX?
THIS IS A COURTESY CALL TO LET YOU KNOW THAT MY PATIENCE IS NOW AT AN END.
THE JOOF BOY...HE'S NOT GONNA MAKE IT.
...
I WOULDN'T ACT PRECIPITATELY, REX. LAST I CHECKED LEO AND JERRY HAD SINGLE-HANDEDLY INCREASED FOOTFALL IN YOUR CORNUTOPIA STORES BY THIRTEEN PER CENT.
YES. AND NOBODY'S BUYING SO MUCH AS A BOX OF MILK DUDS.
BESIDES, THERE'S THE PRINCIPLE TO CONSIDER.
...
I UNDERSTAND, REX. WELL, IT WAS NICE WHILE IT LASTED.
LOOK, CLARENCE... NO HARD FEELINGS.
FOR WHAT IT'S WORTH, YOU HAVE MY RESPECT.
THANK YOU, BUT FOR WHAT?

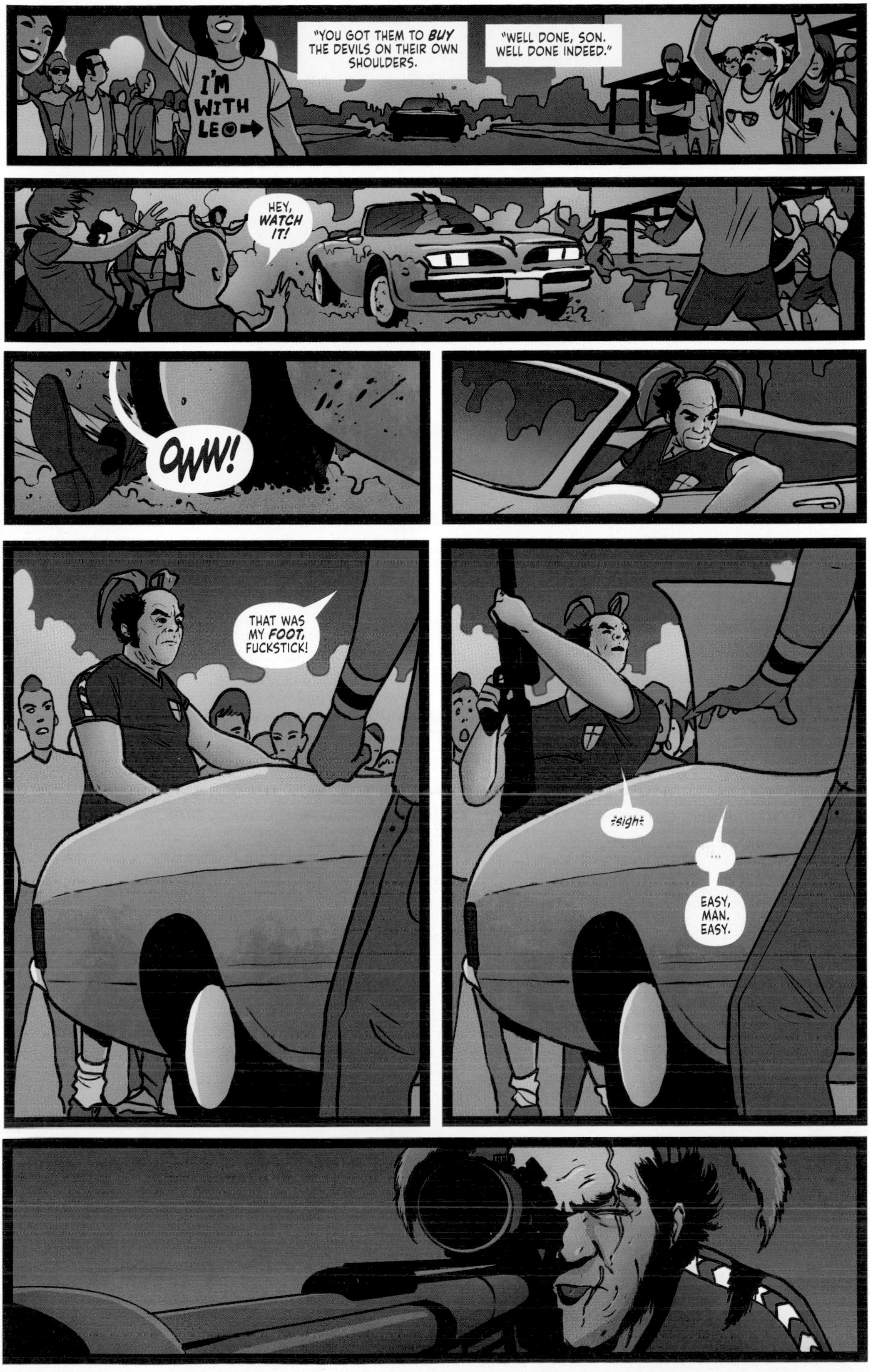
"YOU GOT THEM TO BUY THE DEVILS ON THEIR OWN SHOULDERS.
"WELL DONE, SON. WELL DONE INDEED."
I'M WITH LEO
HEY, WATCH IT!
OWW!
THAT WAS MY FOOT, FUCKSTICK!
sigh
...
EASY, MAN. EASY.

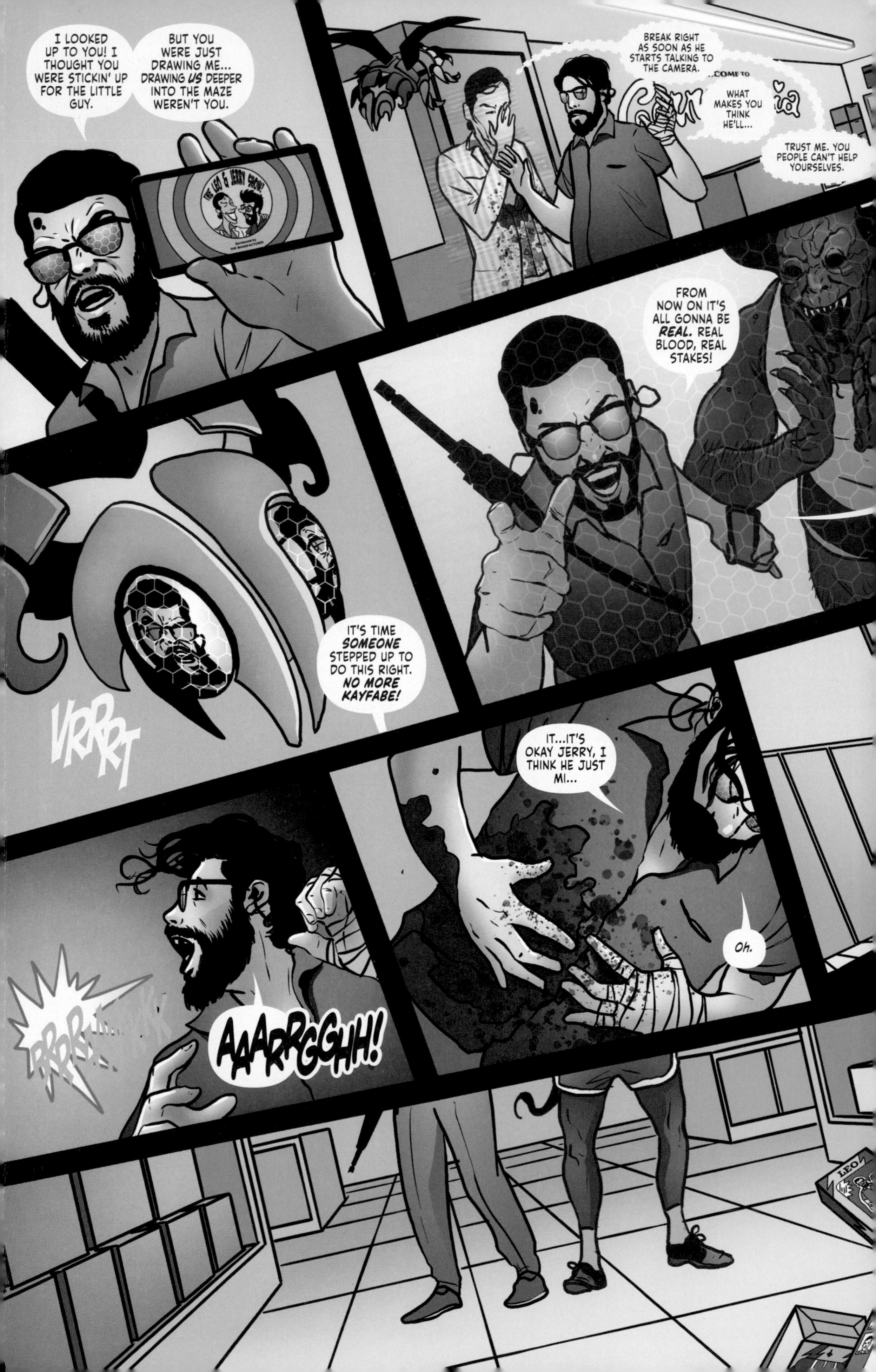
I LOOKED UP TO YOU! I THOUGHT YOU WERE STICKIN' UP FOR THE LITTLE GUY.
BUT YOU WERE JUST DRAWING ME... DRAWING *US* DEEPER INTO THE MAZE WEREN'T YOU.
THE LEO & JERRY SHOW!
BREAK RIGHT AS SOON AS HE STARTS TALKING TO THE CAMERA.
WHAT MAKES YOU THINK HE'LL...
TRUST ME. YOU PEOPLE CAN'T HELP YOURSELVES.
FROM NOW ON IT'S ALL GONNA BE ***REAL.*** REAL BLOOD, REAL STAKES!
IT'S TIME ***SOMEONE*** STEPPED UP TO DO THIS RIGHT. ***NO MORE KAYFABE!***
VRRRT
IT...IT'S OKAY JERRY, I THINK HE JUST MI...
BRRRK
AAARRGGHH!
Oh.
LEO

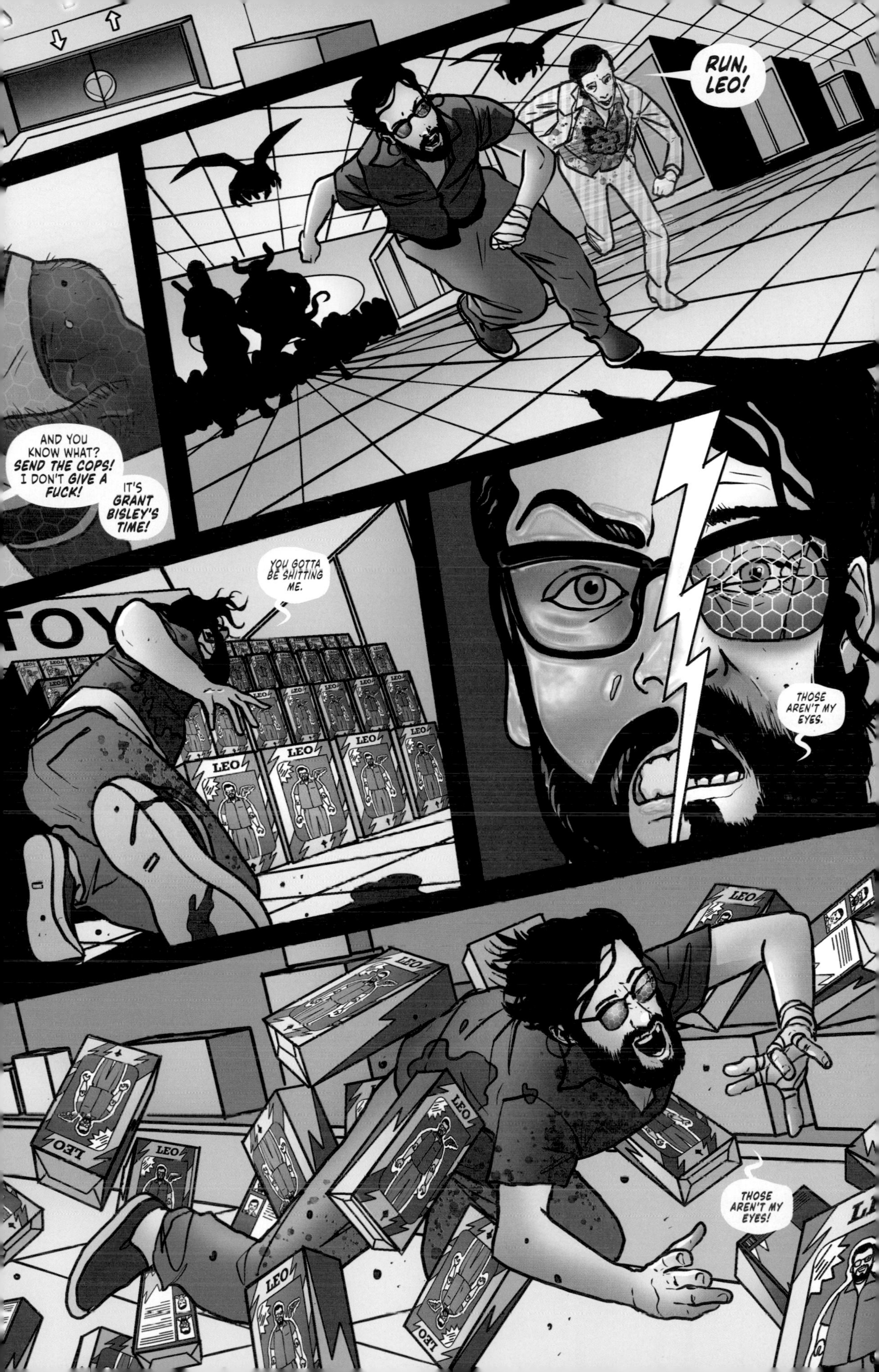
RUN, LEO!
AND YOU KNOW WHAT? SEND THE COPS! I DON'T GIVE A FUCK!
IT'S GRANT BISLEY'S TIME!
YOU GOTTA BE SHITTING ME.
TOY
LEO
THOSE AREN'T MY EYES.
LEO
THOSE AREN'T MY EYES!

YOU'RE *PART* OF IT, AREN'T YOU.

THE THESIS AND THE ANTITHESIS... BOTH CHEEKS OF THE SAME ASS!

THE QUESTION ANSWERS ITSELF AND SELF-DESTRUCTS BEFORE ANY OF US CAN GET A WORD IN EDGEWISE.

I THOUGHT I WAS *YOUR* OFF-BRAND KNOCKOFF, BUT YOU'RE *MINE*, MOTHERFUCKER!

YOU'VE BEEN FOCUS-GROUPED AND POLLED AND MARKET TESTED TO THE POINT WHERE ANYTHING THAT USED TO BE HUMAN'S BEEN SWAPPED OUT FOR...FOR *VAPOR* AND *STATIC!*

I'M THE *REAL* YOU.

Ggggll... JERRY.

DON'T LOOK AT *HIM*, LEO. HE CAN'T HELP YOU NOW.

NO-ONE CAN.

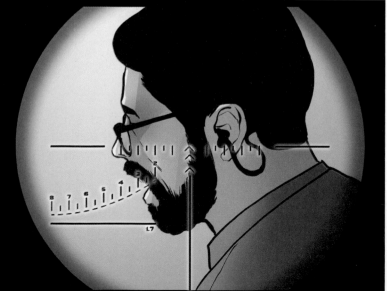

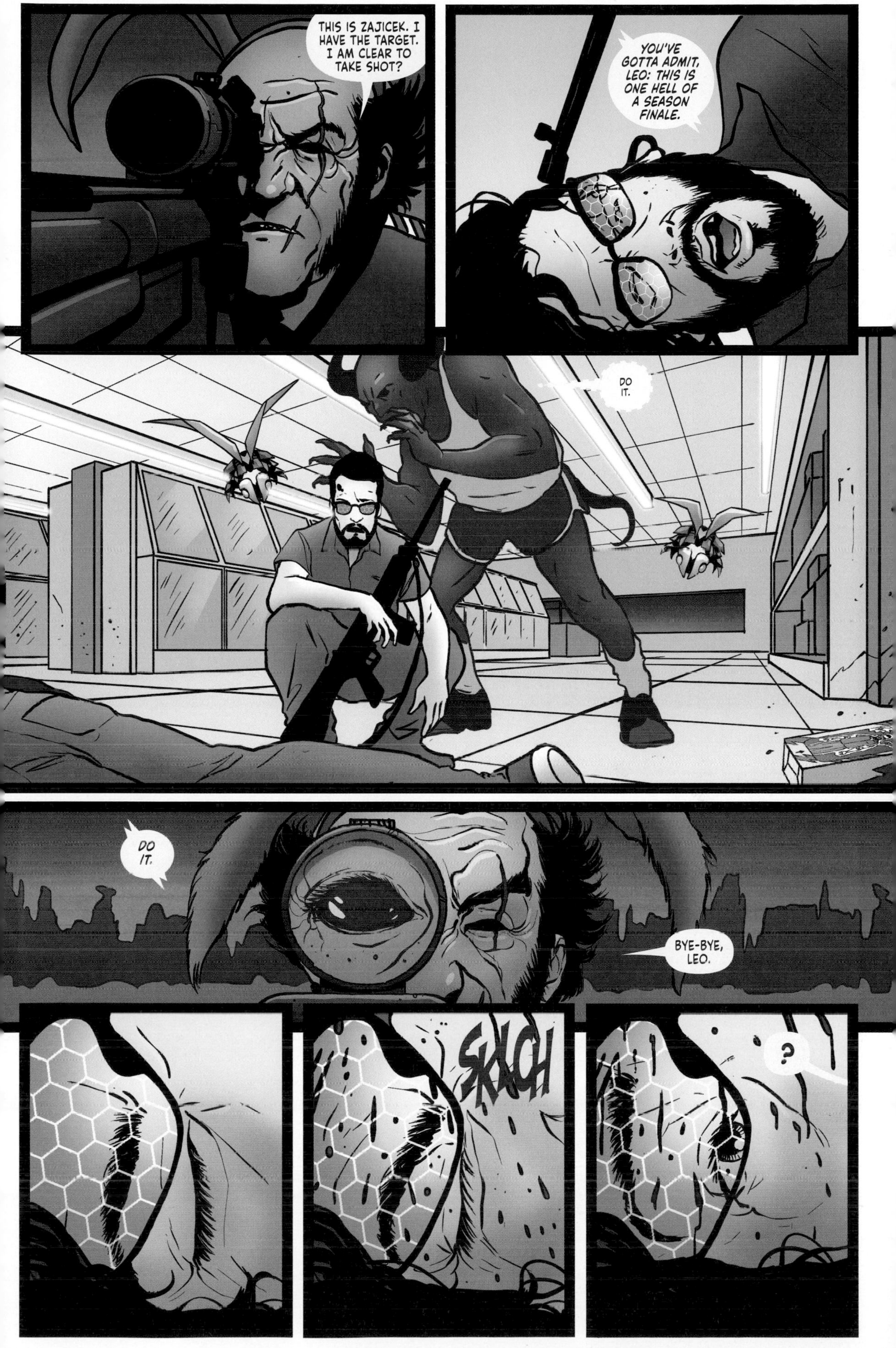

THIS IS ZAJICEK. I HAVE THE TARGET. I AM CLEAR TO TAKE SHOT?
YOU'VE GOTTA ADMIT, LEO: THIS IS ONE HELL OF A SEASON FINALE.
DO IT.
DO IT.
BYE-BYE, LEO.
SKLCH
?

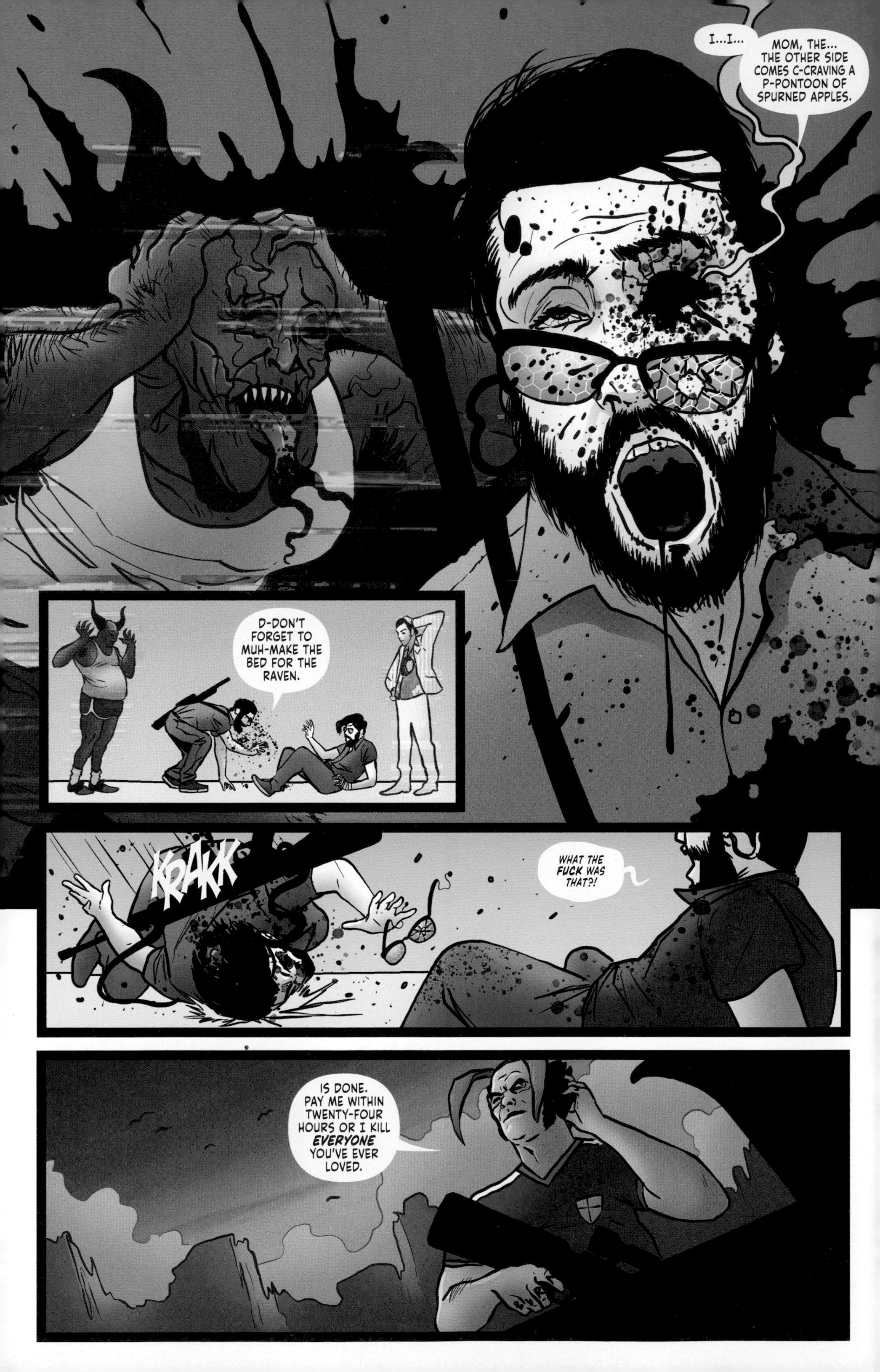
I...I...
MOM, THE... THE OTHER SIDE COMES C-CRAVING A P-PONTOON OF SPURNED APPLES.
D-DON'T FORGET TO MUH-MAKE THE BED FOR THE RAVEN.
KRAKK
WHAT THE *FUCK* WAS THAT?!
IS DONE. PAY ME WITHIN TWENTY-FOUR HOURS OR I KILL ***EVERYONE*** YOU'VE EVER LOVED.

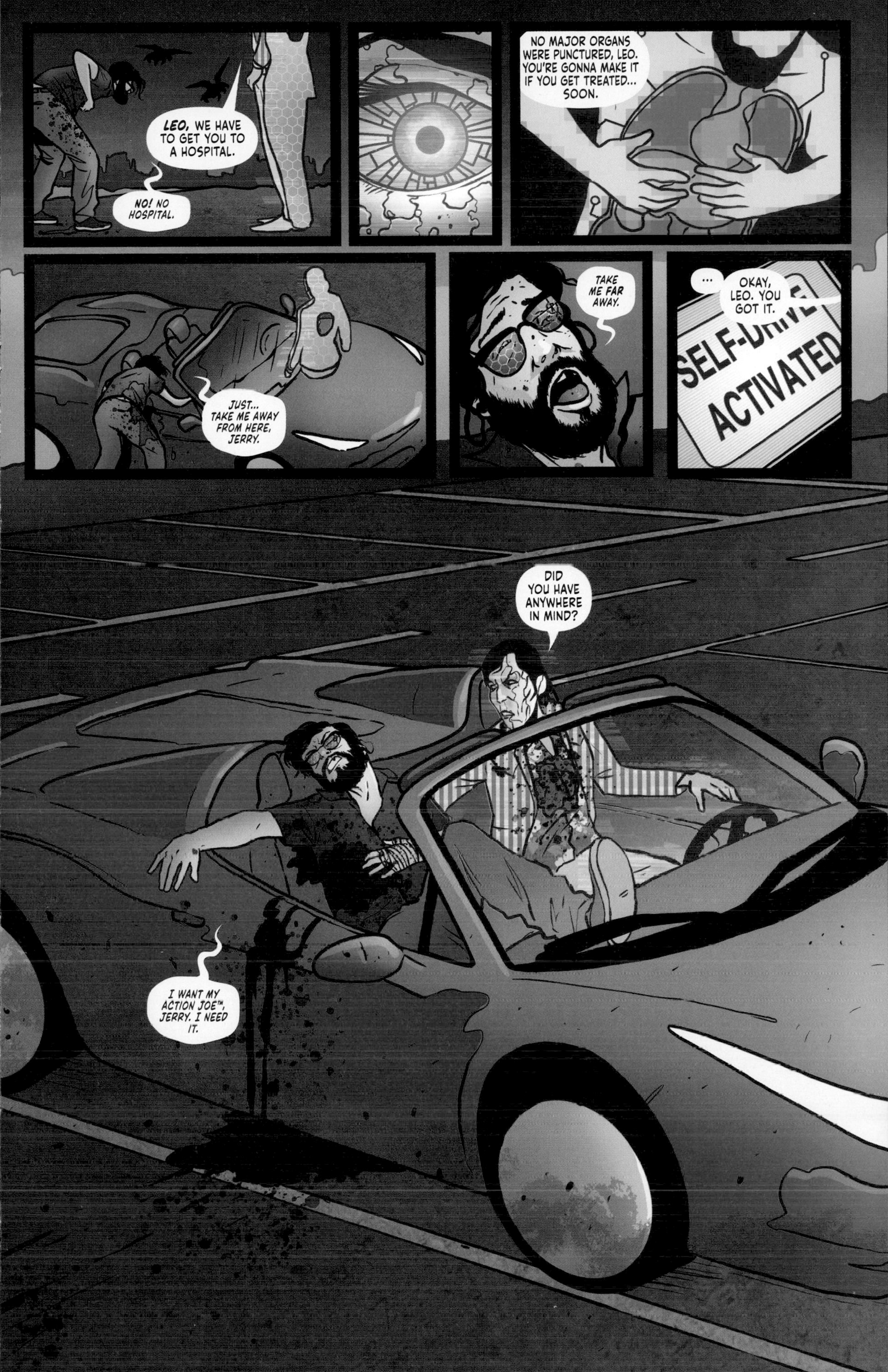
LEO, WE HAVE TO GET YOU TO A HOSPITAL.
NO! NO HOSPITAL.
NO MAJOR ORGANS WERE PUNCTURED, LEO. YOU'RE GONNA MAKE IT IF YOU GET TREATED... SOON.
JUST... TAKE ME AWAY FROM HERE, JERRY.
TAKE ME FAR AWAY.
...
OKAY, LEO. YOU GOT IT.
SELF-DRIVE ACTIVATED
DID YOU HAVE ANYWHERE IN MIND?
I WANT MY ACTION JOE™, JERRY. I NEED IT.

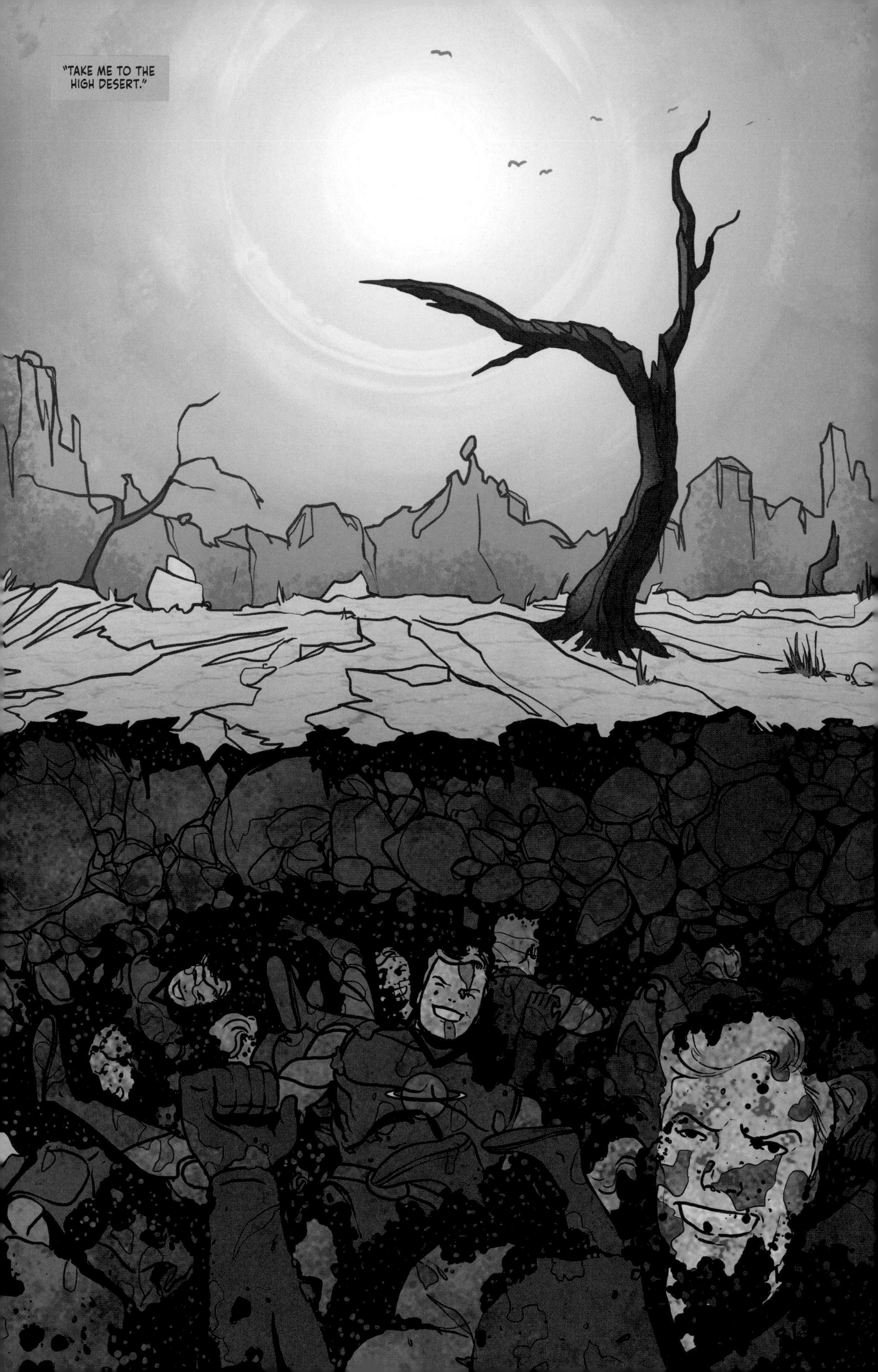
"TAKE ME TO THE HIGH DESERT."

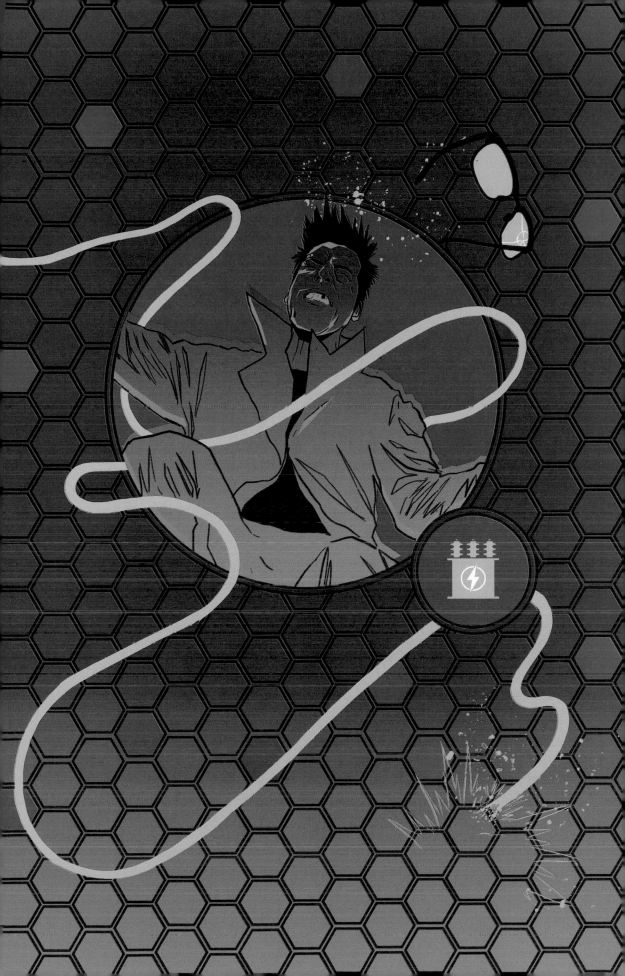

FIVE

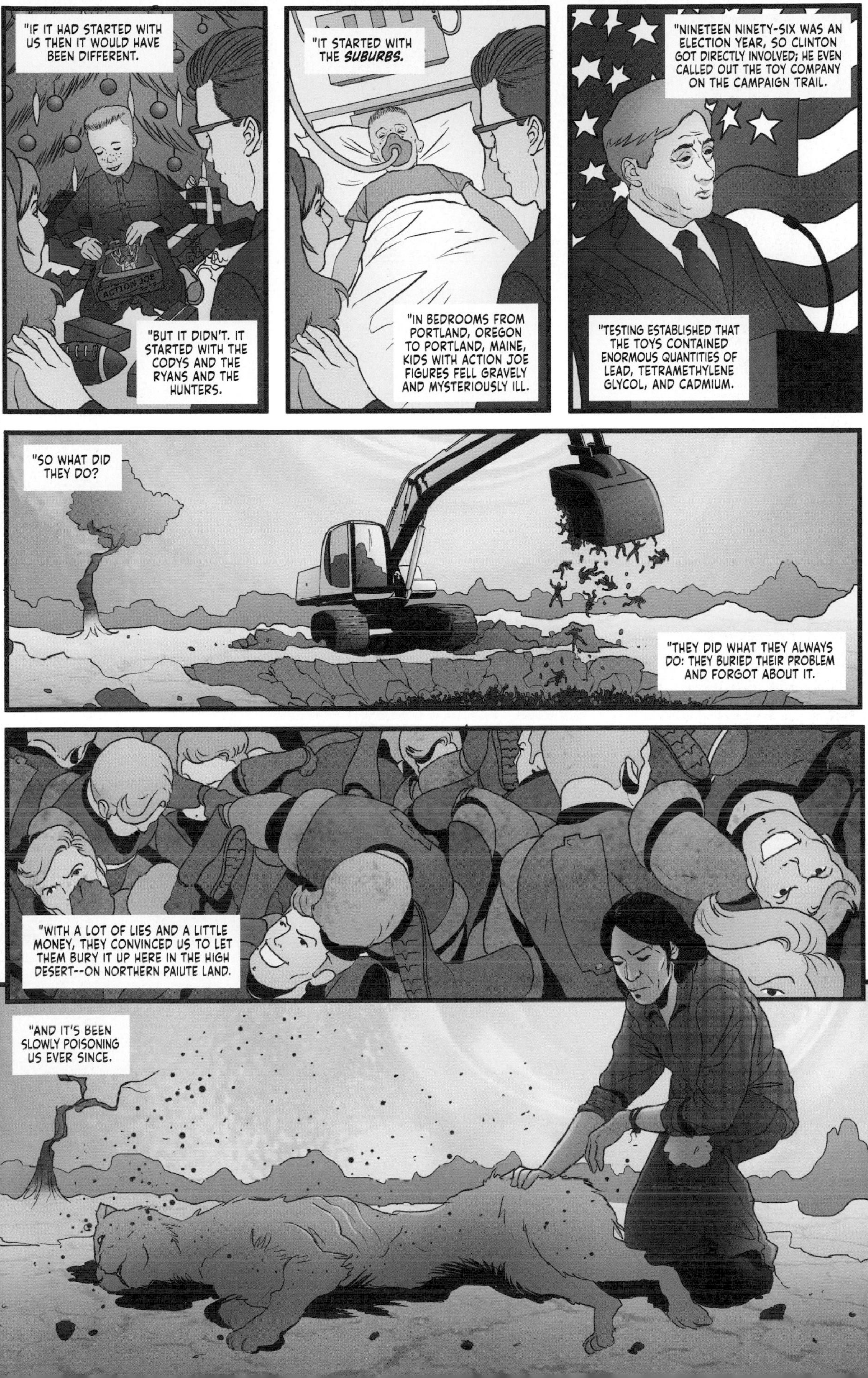
"IF IT HAD STARTED WITH US THEN IT WOULD HAVE BEEN DIFFERENT.
ACTION JOE
"BUT IT DIDN'T. IT STARTED WITH THE CODYS AND THE RYANS AND THE HUNTERS.
"IT STARTED WITH THE SUBURBS.
"IN BEDROOMS FROM PORTLAND, OREGON TO PORTLAND, MAINE, KIDS WITH ACTION JOE FIGURES FELL GRAVELY AND MYSTERIOUSLY ILL.
"NINETEEN NINETY-SIX WAS AN ELECTION YEAR, SO CLINTON GOT DIRECTLY INVOLVED; HE EVEN CALLED OUT THE TOY COMPANY ON THE CAMPAIGN TRAIL.
"TESTING ESTABLISHED THAT THE TOYS CONTAINED ENORMOUS QUANTITIES OF LEAD, TETRAMETHYLENE GLYCOL, AND CADMIUM.
"SO WHAT DID THEY DO?
"THEY DID WHAT THEY ALWAYS DO: THEY BURIED THEIR PROBLEM AND FORGOT ABOUT IT.
"WITH A LOT OF LIES AND A LITTLE MONEY, THEY CONVINCED US TO LET THEM BURY IT UP HERE IN THE HIGH DESERT--ON NORTHERN PAIUTE LAND.
"AND IT'S BEEN SLOWLY POISONING US EVER SINCE.

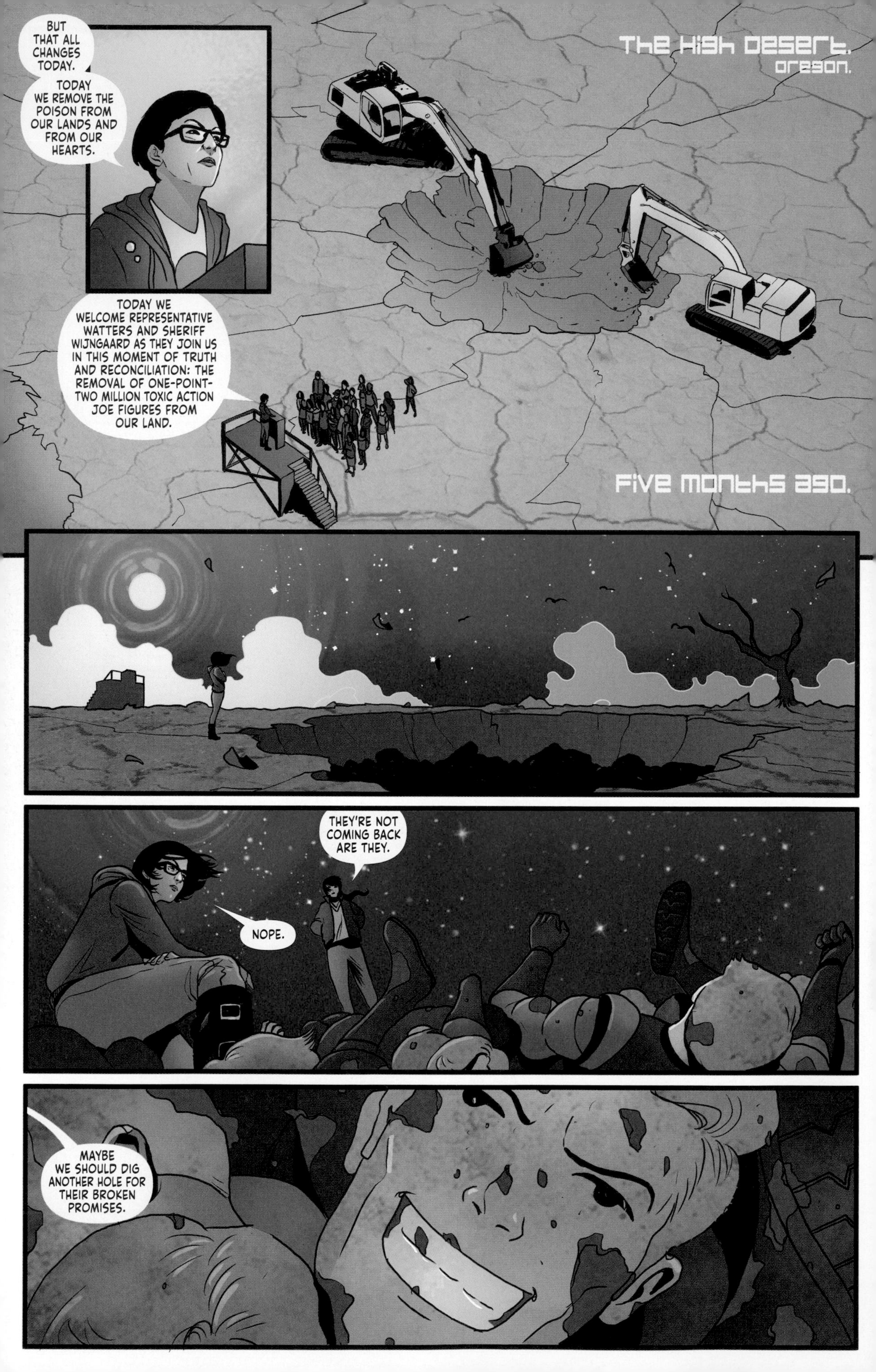
The High Desert.
Oregon.
BUT THAT ALL CHANGES TODAY.
TODAY WE REMOVE THE POISON FROM OUR LANDS AND FROM OUR HEARTS.
TODAY WE WELCOME REPRESENTATIVE WATTERS AND SHERIFF WIJNGAARD AS THEY JOIN US IN THIS MOMENT OF TRUTH AND RECONCILIATION: THE REMOVAL OF ONE-POINT-TWO MILLION TOXIC ACTION JOE FIGURES FROM OUR LAND.
Five months ago.
THEY'RE NOT COMING BACK ARE THEY.
NOPE.
MAYBE WE SHOULD DIG ANOTHER HOLE FOR THEIR BROKEN PROMISES.

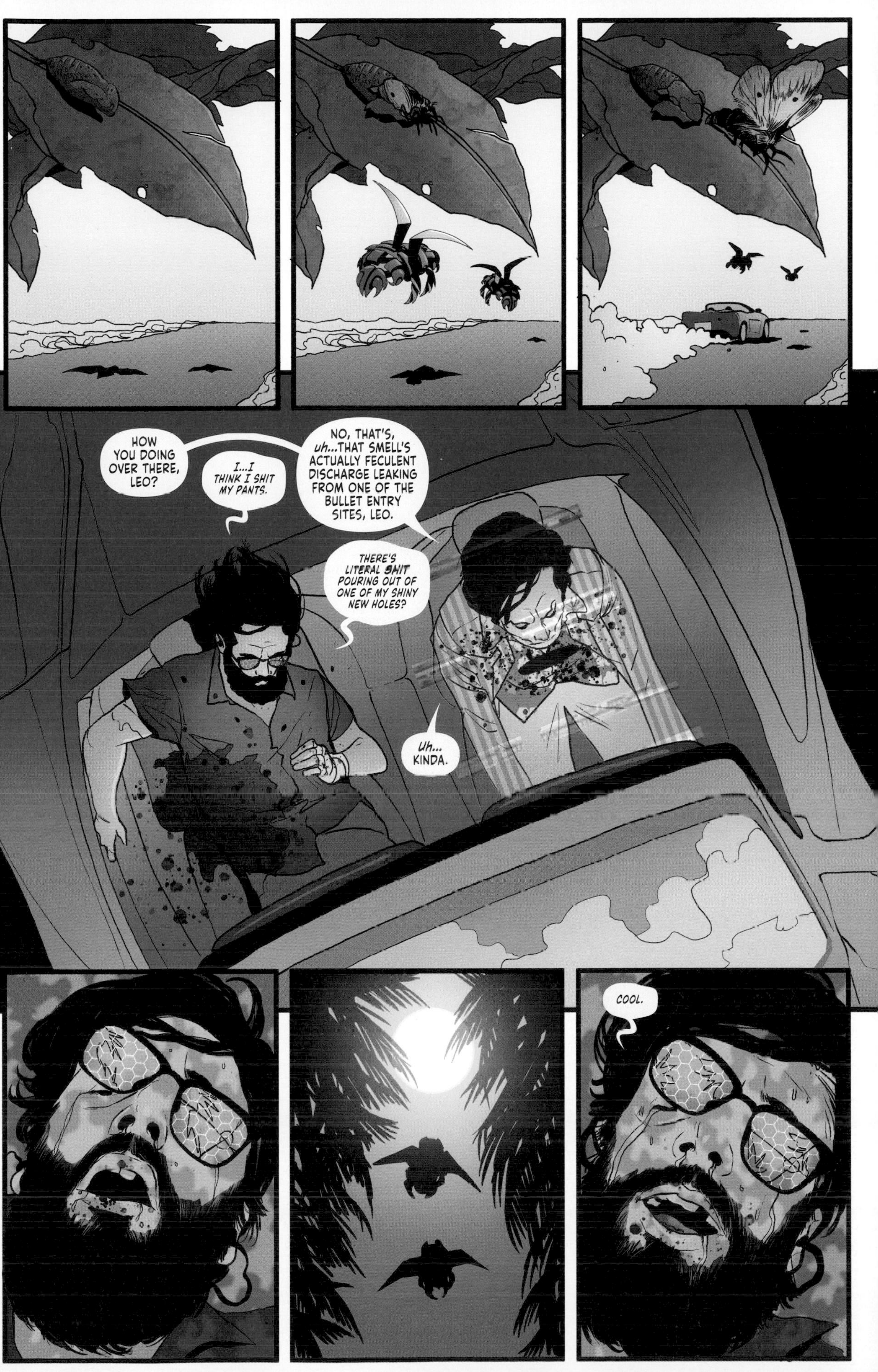
HOW YOU DOING OVER THERE, LEO?
I...I THINK I SHIT MY PANTS.
NO, THAT'S, uh...THAT SMELL'S ACTUALLY FECULENT DISCHARGE LEAKING FROM ONE OF THE BULLET ENTRY SITES, LEO.
THERE'S LITERAL SHIT POURING OUT OF ONE OF MY SHINY NEW HOLES?
Uh... KINDA.
COOL.

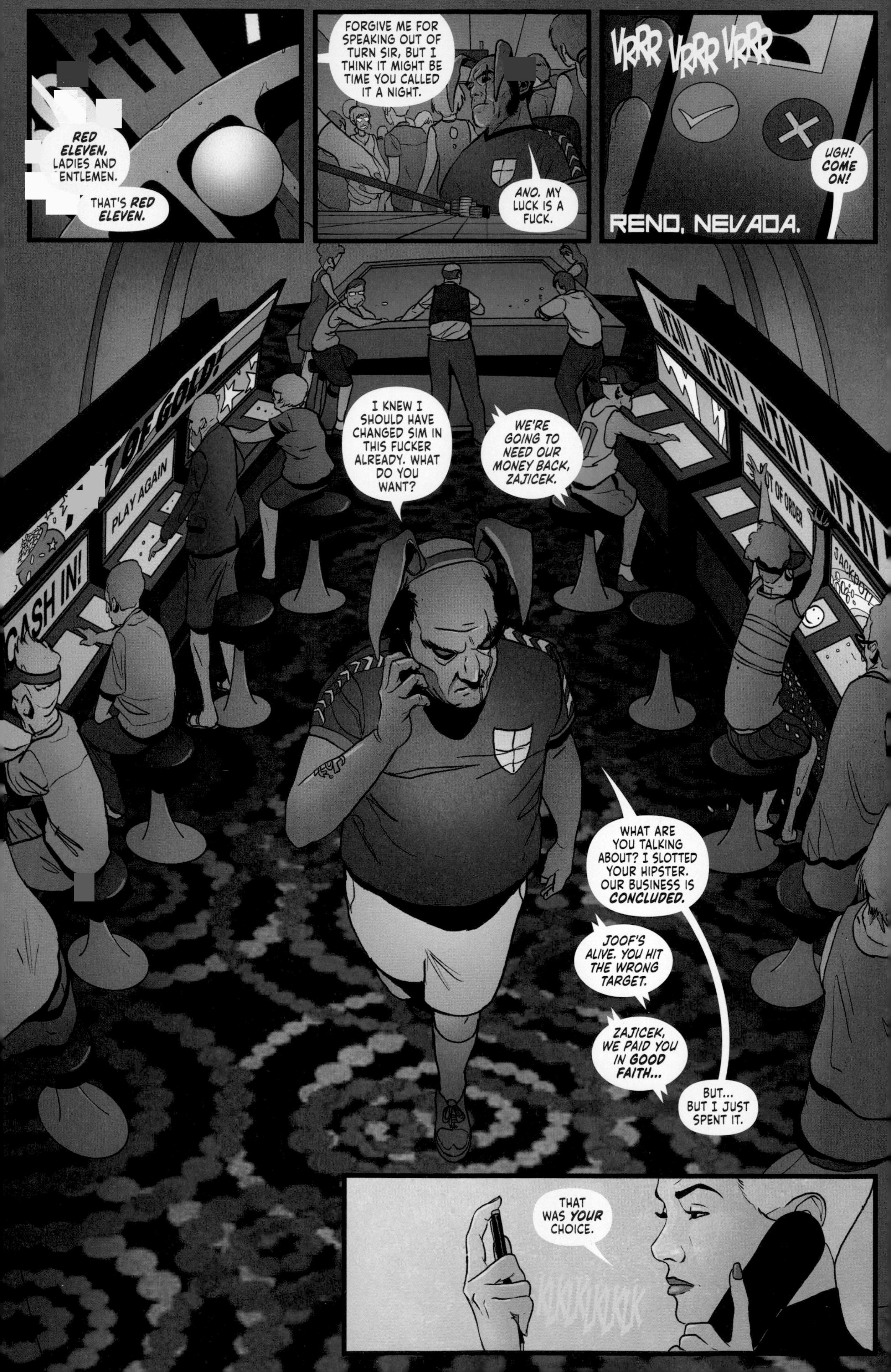
RED ELEVEN, LADIES AND ENTLEMEN.
THAT'S RED ELEVEN.
FORGIVE ME FOR SPEAKING OUT OF TURN SIR, BUT I THINK IT MIGHT BE TIME YOU CALLED IT A NIGHT.
ANO. MY LUCK IS A FUCK.
VRRR VRRR VRRR
UGH! COME ON!
RENO, NEVADA.
OF GOLD!
PLAY AGAIN
CASH IN!
WIN! WIN! WIN! WIN!
OUT OF ORDER
JACKPOT!
I KNEW I SHOULD HAVE CHANGED SIM IN THIS FUCKER ALREADY. WHAT DO YOU WANT?
WE'RE GOING TO NEED OUR MONEY BACK, ZAJICEK.
WHAT ARE YOU TALKING ABOUT? I SLOTTED YOUR HIPSTER. OUR BUSINESS IS CONCLUDED.
JOOF'S ALIVE. YOU HIT THE WRONG TARGET.
ZAJICEK, WE PAID YOU IN GOOD FAITH...
BUT... BUT I JUST SPENT IT.
THAT WAS YOUR CHOICE.
KLIKLIKLIKLIK

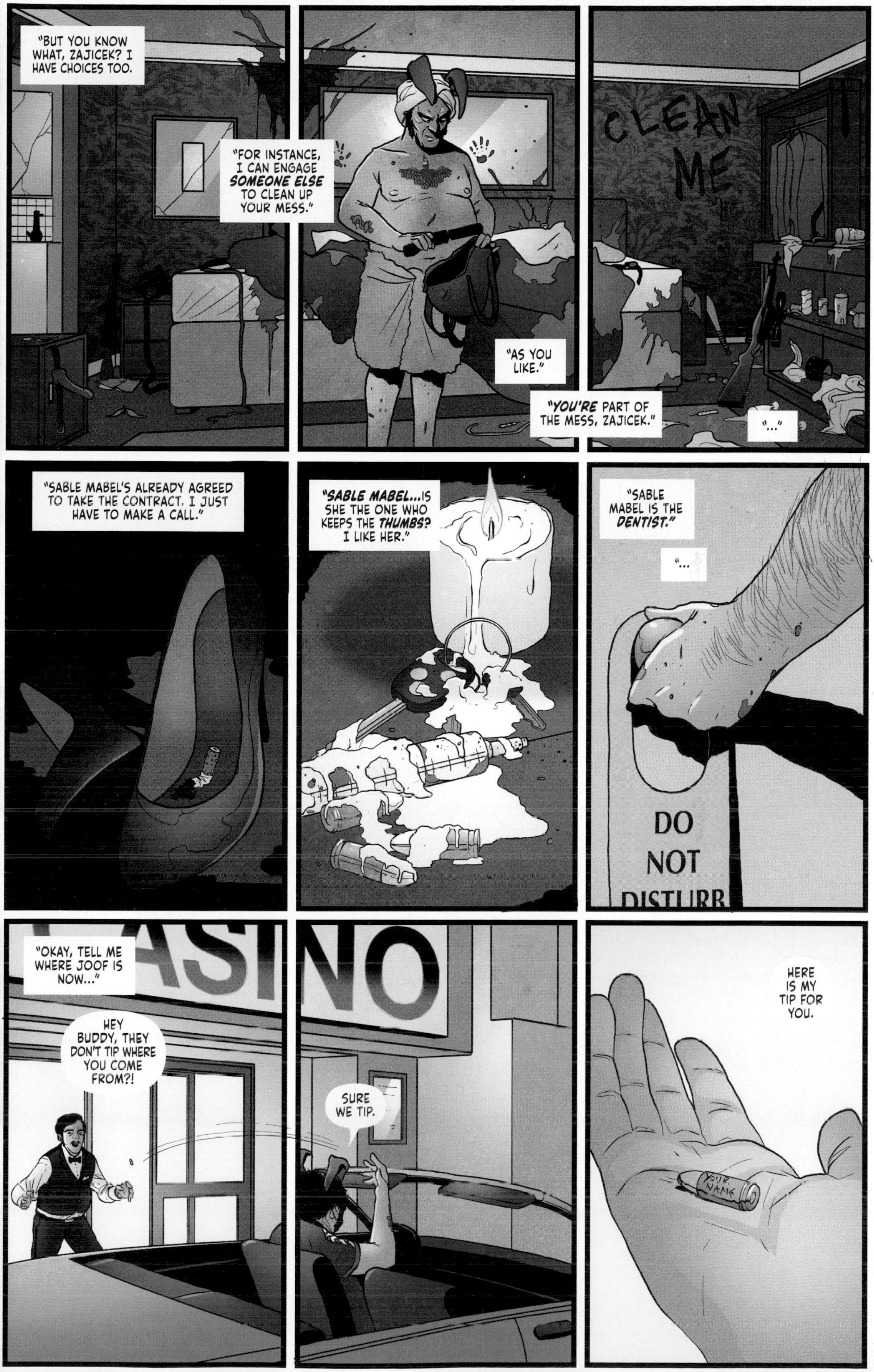

"BUT YOU KNOW WHAT, ZAJICEK? I HAVE CHOICES TOO.
"FOR INSTANCE, I CAN ENGAGE SOMEONE ELSE TO CLEAN UP YOUR MESS."
"AS YOU LIKE."
CLEAN ME
"YOU'RE PART OF THE MESS, ZAJICEK."
"..."
"SABLE MABEL'S ALREADY AGREED TO TAKE THE CONTRACT. I JUST HAVE TO MAKE A CALL."
"SABLE MABEL...IS SHE THE ONE WHO KEEPS THE THUMBS? I LIKE HER."
"SABLE MABEL IS THE DENTIST."
"...
DO NOT DISTURB
"OKAY, TELL ME WHERE JOOF IS NOW..."
ASINO
HEY BUDDY, THEY DON'T TIP WHERE YOU COME FROM?!
SURE WE TIP.
HERE IS MY TIP FOR YOU.
YOUR NAME

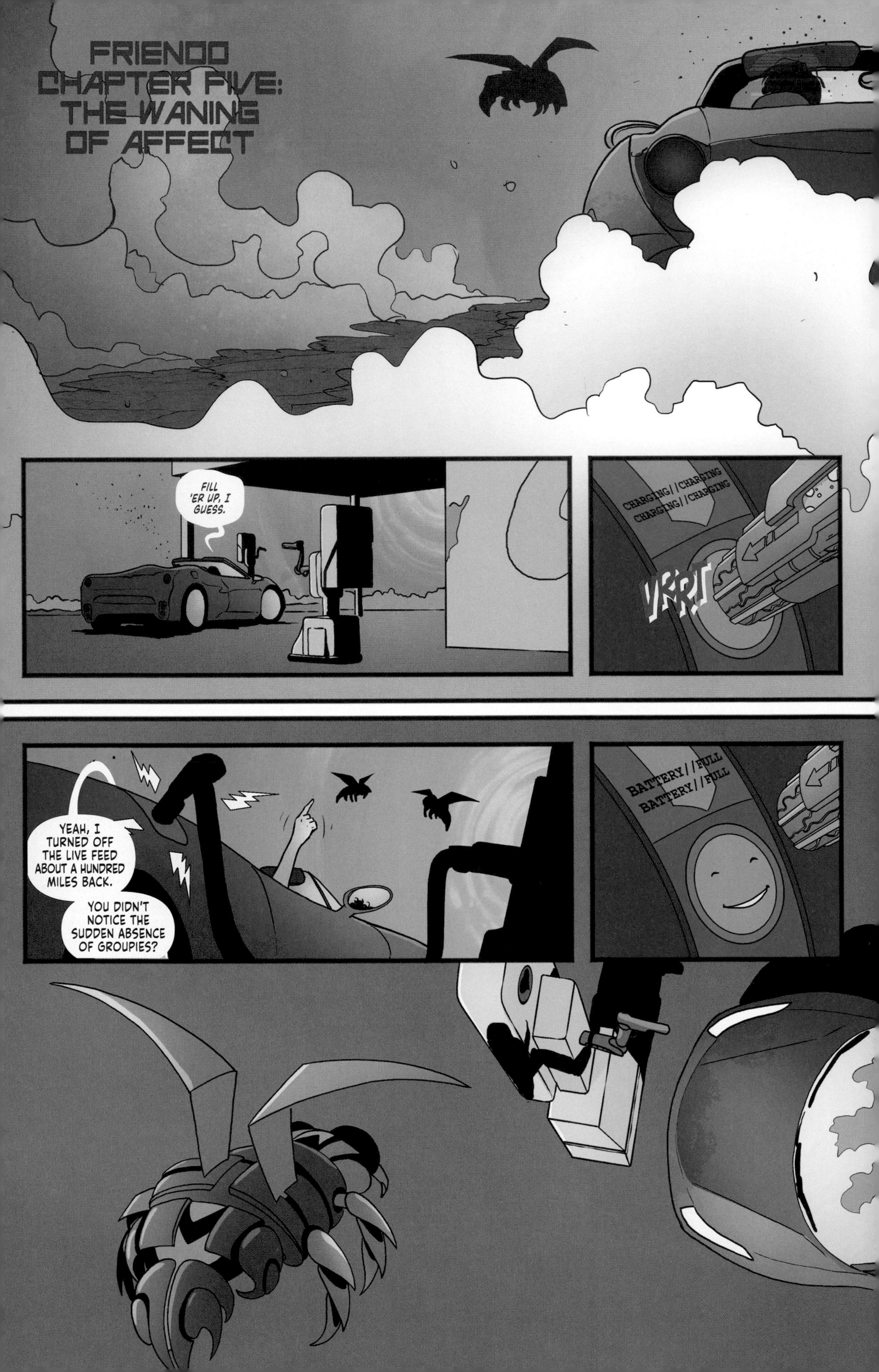
FRIENDO
CHAPTER FIVE:
THE WANING
OF AFFECT
FILL 'ER UP, I GUESS.
CHARGING//CHARGING
CHARGING//CHARGING
VRRT
YEAH, I TURNED OFF THE LIVE FEED ABOUT A HUNDRED MILES BACK.
YOU DIDN'T NOTICE THE SUDDEN ABSENCE OF GROUPIES?
BATTERY//FULL
BATTERY//FULL

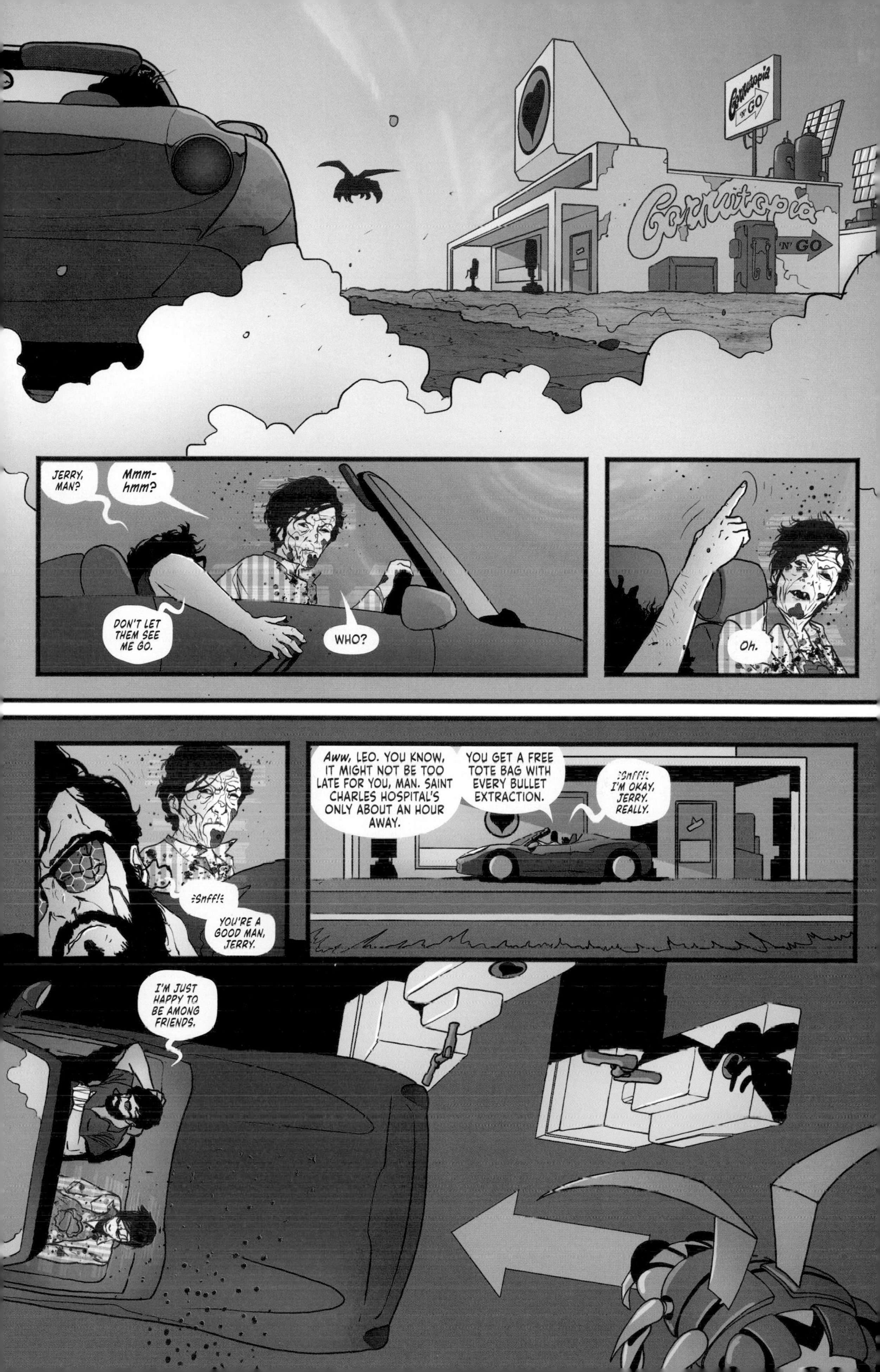
Cornutopia 'N' GO
Cornutopia
'N' GO
JERRY, MAN?
Mmm-hmm?
DON'T LET THEM SEE ME GO.
WHO?
Oh.
Aww, LEO. YOU KNOW, IT MIGHT NOT BE TOO LATE FOR YOU, MAN. SAINT CHARLES HOSPITAL'S ONLY ABOUT AN HOUR AWAY.
YOU GET A FREE TOTE BAG WITH EVERY BULLET EXTRACTION.
SNFF!
I'M OKAY, JERRY. REALLY.
SNFF!
YOU'RE A GOOD MAN, JERRY.
I'M JUST HAPPY TO BE AMONG FRIENDS.

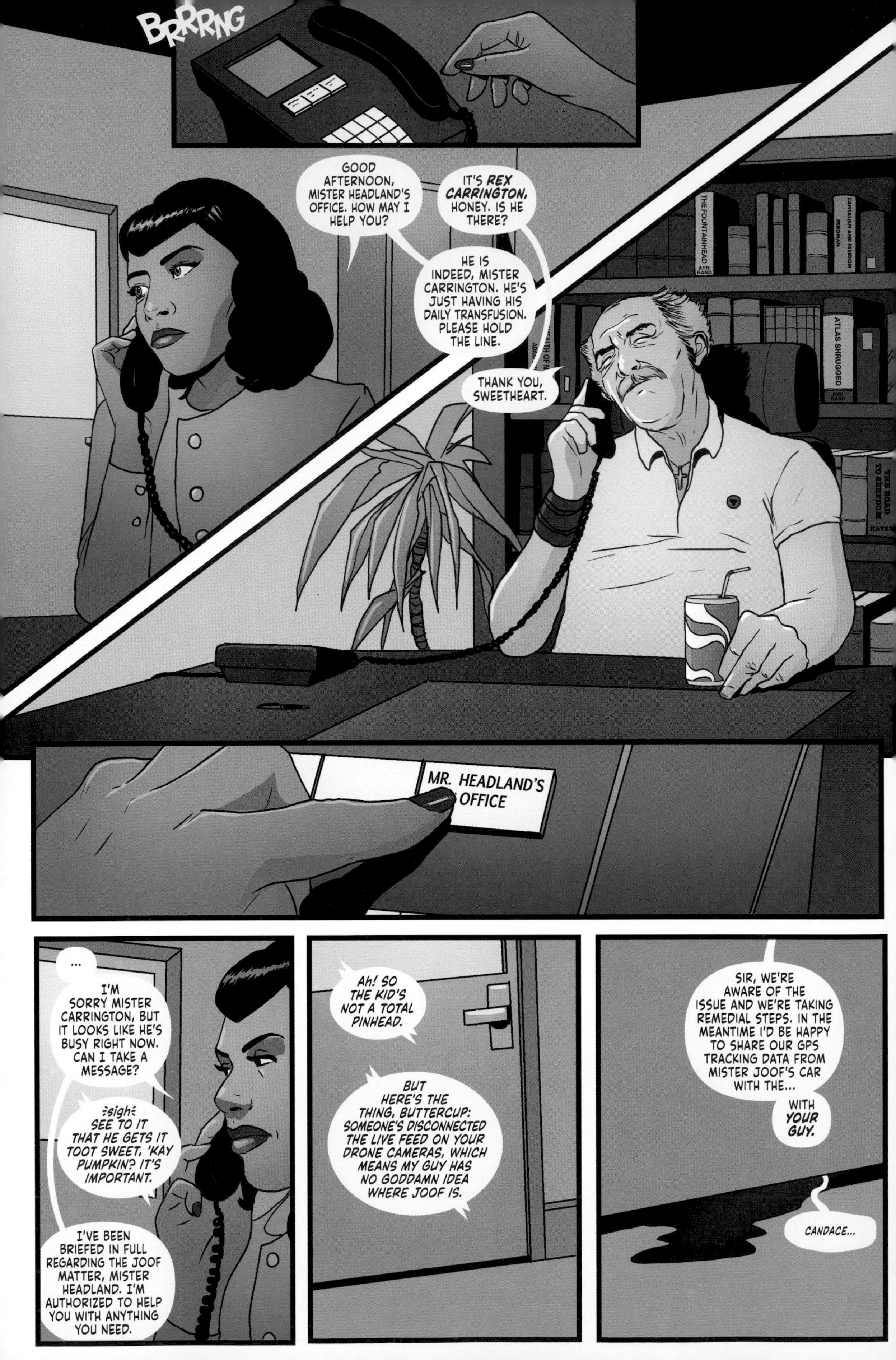
BRRRNG
GOOD AFTERNOON, MISTER HEADLAND'S OFFICE. HOW MAY I HELP YOU?
IT'S REX CARRINGTON, HONEY. IS HE THERE?
HE IS INDEED, MISTER CARRINGTON. HE'S JUST HAVING HIS DAILY TRANSFUSION. PLEASE HOLD THE LINE.
THANK YOU, SWEETHEART.
THE FOUNTAINHEAD AYN RAND
CAPITALISM AND FREEDOM FRIEDMAN
ATLAS SHRUGGED AYN RAND
THE ROAD TO SERFDOM
MR. HEADLAND'S OFFICE
...
I'M SORRY MISTER CARRINGTON, BUT IT LOOKS LIKE HE'S BUSY RIGHT NOW. CAN I TAKE A MESSAGE?
sigh SEE TO IT THAT HE GETS IT TOOT SWEET, 'KAY PUMPKIN? IT'S IMPORTANT.
I'VE BEEN BRIEFED IN FULL REGARDING THE JOOF MATTER, MISTER HEADLAND. I'M AUTHORIZED TO HELP YOU WITH ANYTHING YOU NEED.
AH! SO THE KID'S NOT A TOTAL PINHEAD.
BUT HERE'S THE THING, BUTTERCUP: SOMEONE'S DISCONNECTED THE LIVE FEED ON YOUR DRONE CAMERAS, WHICH MEANS MY GUY HAS NO GODDAMN IDEA WHERE JOOF IS.
SIR, WE'RE AWARE OF THE ISSUE AND WE'RE TAKING REMEDIAL STEPS. IN THE MEANTIME I'D BE HAPPY TO SHARE OUR GPS TRACKING DATA FROM MISTER JOOF'S CAR WITH THE...
WITH YOUR GUY.
CANDACE...

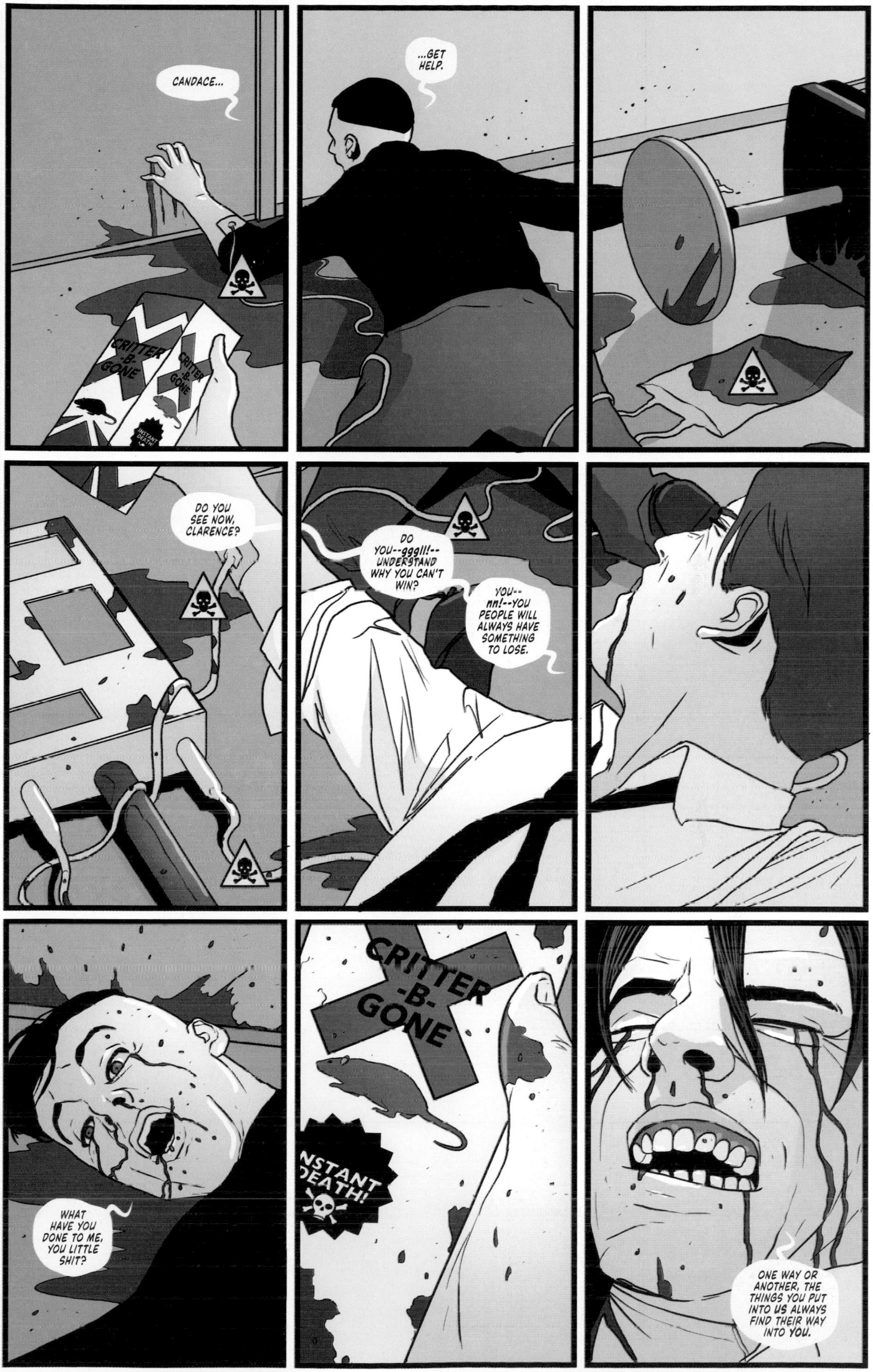

CANDACE...
CRITTER -B- GONE
CRITTER -B- GONE
...GET HELP.
DO YOU SEE NOW, CLARENCE?
DO YOU--gggll!--UNDERSTAND WHY YOU CAN'T WIN?
YOU--nn!--YOU PEOPLE WILL ALWAYS HAVE SOMETHING TO LOSE.
WHAT HAVE YOU DONE TO ME, YOU LITTLE SHIT?
CRITTER -B- GONE
NSTANT DEATH!
ONE WAY OR ANOTHER, THE THINGS YOU PUT INTO US ALWAYS FIND THEIR WAY INTO YOU.

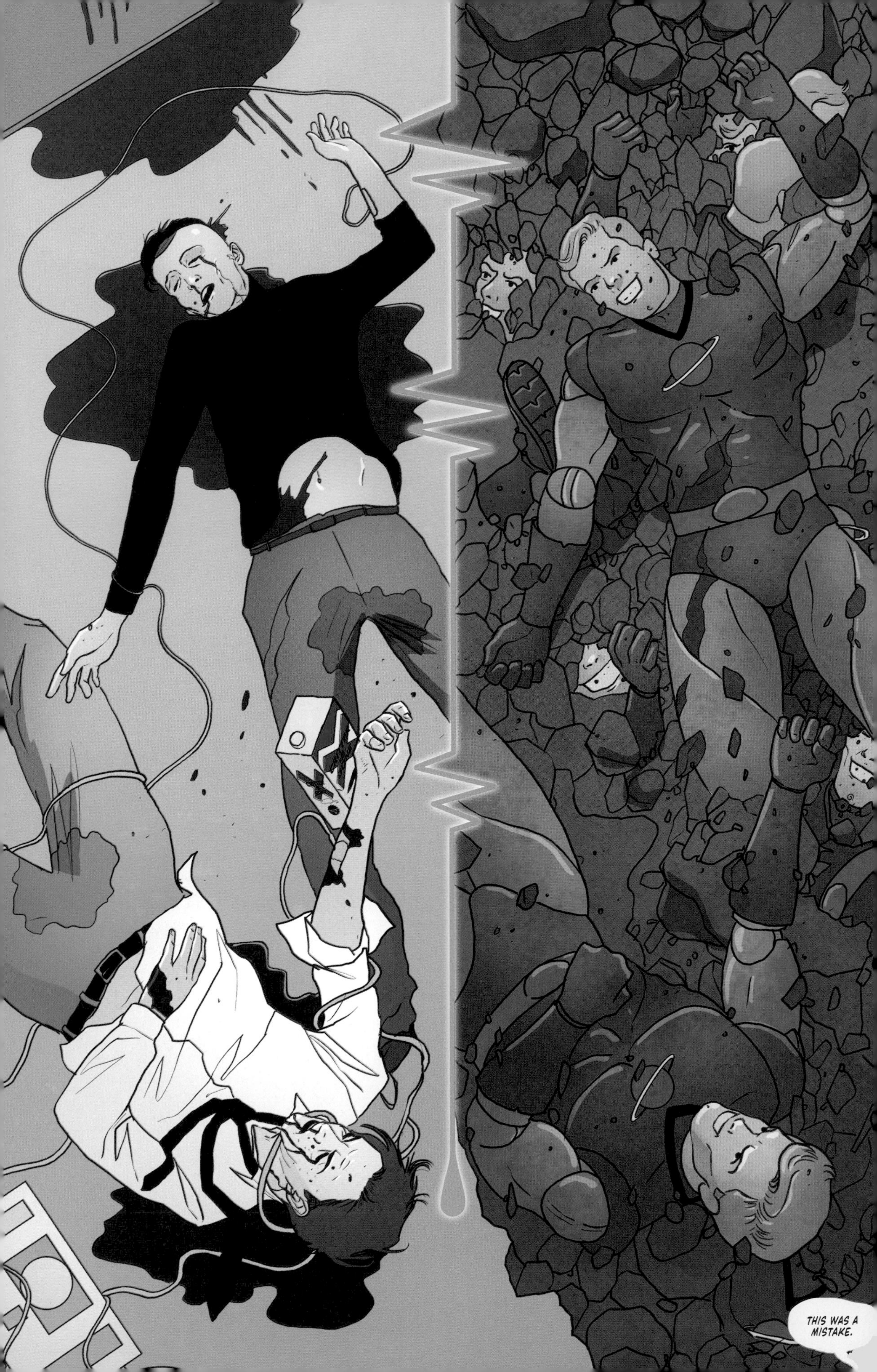
THIS WAS A MISTAKE.

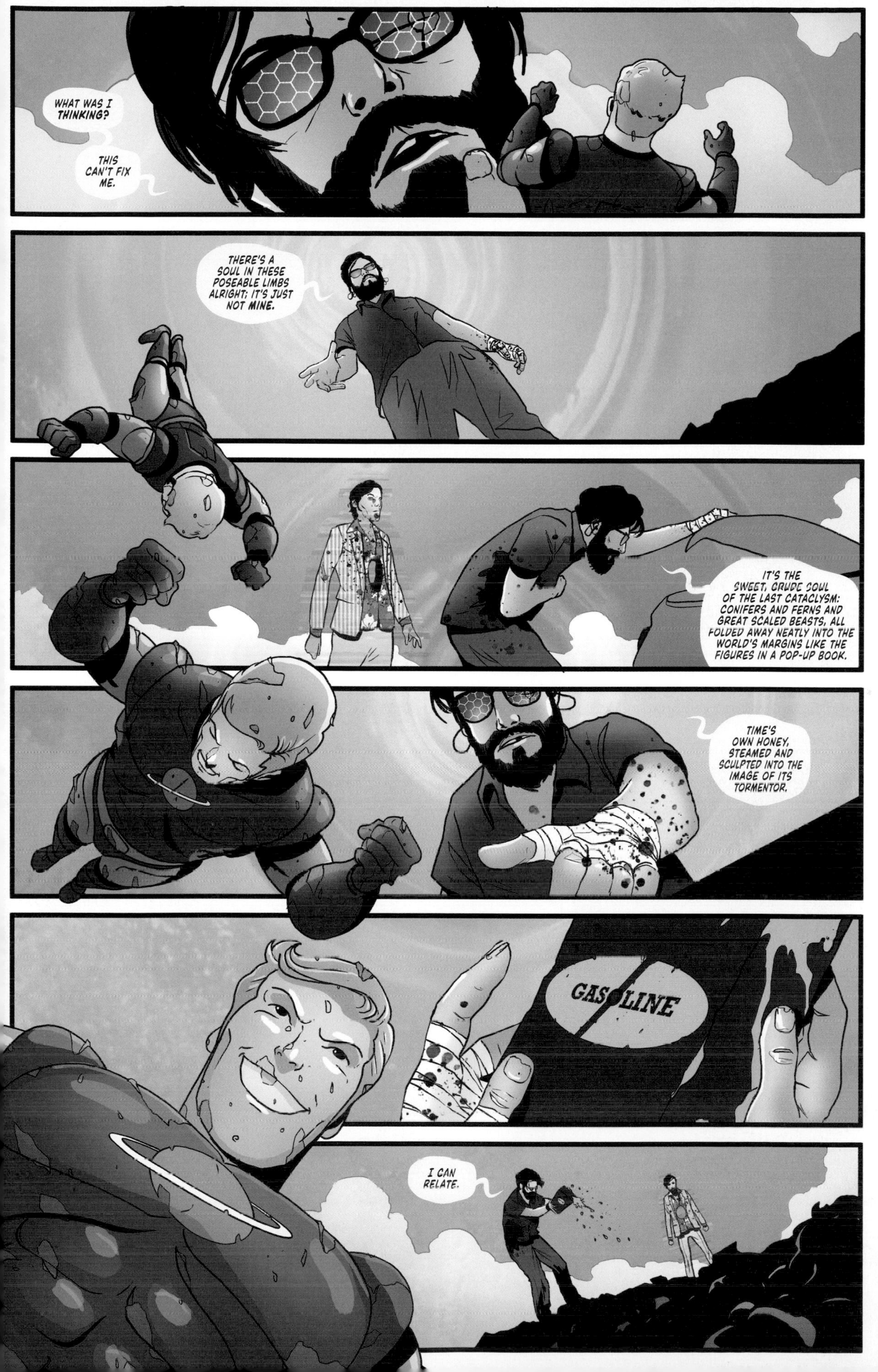

WHAT WAS I THINKING?
THIS CAN'T FIX ME.
THERE'S A SOUL IN THESE POSEABLE LIMBS ALRIGHT; IT'S JUST NOT MINE.
IT'S THE SWEET, CRUDE SOUL OF THE LAST CATACLYSM: CONIFERS AND FERNS AND GREAT SCALED BEASTS, ALL FOLDED AWAY NEATLY INTO THE WORLD'S MARGINS LIKE THE FIGURES IN A POP-UP BOOK.
TIME'S OWN HONEY, STEAMED AND SCULPTED INTO THE IMAGE OF ITS TORMENTOR.
GASOLINE
I CAN RELATE.

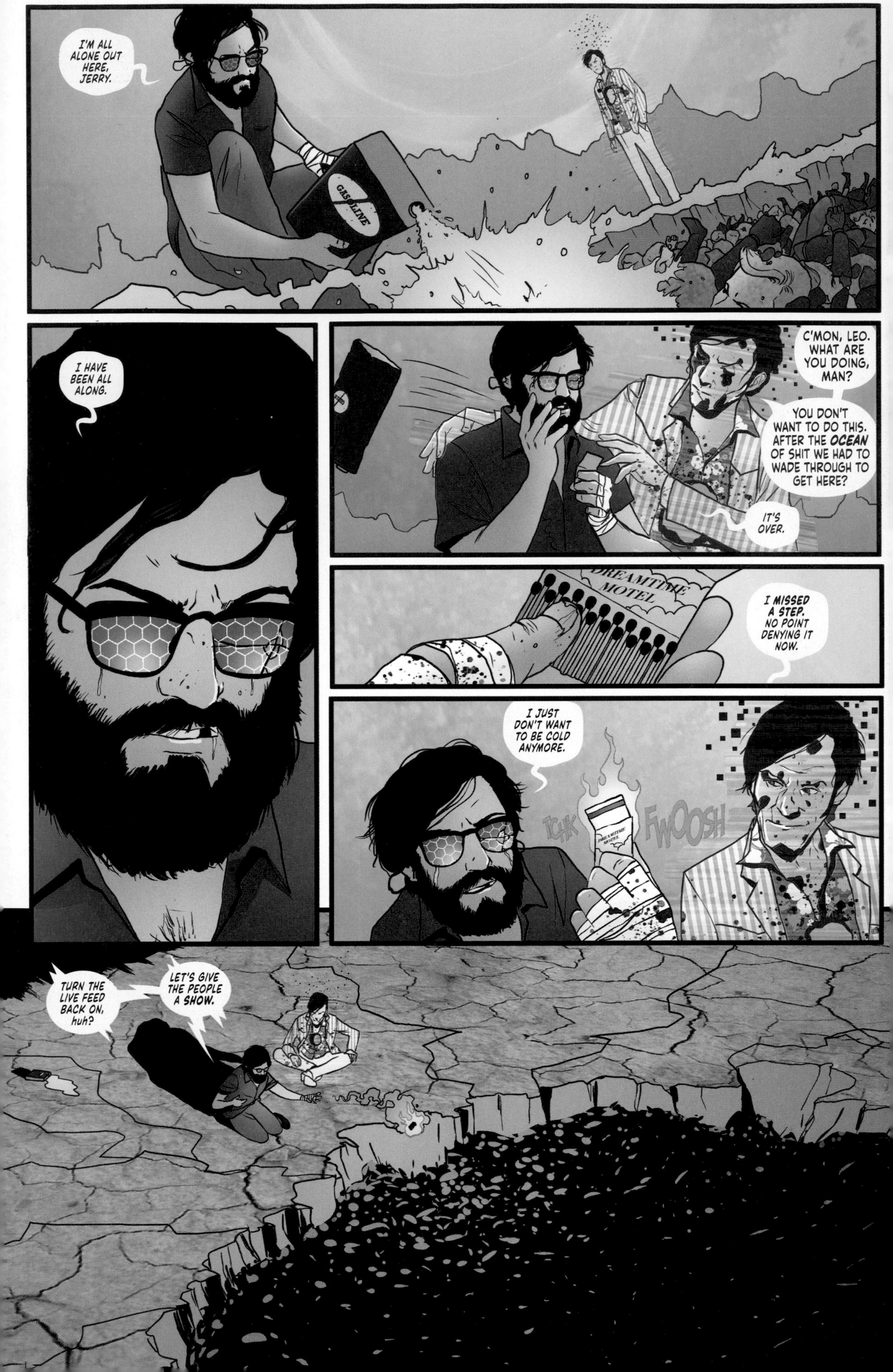
I'M ALL ALONE OUT HERE, JERRY.
I HAVE BEEN ALL ALONG.
C'MON, LEO. WHAT ARE YOU DOING, MAN?
YOU DON'T WANT TO DO THIS. AFTER THE OCEAN OF SHIT WE HAD TO WADE THROUGH TO GET HERE?
IT'S OVER.
DREAMTIME MOTEL
I MISSED A STEP. NO POINT DENYING IT NOW.
I JUST DON'T WANT TO BE COLD ANYMORE.
TCHK
FWOOSH
DREAMTIME MOTEL
TURN THE LIVE FEED BACK ON, huh?
LET'S GIVE THE PEOPLE A SHOW.

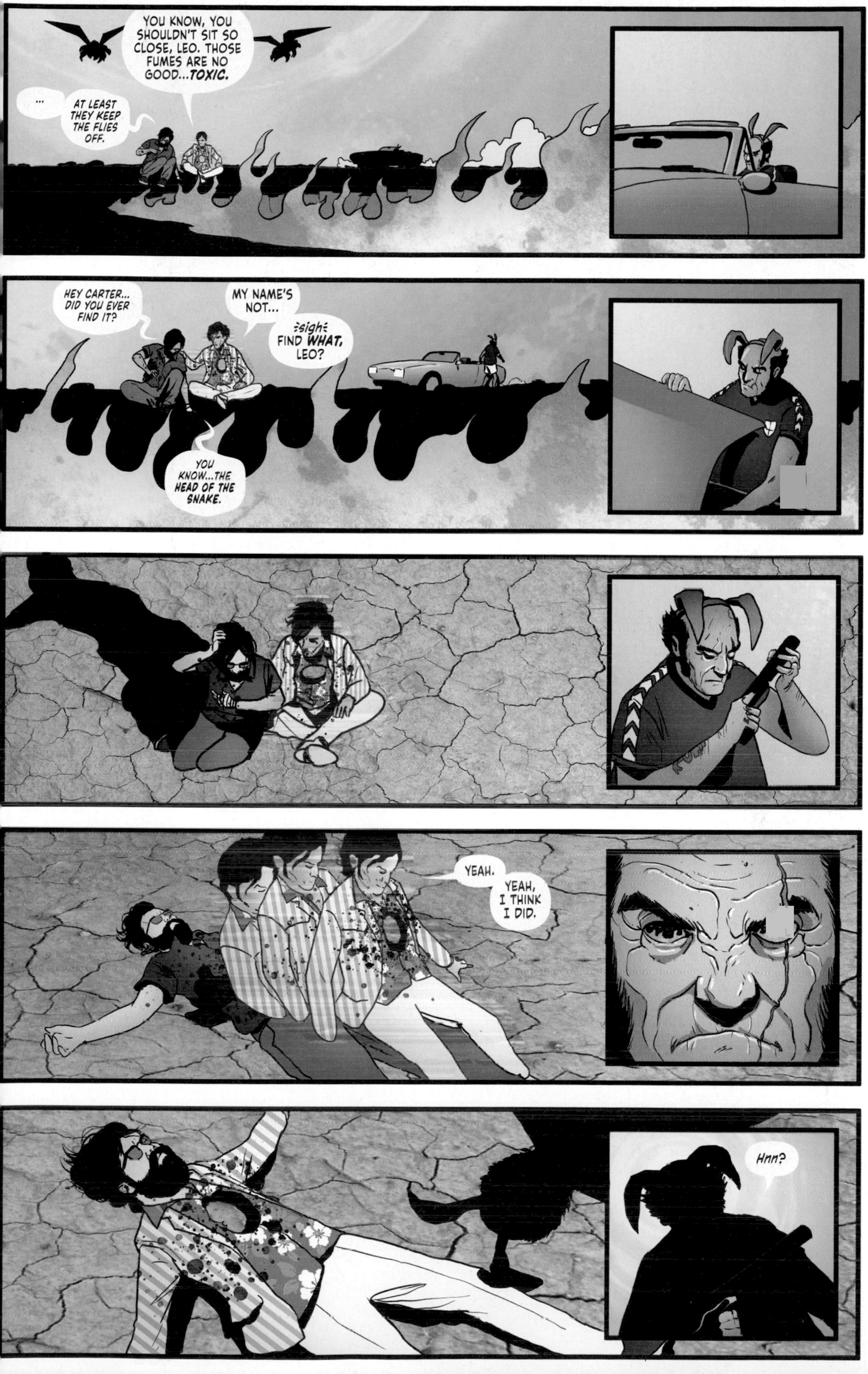

YOU KNOW, YOU SHOULDN'T SIT SO CLOSE, LEO. THOSE FUMES ARE NO GOOD...TOXIC.
...
AT LEAST THEY KEEP THE FLIES OFF.
HEY CARTER... DID YOU EVER FIND IT?
MY NAME'S NOT...
sigh
FIND WHAT, LEO?
YOU KNOW...THE HEAD OF THE SNAKE.
YEAH.
YEAH, I THINK I DID.
Hnn?

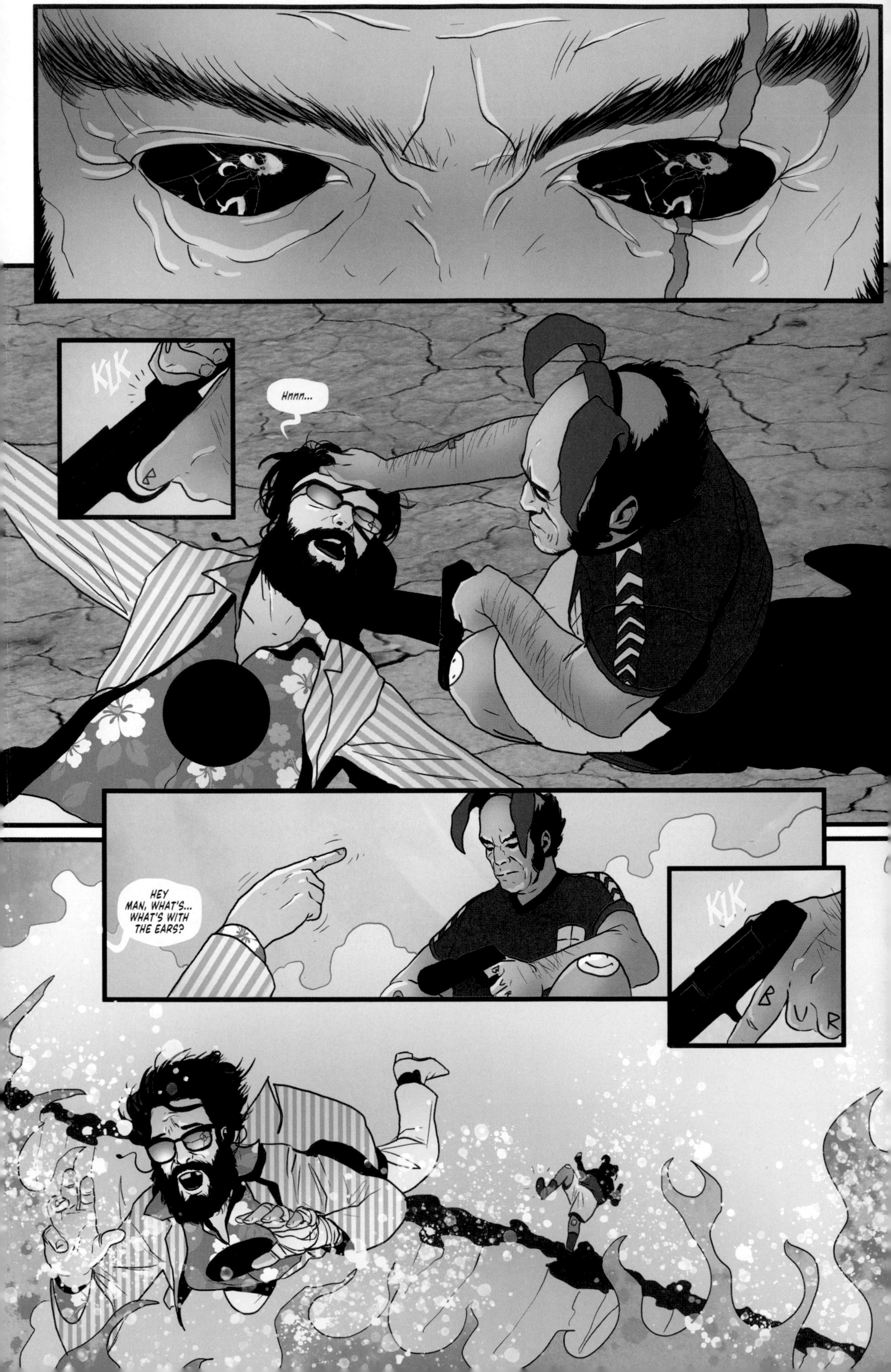
KLK
Hnnn...
HEY MAN, WHAT'S... WHAT'S WITH THE EARS?
KLK
B U R

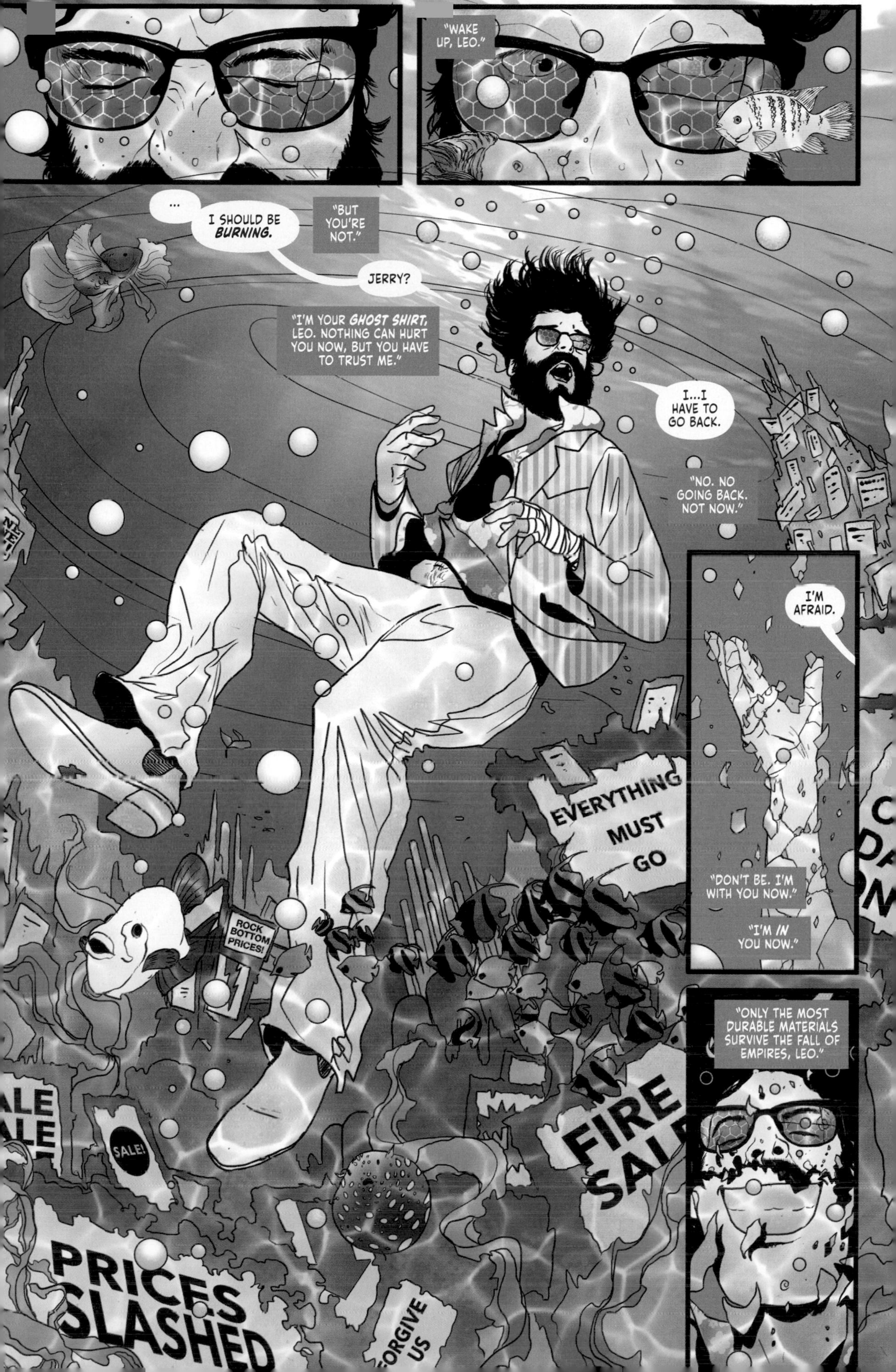
"WAKE UP, LEO."
...
I SHOULD BE BURNING.
"BUT YOU'RE NOT."
JERRY?
"I'M YOUR GHOST SHIRT, LEO. NOTHING CAN HURT YOU NOW, BUT YOU HAVE TO TRUST ME."
I...I HAVE TO GO BACK.
"NO. NO GOING BACK. NOT NOW."
I'M AFRAID.
"DON'T BE. I'M WITH YOU NOW."
"I'M IN YOU NOW."
"ONLY THE MOST DURABLE MATERIALS SURVIVE THE FALL OF EMPIRES, LEO."
EVERYTHING MUST GO
ROCK BOTTOM PRICES!
SALE!
FIRE SAL
PRICES SLASHED
FORGIVE US

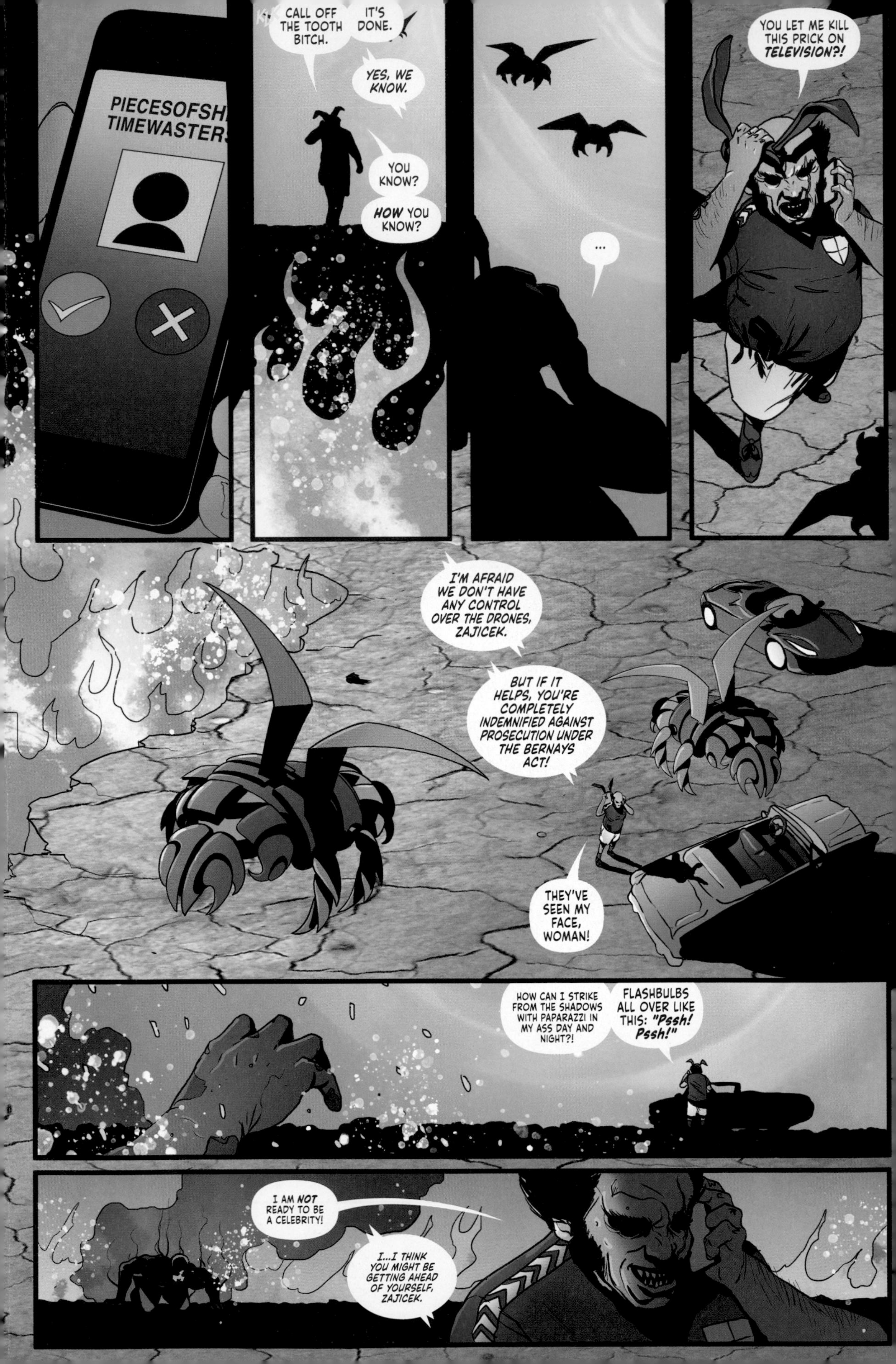
PIECESOFSH
TIMEWASTERS
CALL OFF THE TOOTH BITCH.
IT'S DONE.
YES, WE KNOW.
YOU KNOW?
HOW YOU KNOW?
...
YOU LET ME KILL THIS PRICK ON TELEVISION?!
I'M AFRAID WE DON'T HAVE ANY CONTROL OVER THE DRONES, ZAJICEK.
BUT IF IT HELPS, YOU'RE COMPLETELY INDEMNIFIED AGAINST PROSECUTION UNDER THE BERNAYS ACT!
THEY'VE SEEN MY FACE, WOMAN!
HOW CAN I STRIKE FROM THE SHADOWS WITH PAPARAZZI IN MY ASS DAY AND NIGHT?!
FLASHBULBS ALL OVER LIKE THIS: "Pssh! Pssh!"
I AM NOT READY TO BE A CELEBRITY!
I...I THINK YOU MIGHT BE GETTING AHEAD OF YOURSELF, ZAJICEK.

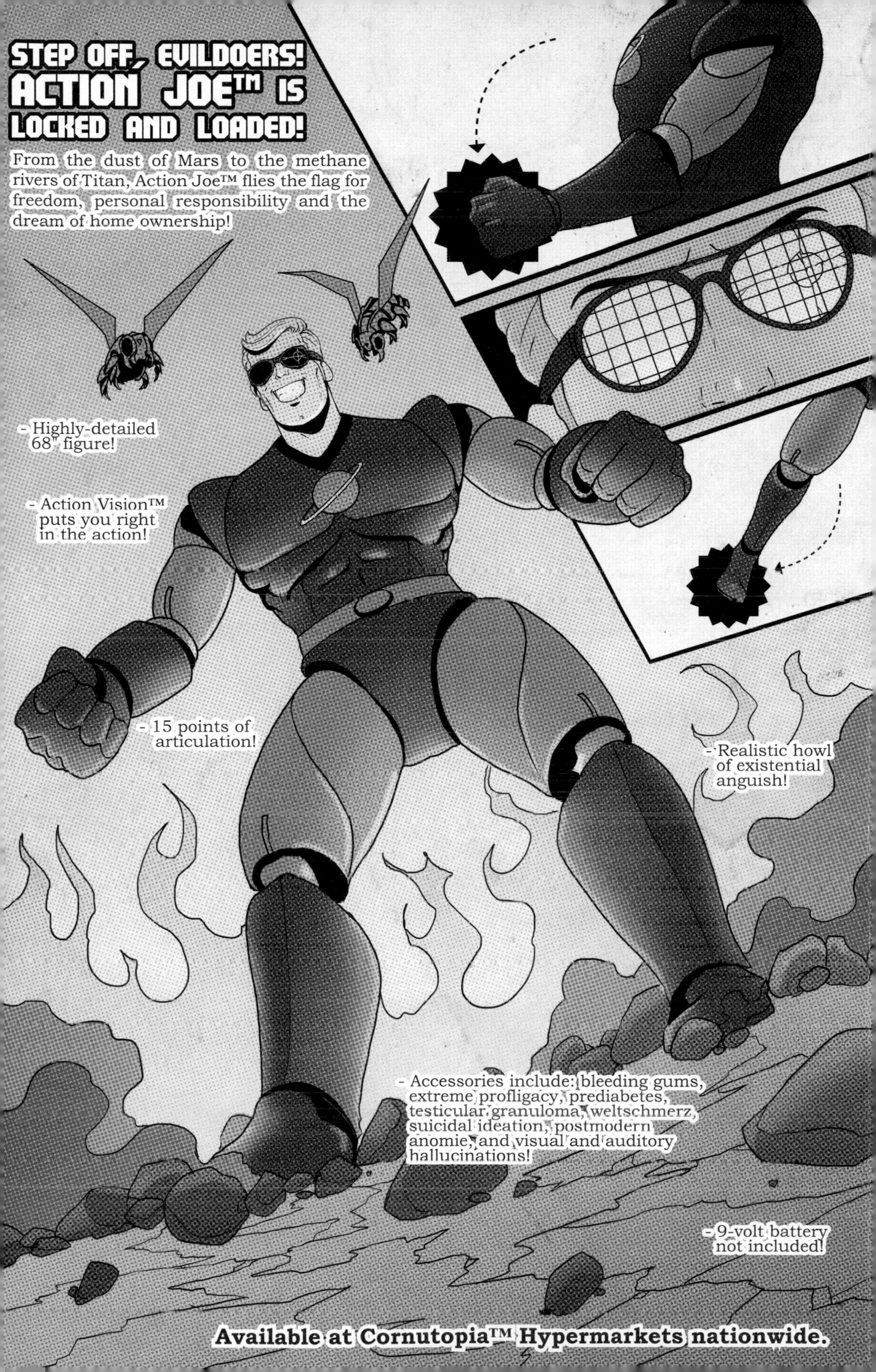
STEP OFF, EVILDOERS! ACTION JOE™ IS LOCKED AND LOADED!
From the dust of Mars to the methane rivers of Titan, Action Joe™ flies the flag for freedom, personal responsibility and the dream of home ownership!
- Highly-detailed 68" figure!
- Action Vision™ puts you right in the action!
- 15 points of articulation!
- Realistic howl of existential anguish!
- Accessories include: bleeding gums, extreme profligacy, prediabetes, testicular granuloma, weltschmerz, suicidal ideation, postmodern anomie, and visual and auditory hallucinations!
- 9-volt battery not included!
Available at Cornutopia™ Hypermarkets nationwide.

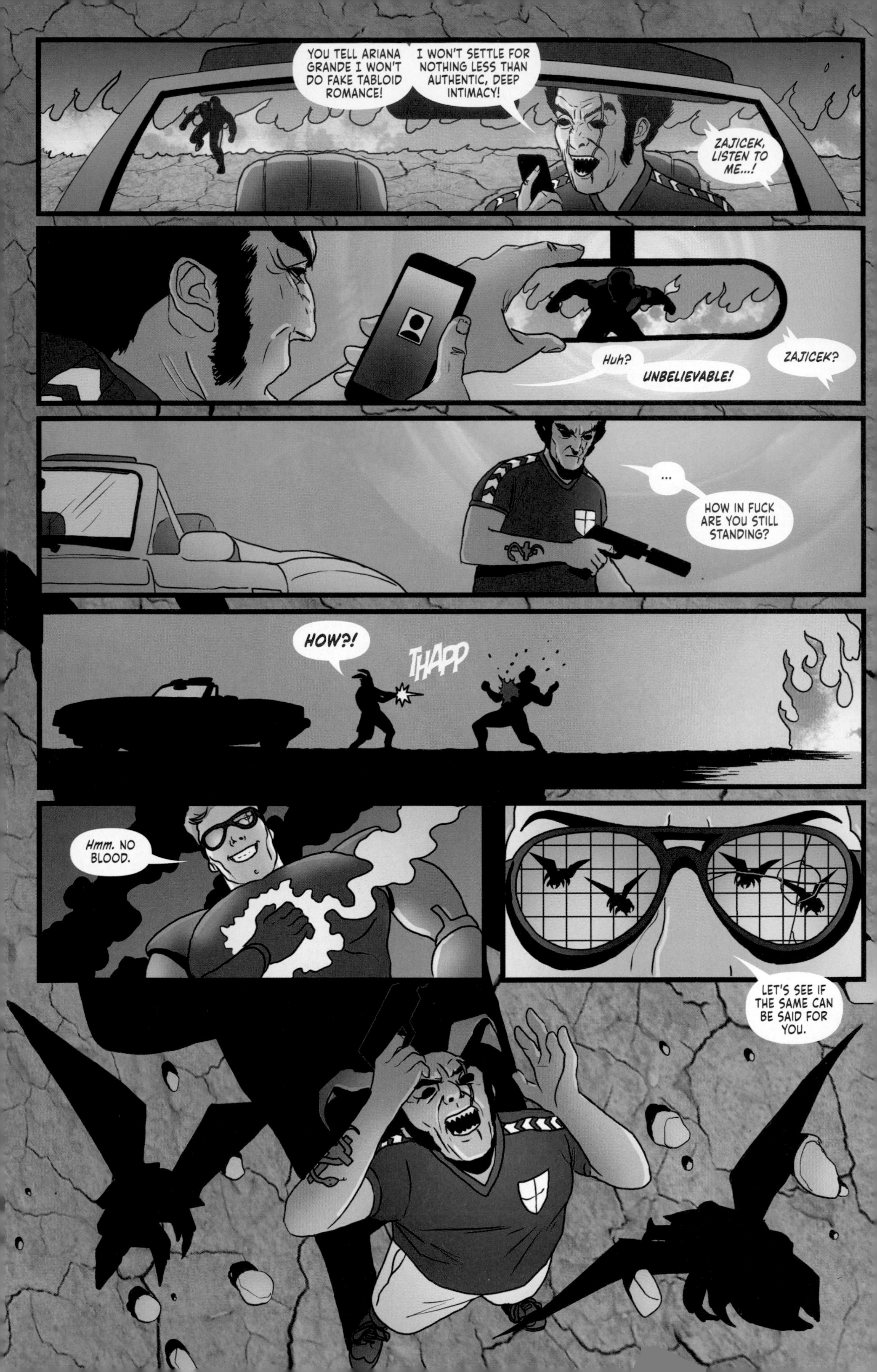
YOU TELL ARIANA GRANDE I WON'T DO FAKE TABLOID ROMANCE!
I WON'T SETTLE FOR NOTHING LESS THAN AUTHENTIC, DEEP INTIMACY!
ZAJICEK, LISTEN TO ME...!
Huh?
UNBELIEVABLE!
ZAJICEK?
...
HOW IN FUCK ARE YOU STILL STANDING?
HOW?!
THAPP
Hmm. NO BLOOD.
LET'S SEE IF THE SAME CAN BE SAID FOR YOU.

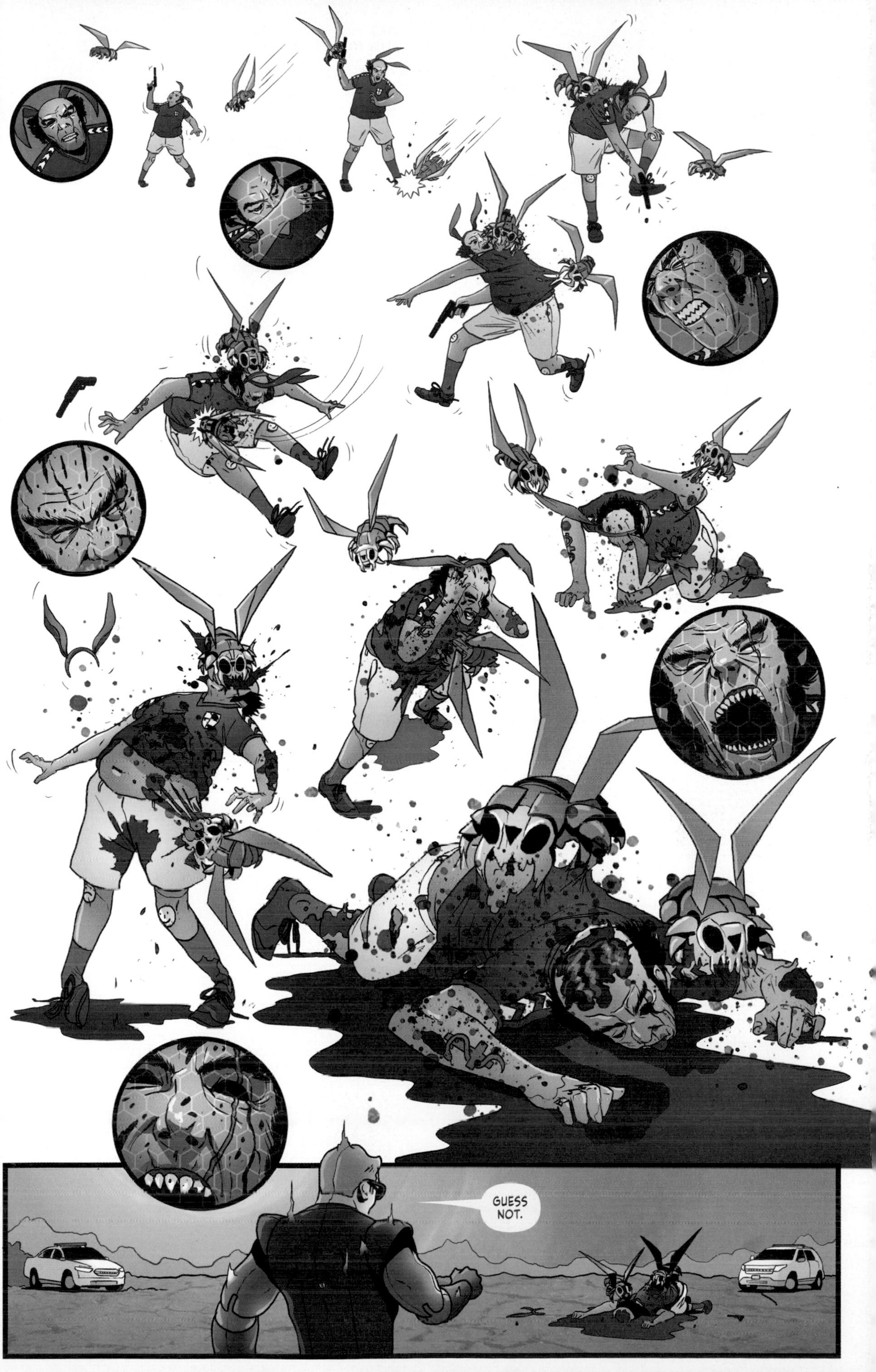
GUESS NOT.

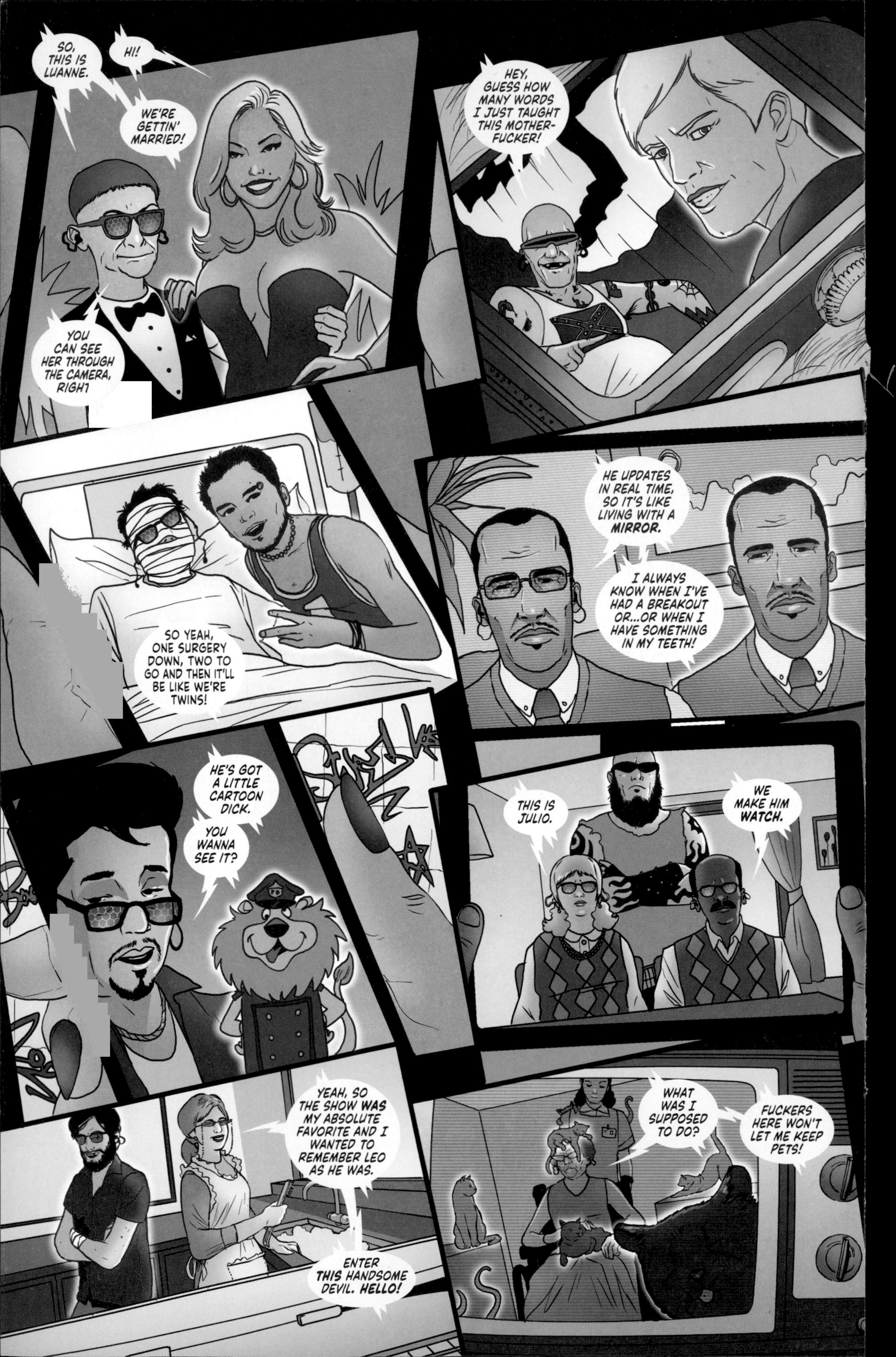
SO, THIS IS LUANNE.
HI!
WE'RE GETTIN' MARRIED!
YOU CAN SEE HER THROUGH THE CAMERA, RIGH
HEY, GUESS HOW MANY WORDS I JUST TAUGHT THIS MOTHER-FUCKER!
SO YEAH, ONE SURGERY DOWN, TWO TO GO AND THEN IT'LL BE LIKE WE'RE TWINS!
HE UPDATES IN REAL TIME, SO IT'S LIKE LIVING WITH A MIRROR.
I ALWAYS KNOW WHEN I'VE HAD A BREAKOUT OR...OR WHEN I HAVE SOMETHING IN MY TEETH!
HE'S GOT A LITTLE CARTOON DICK.
YOU WANNA SEE IT?
THIS IS JULIO.
WE MAKE HIM WATCH.
YEAH, SO THE SHOW WAS MY ABSOLUTE FAVORITE AND I WANTED TO REMEMBER LEO AS HE WAS.
ENTER THIS HANDSOME DEVIL. HELLO!
WHAT WAS I SUPPOSED TO DO?
FUCKERS HERE WON'T LET ME KEEP PETS!

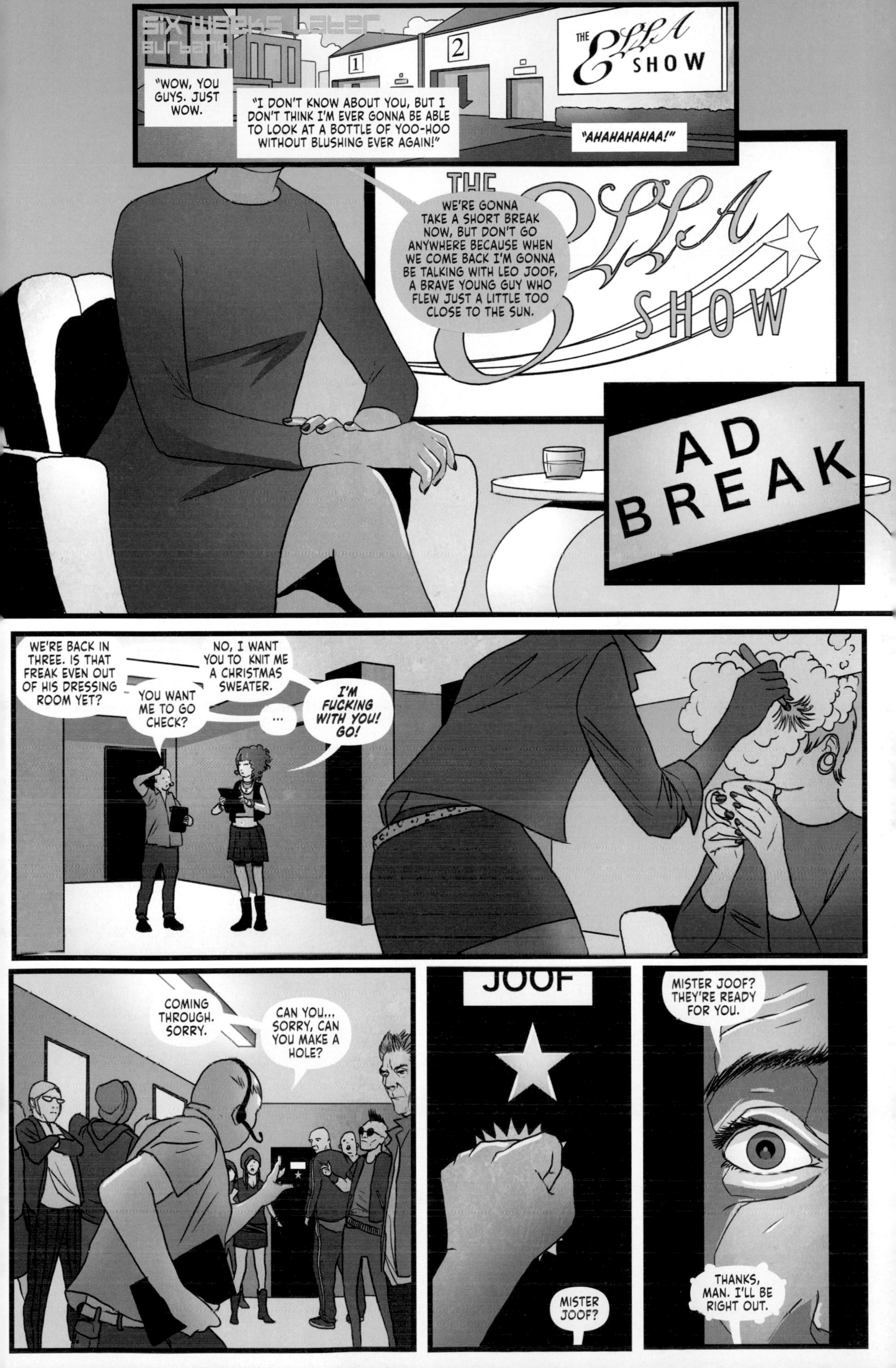

SIX WEEKS LATER,
BURBANK.
"WOW, YOU GUYS. JUST WOW.
"I DON'T KNOW ABOUT YOU, BUT I DON'T THINK I'M EVER GONNA BE ABLE TO LOOK AT A BOTTLE OF YOO-HOO WITHOUT BLUSHING EVER AGAIN!"
THE ELLA SHOW
1
2
"AHAHAHAHAA!"
WE'RE GONNA TAKE A SHORT BREAK NOW, BUT DON'T GO ANYWHERE BECAUSE WHEN WE COME BACK I'M GONNA BE TALKING WITH LEO JOOF, A BRAVE YOUNG GUY WHO FLEW JUST A LITTLE TOO CLOSE TO THE SUN.
THE ELLA SHOW
AD BREAK
WE'RE BACK IN THREE. IS THAT FREAK EVEN OUT OF HIS DRESSING ROOM YET?
YOU WANT ME TO GO CHECK?
NO, I WANT YOU TO KNIT ME A CHRISTMAS SWEATER.
...
I'M FUCKING WITH YOU! GO!
COMING THROUGH. SORRY.
CAN YOU... SORRY, CAN YOU MAKE A HOLE?
JOOF
MISTER JOOF?
MISTER JOOF? THEY'RE READY FOR YOU.
THANKS, MAN. I'LL BE RIGHT OUT.

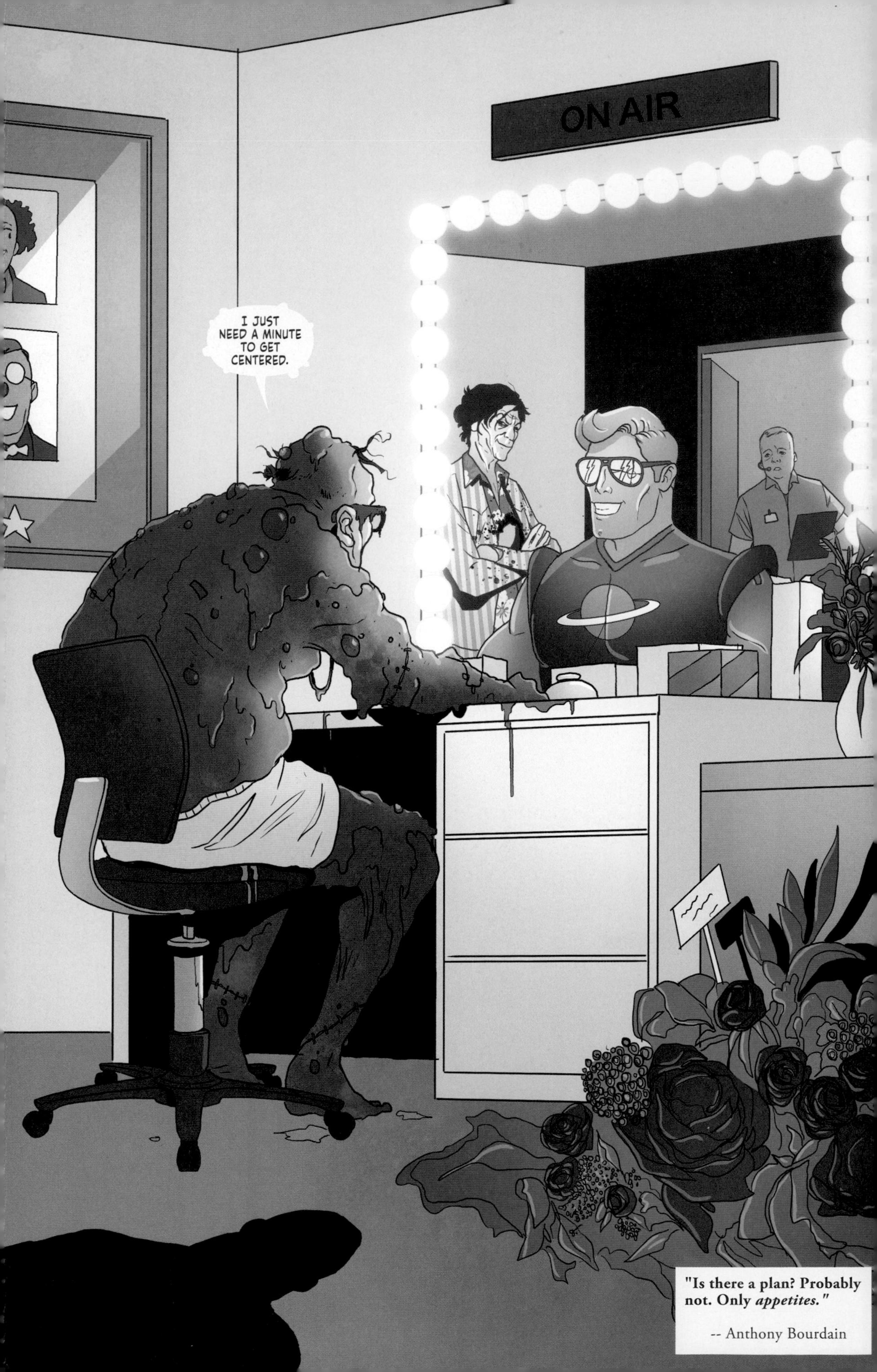
ON AIR
I JUST NEED A MINUTE TO GET CENTERED.

"Is there a plan? Probably not. Only *appetites.*"

-- Anthony Bourdain

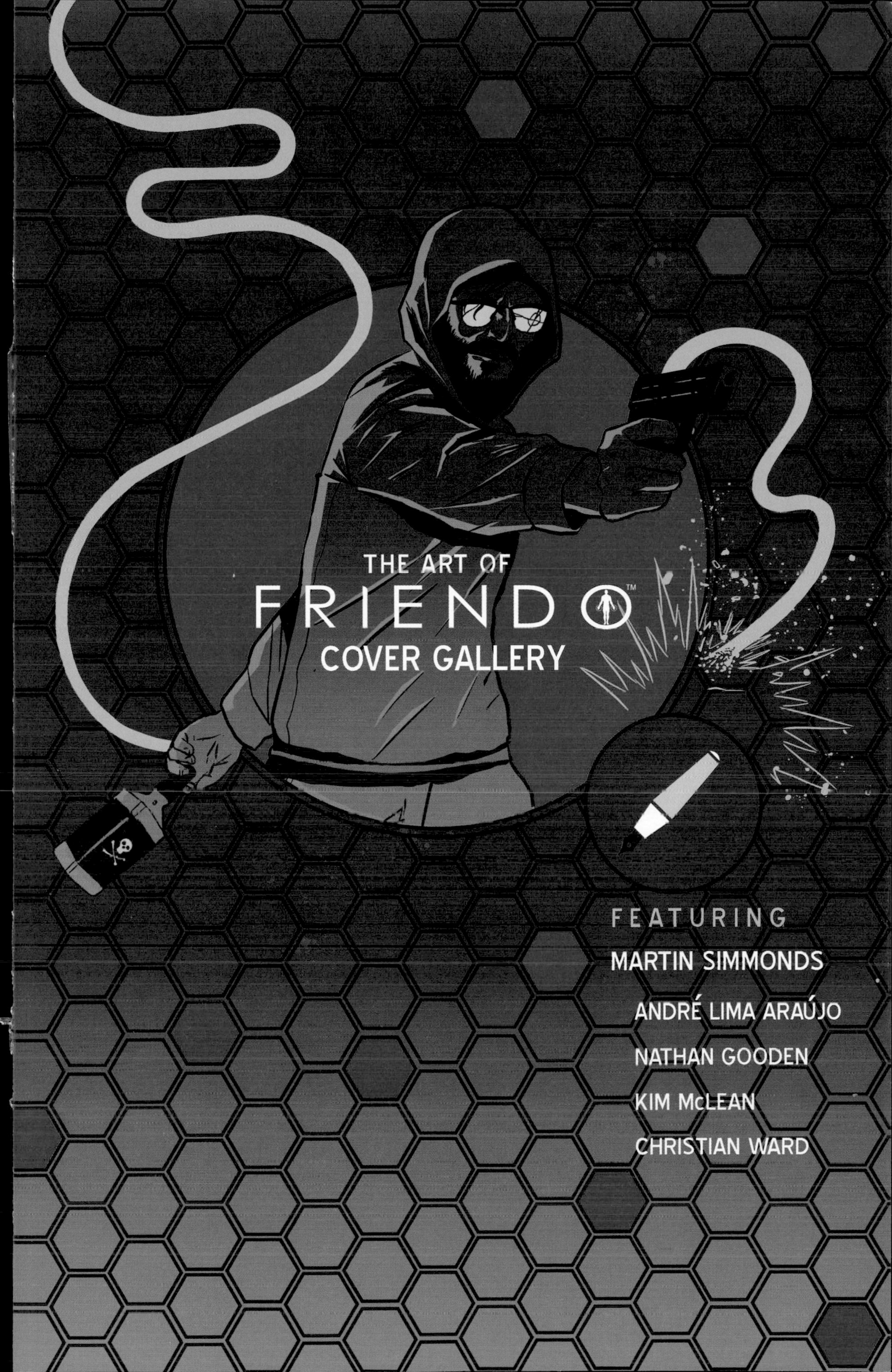
THE ART OF
FRIENDO™
COVER GALLERY
FEATURING
MARTIN SIMMONDS
ANDRÉ LIMA ARAÚJO
NATHAN GOODEN
KIM McLEAN
CHRISTIAN WARD

1

MARTIN SIMMONDS

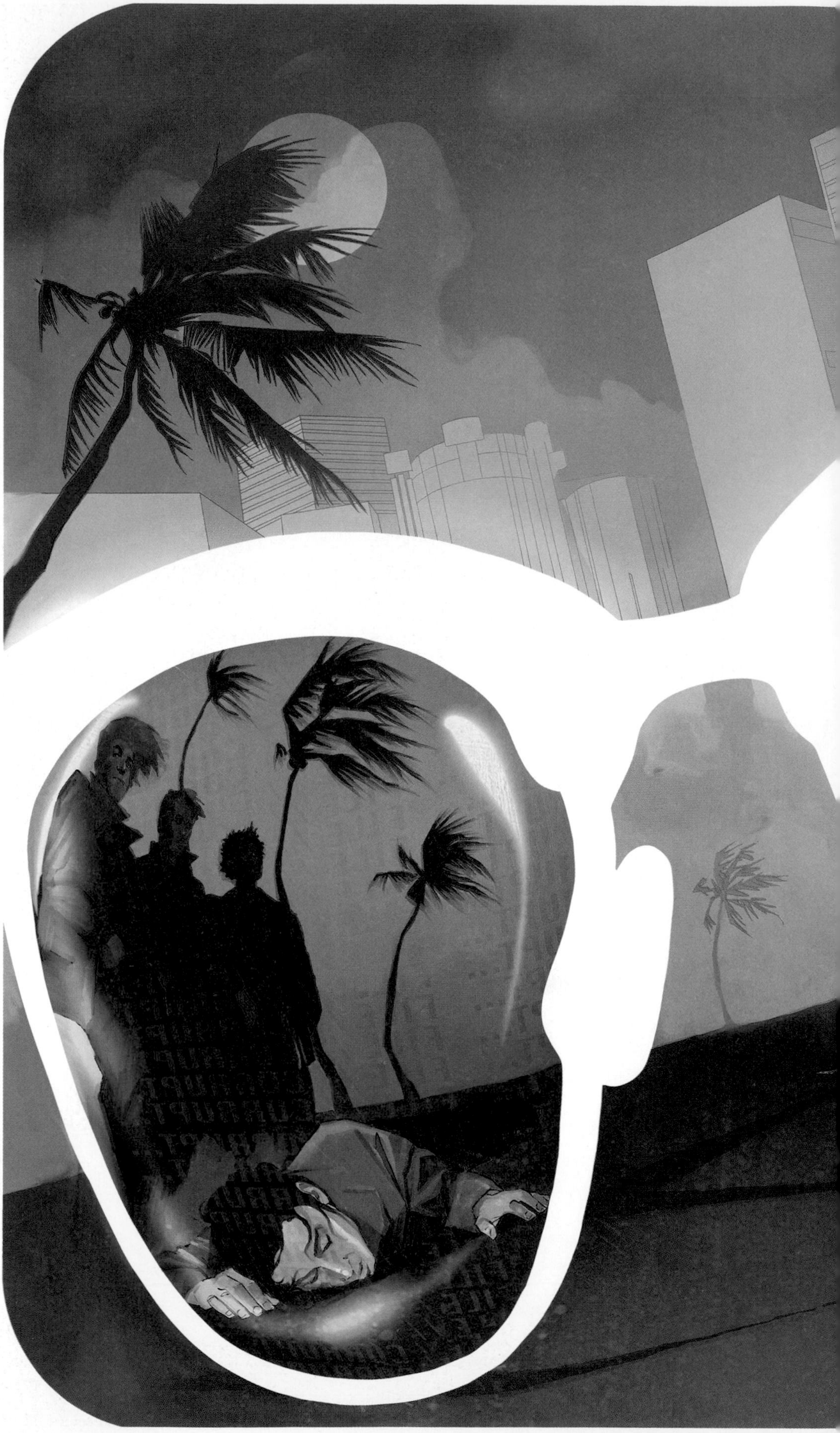

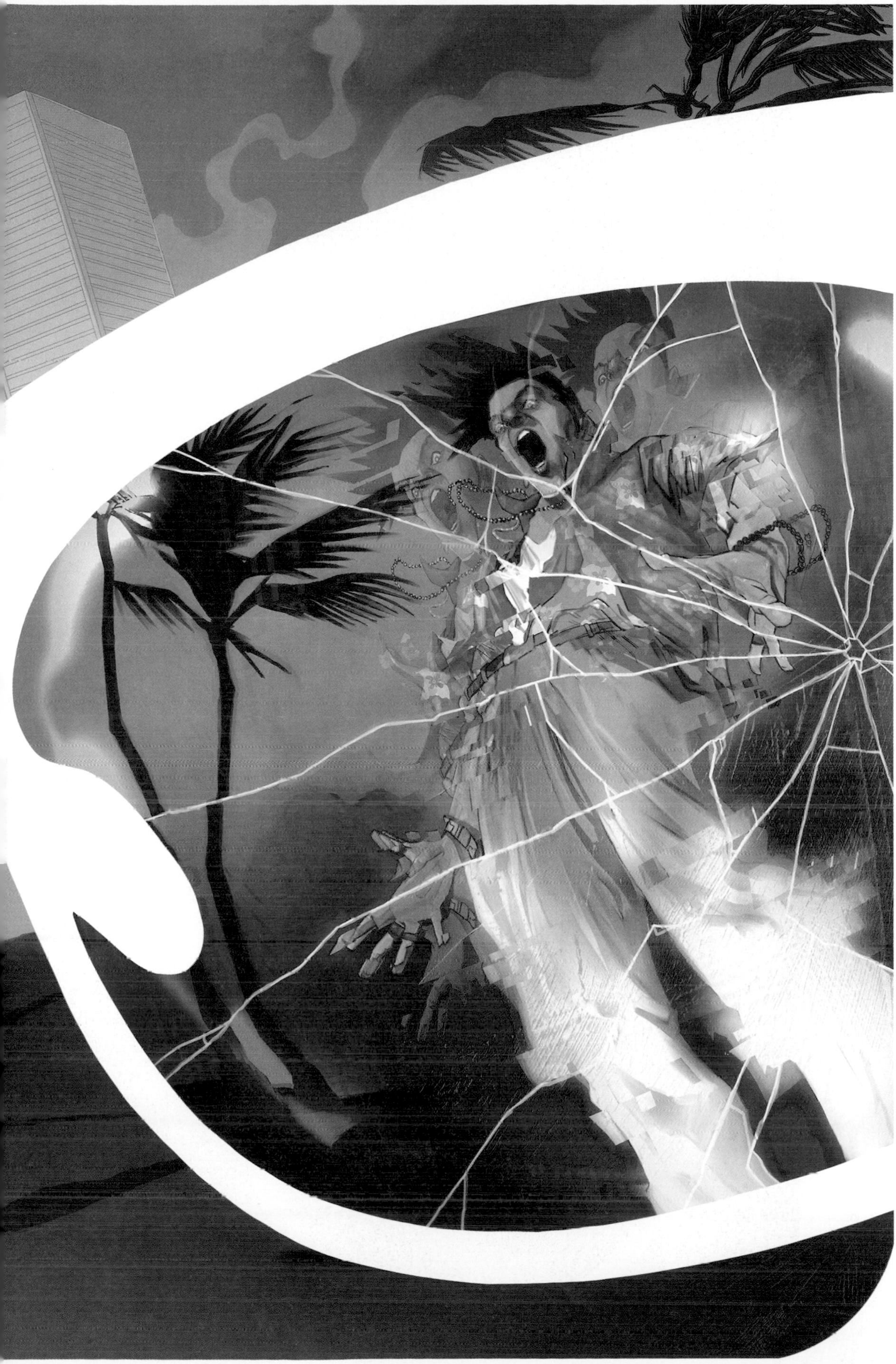

2

MARTIN SIMMONDS

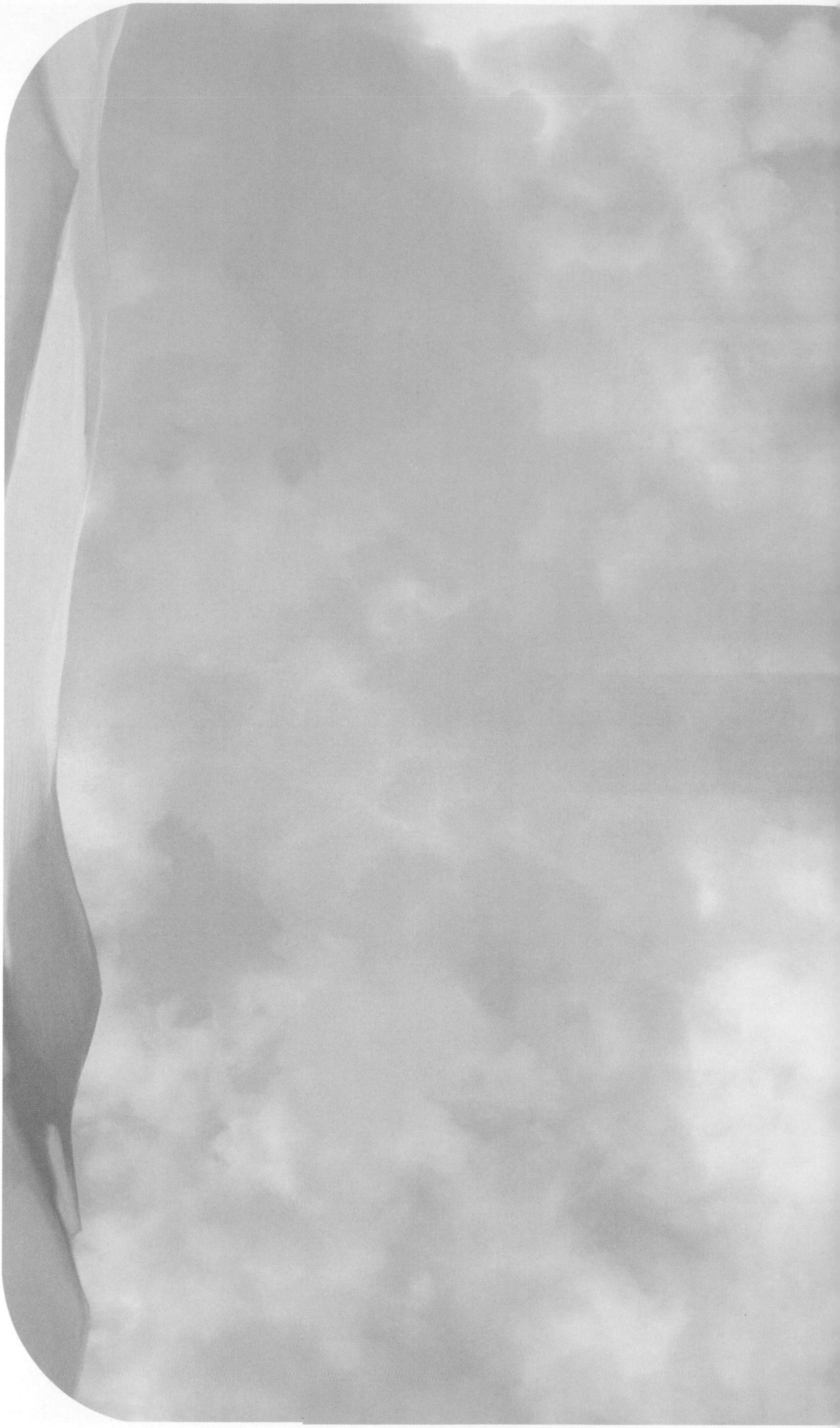

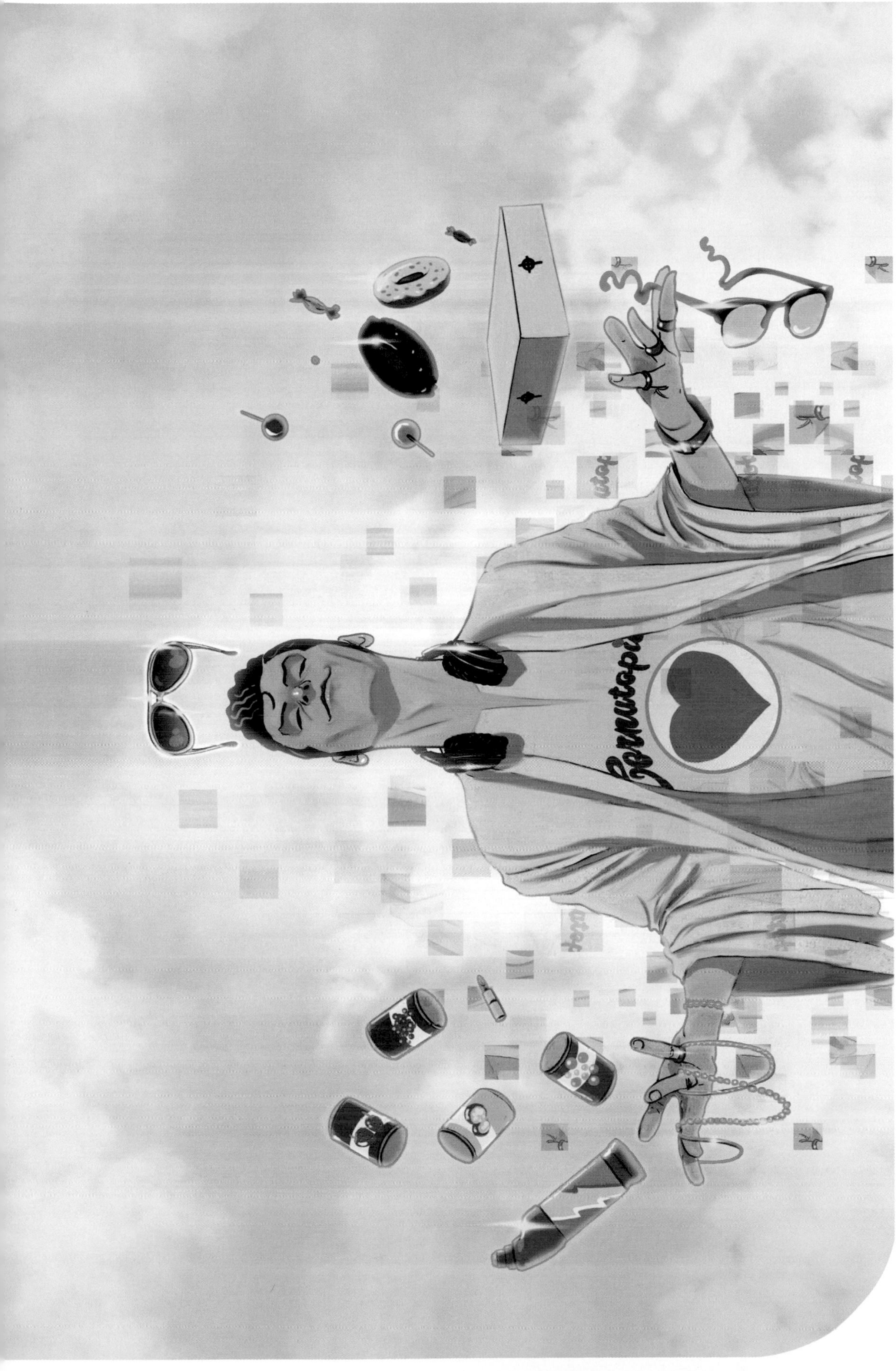
Cornutopi

3

MARTIN SIMMONDS

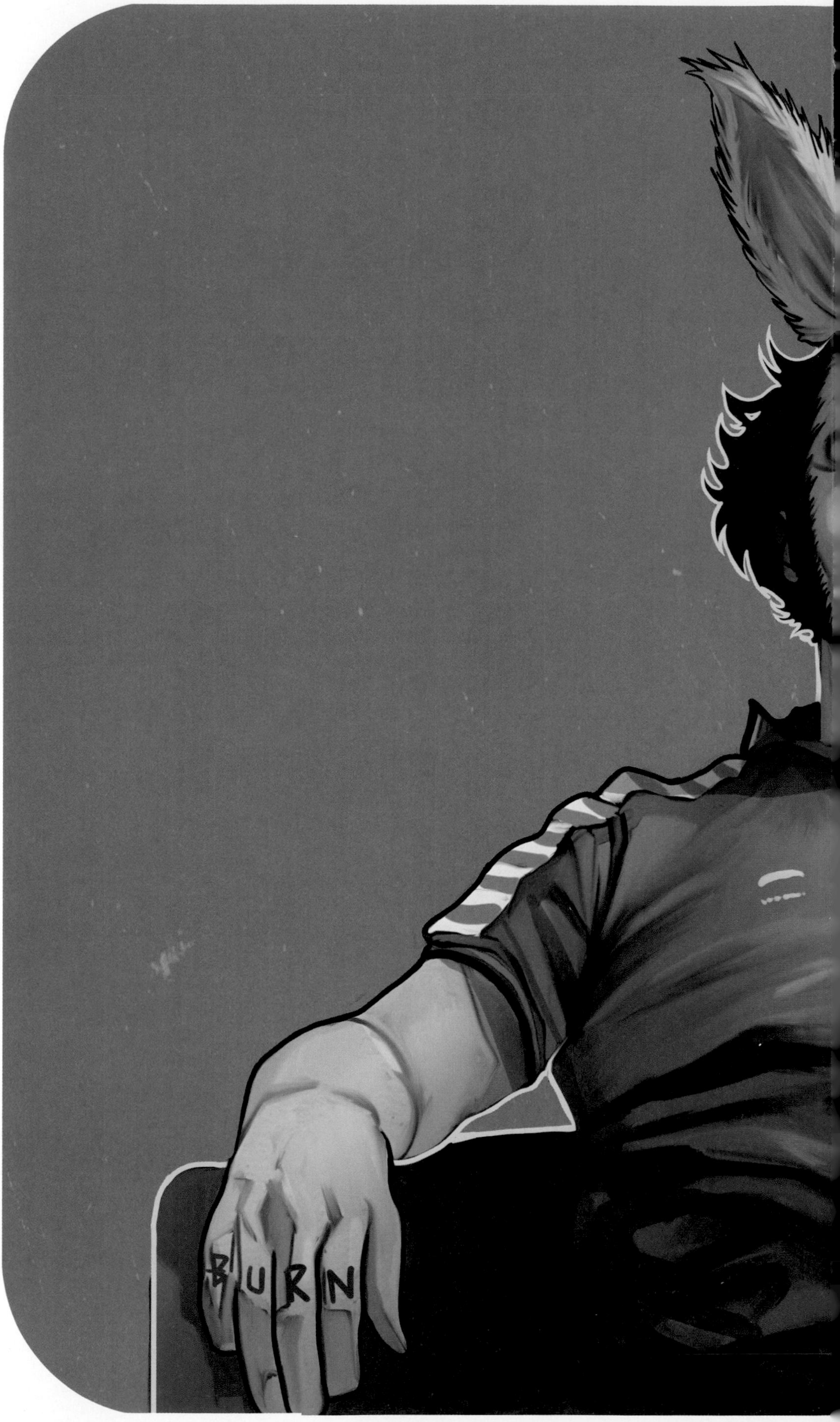
BURN

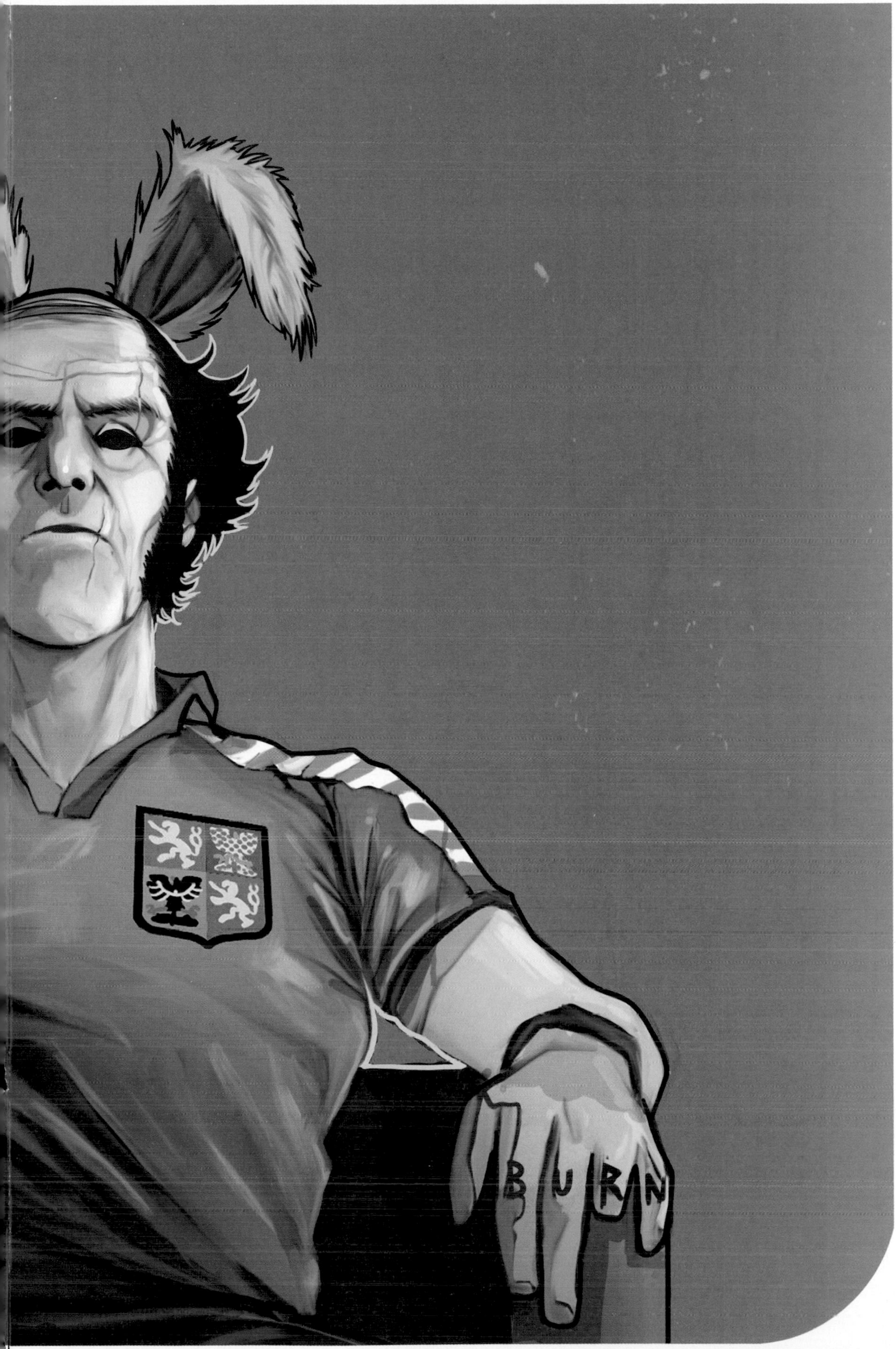
B U R N

4

MARTIN SIMMONDS

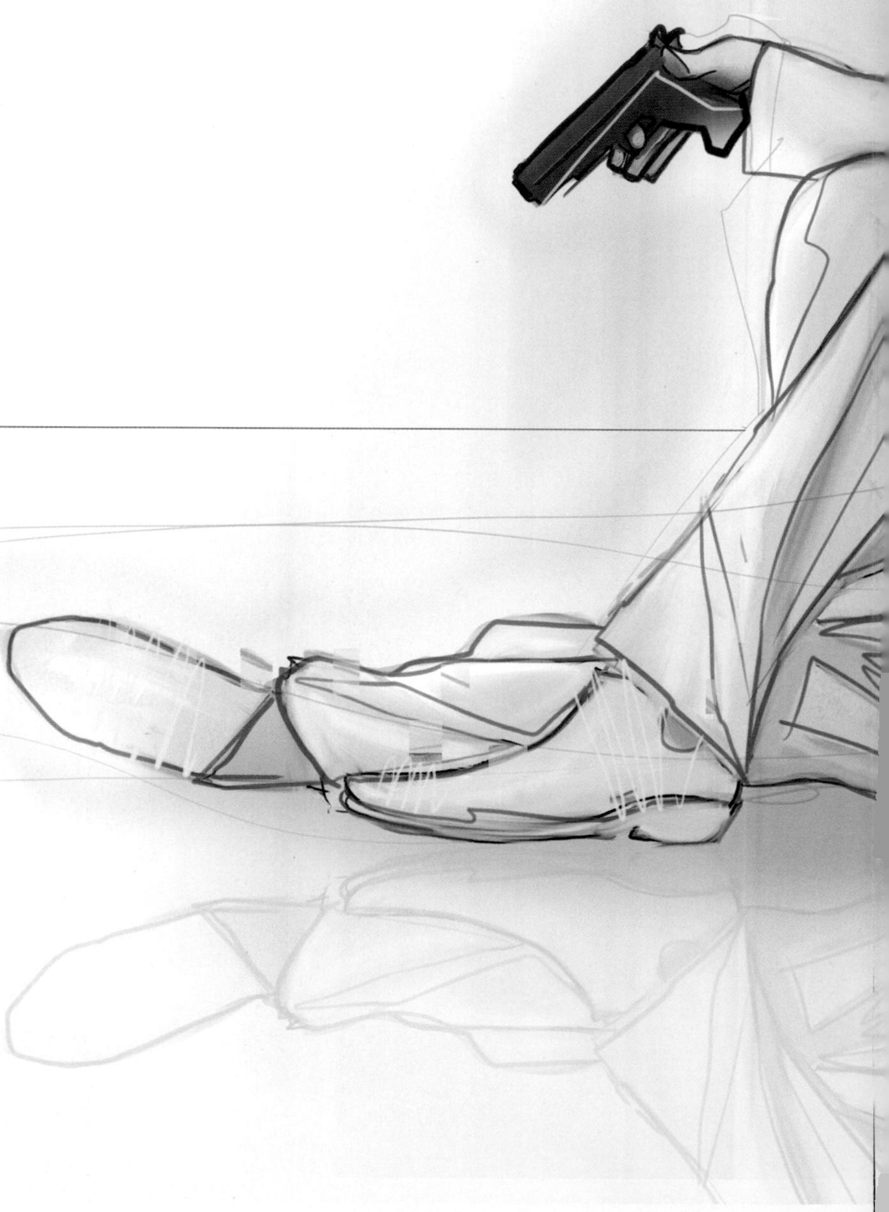

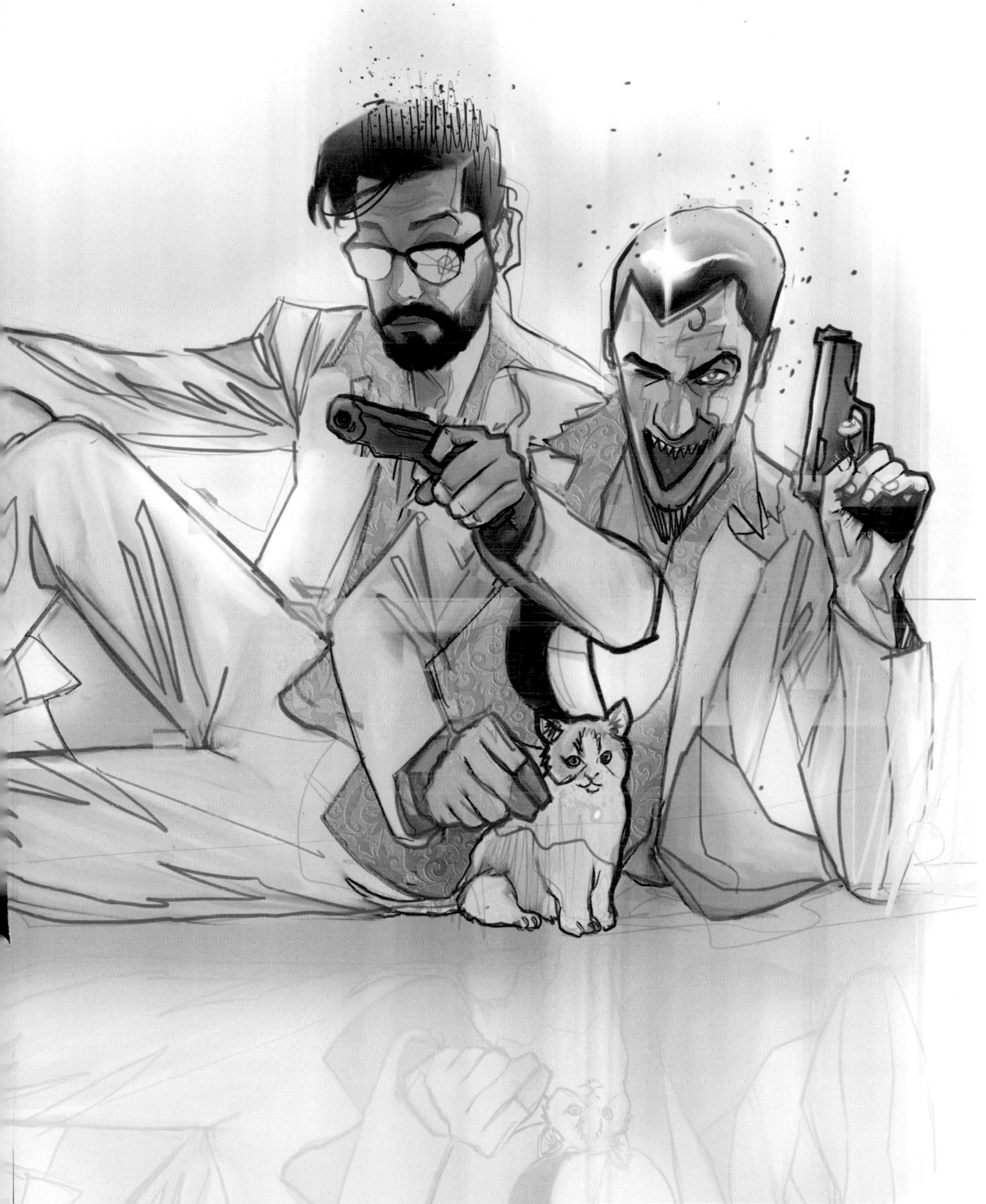

5

MARTIN SIMMONDS

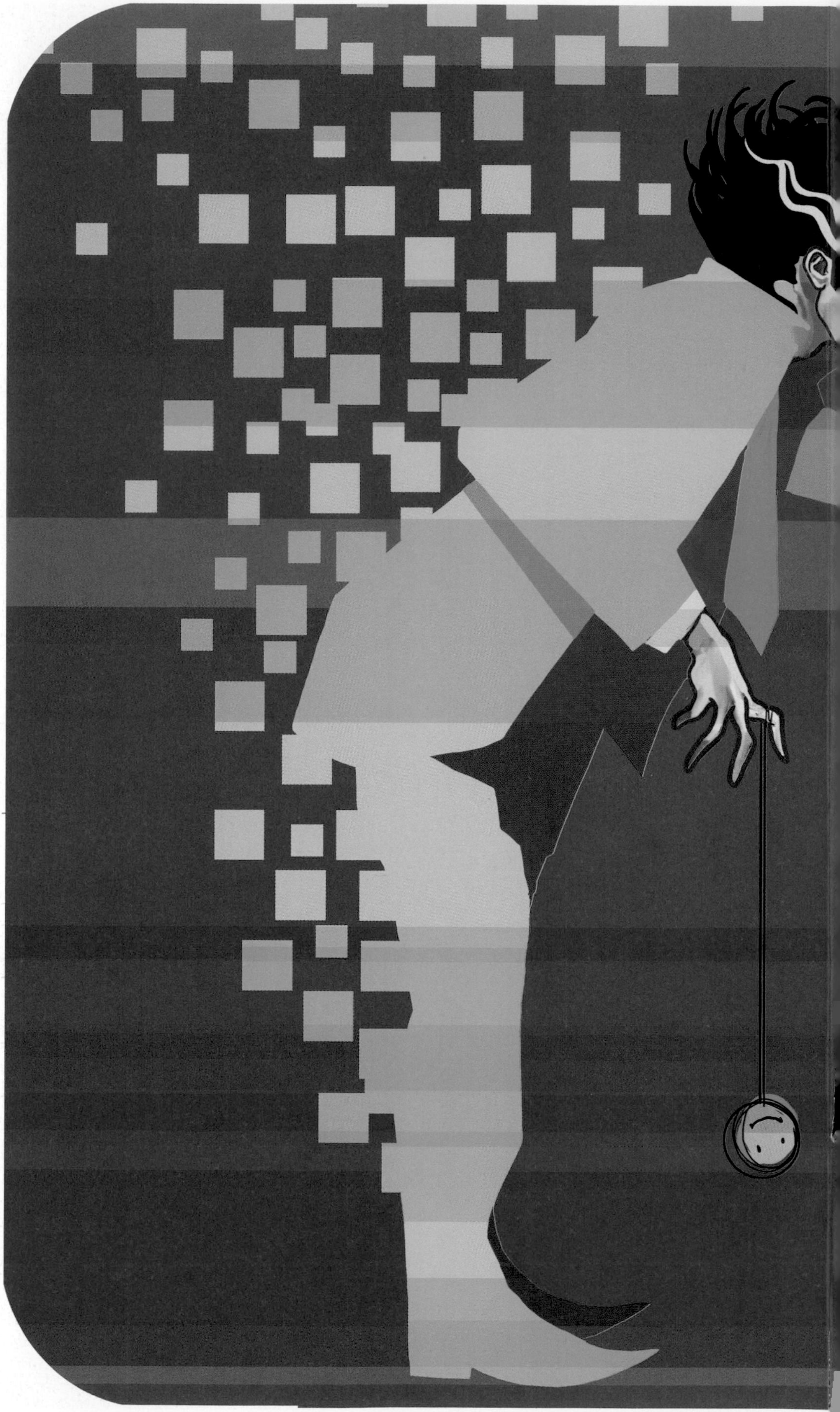

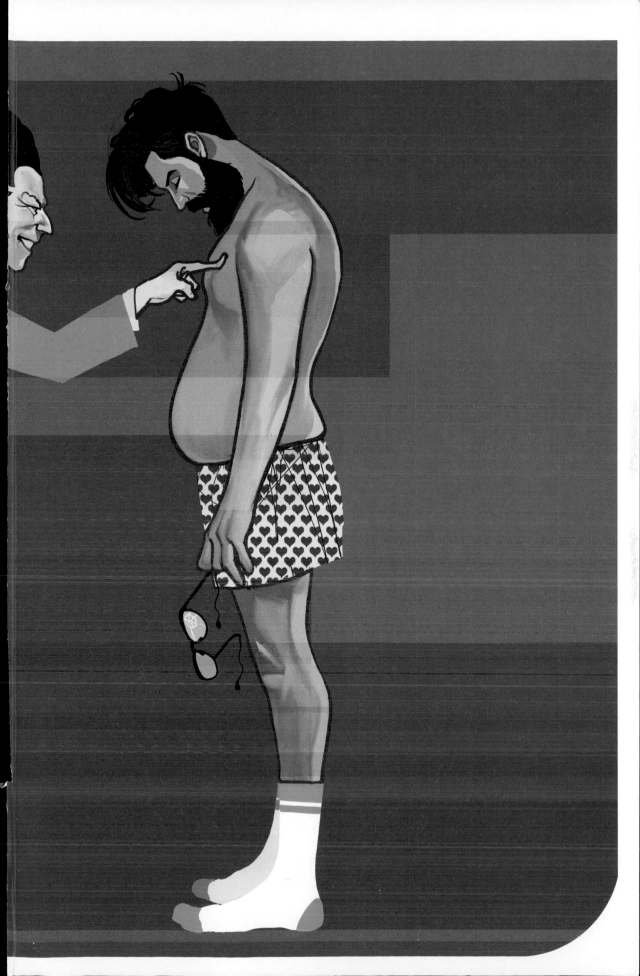

1

KIM McLEAN

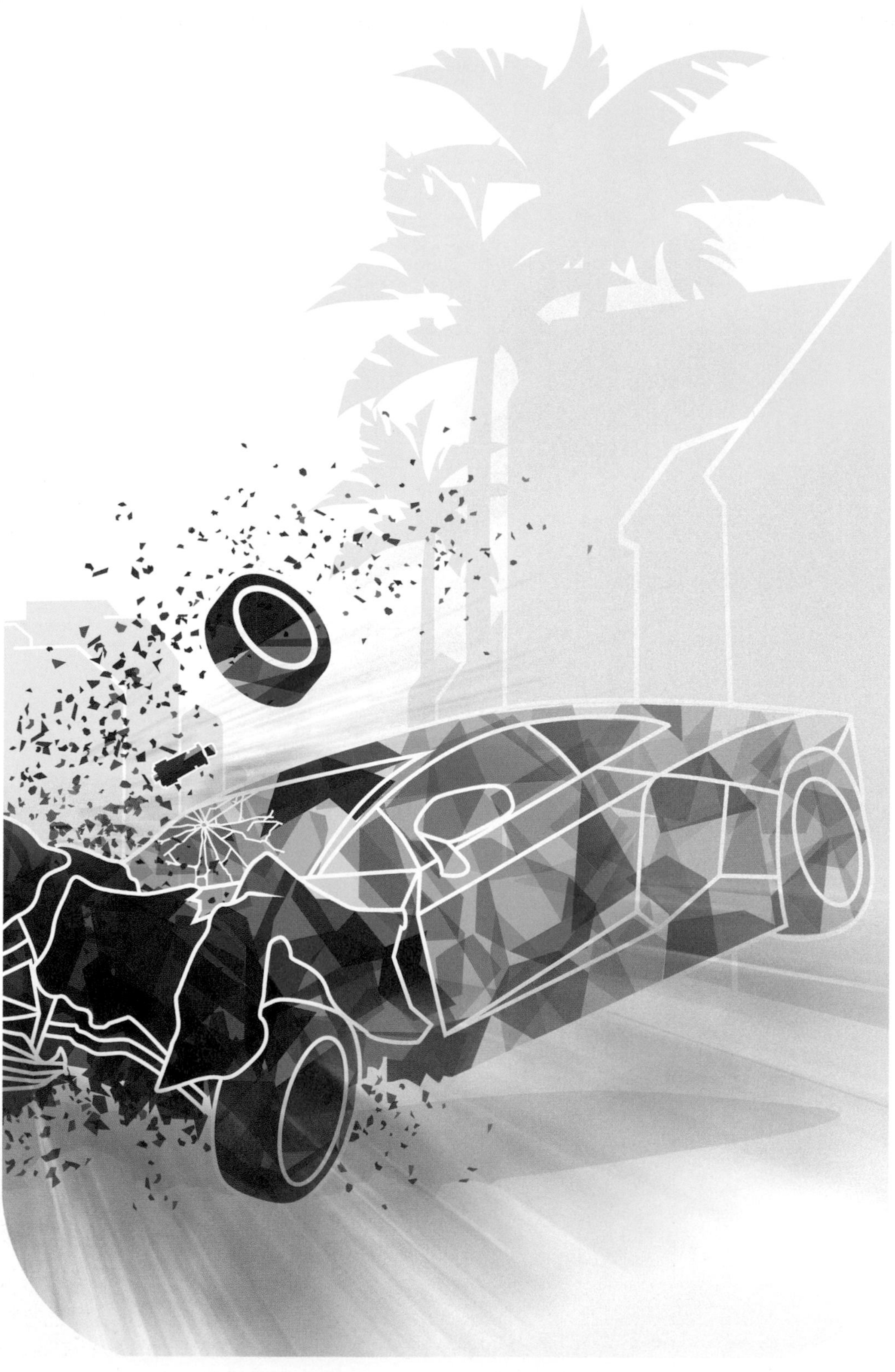

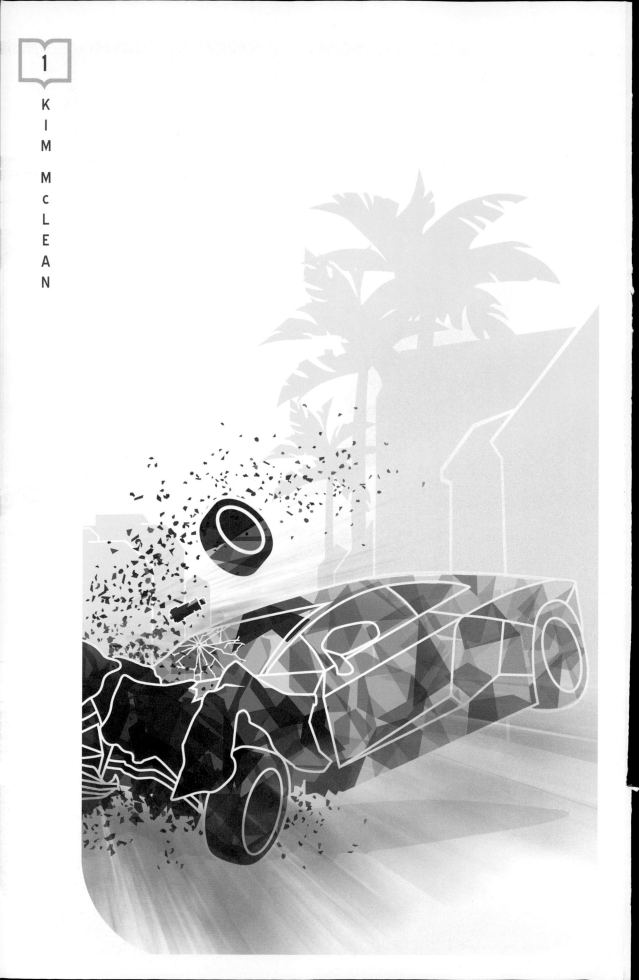

2

KIM McLEAN

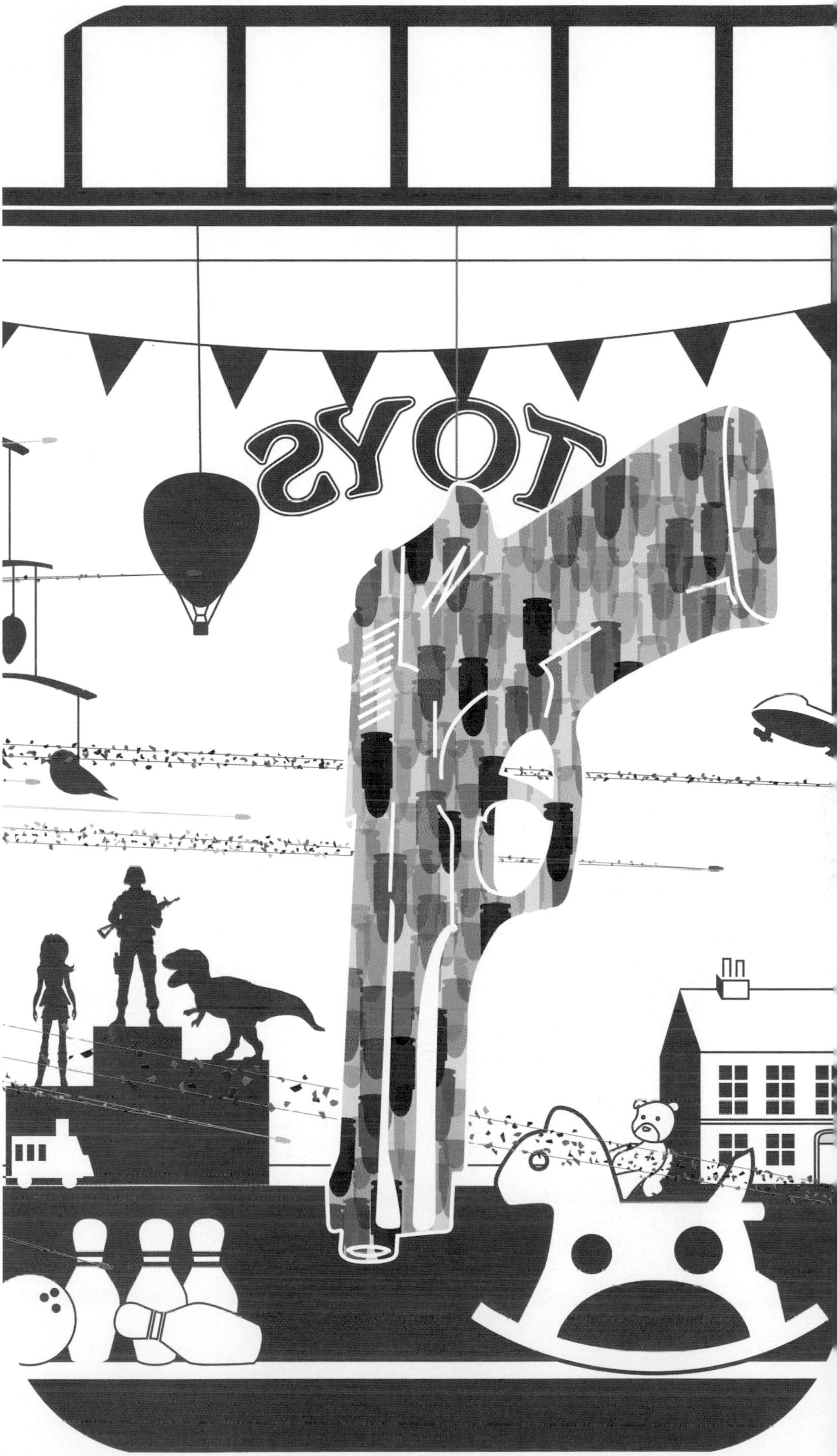

KIM MCLEAN

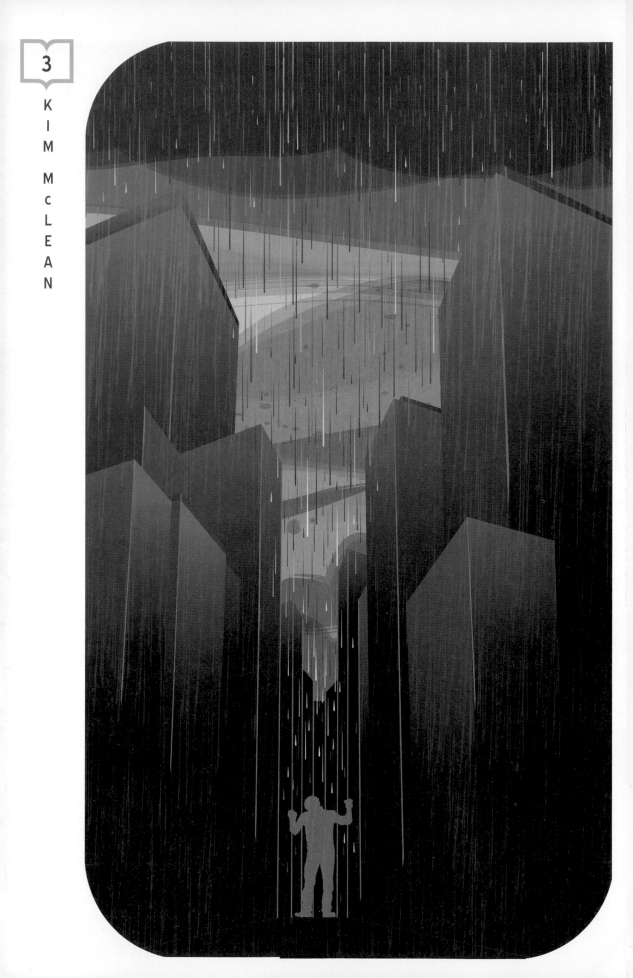

4

K I M M c L E A N

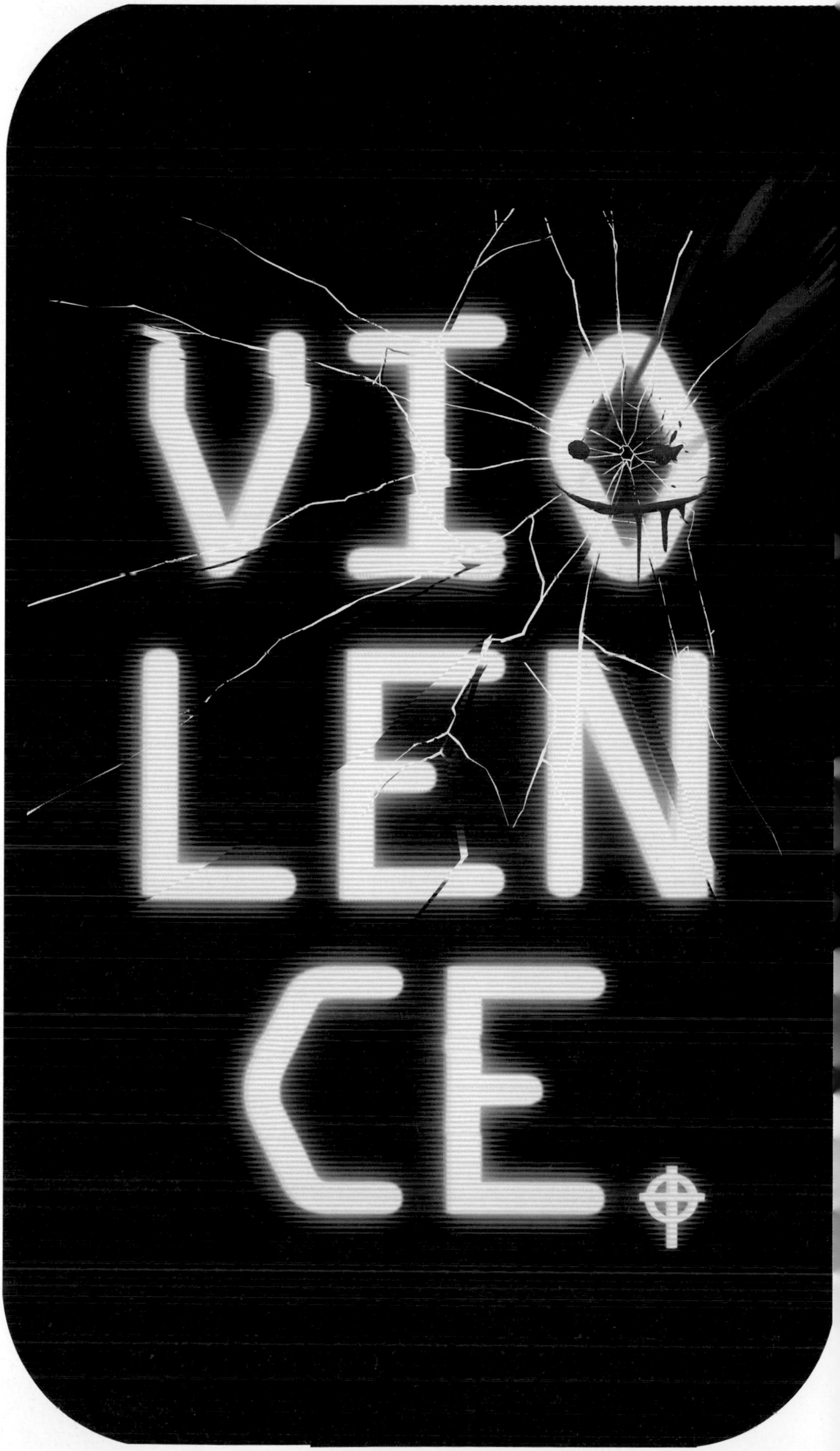
VIO
LEN
CE.

KIM McLEAN

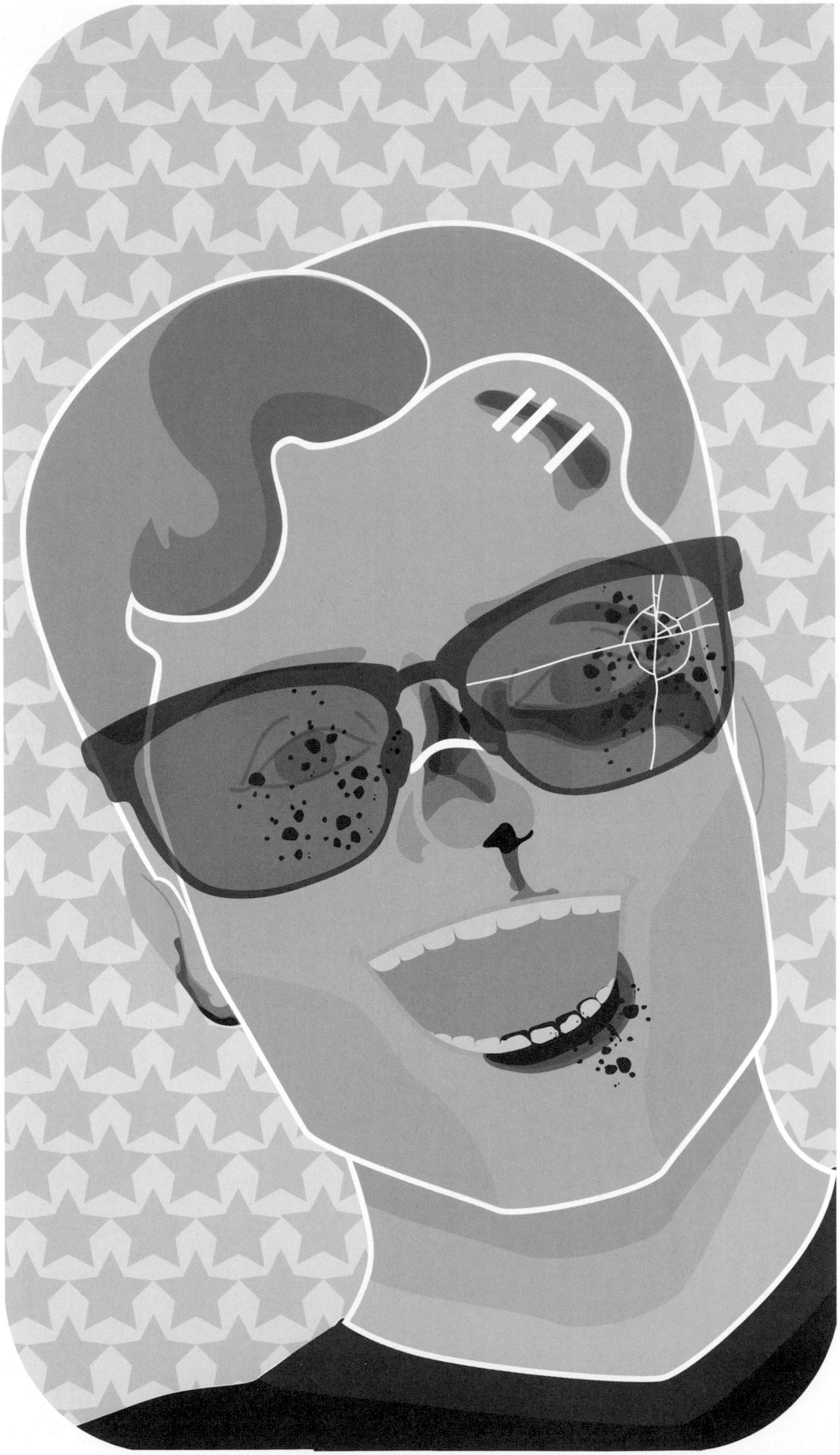

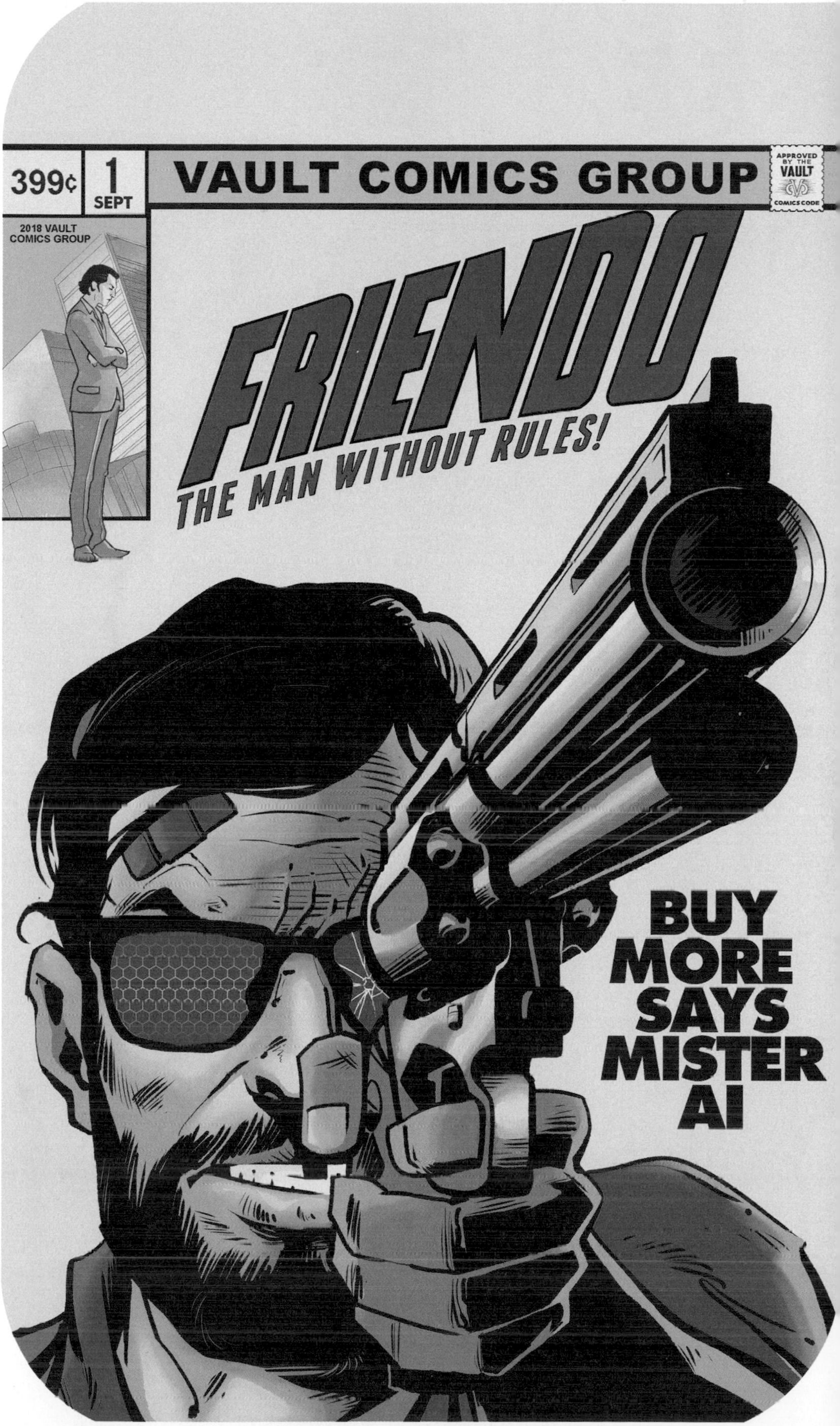
399¢
1
SEPT
VAULT COMICS GROUP
APPROVED BY THE VAULT COMICS CODE
2018 VAULT COMICS GROUP
FRIENDO
THE MAN WITHOUT RULES!
BUY MORE SAYS MISTER AI

1

ANDRE LIMA ARAUJO

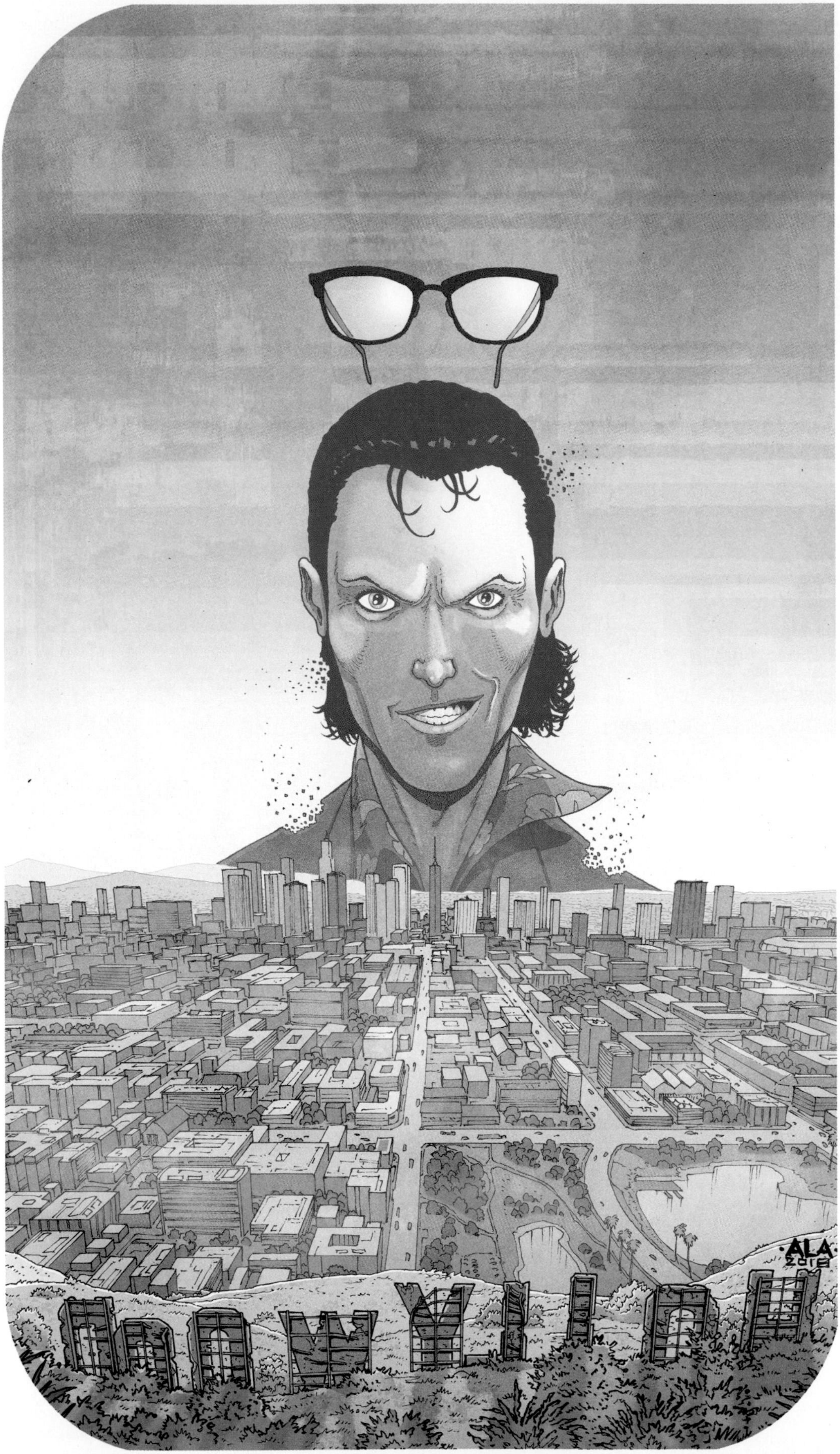
ALA 2018

1

CHRISTIAN WARD

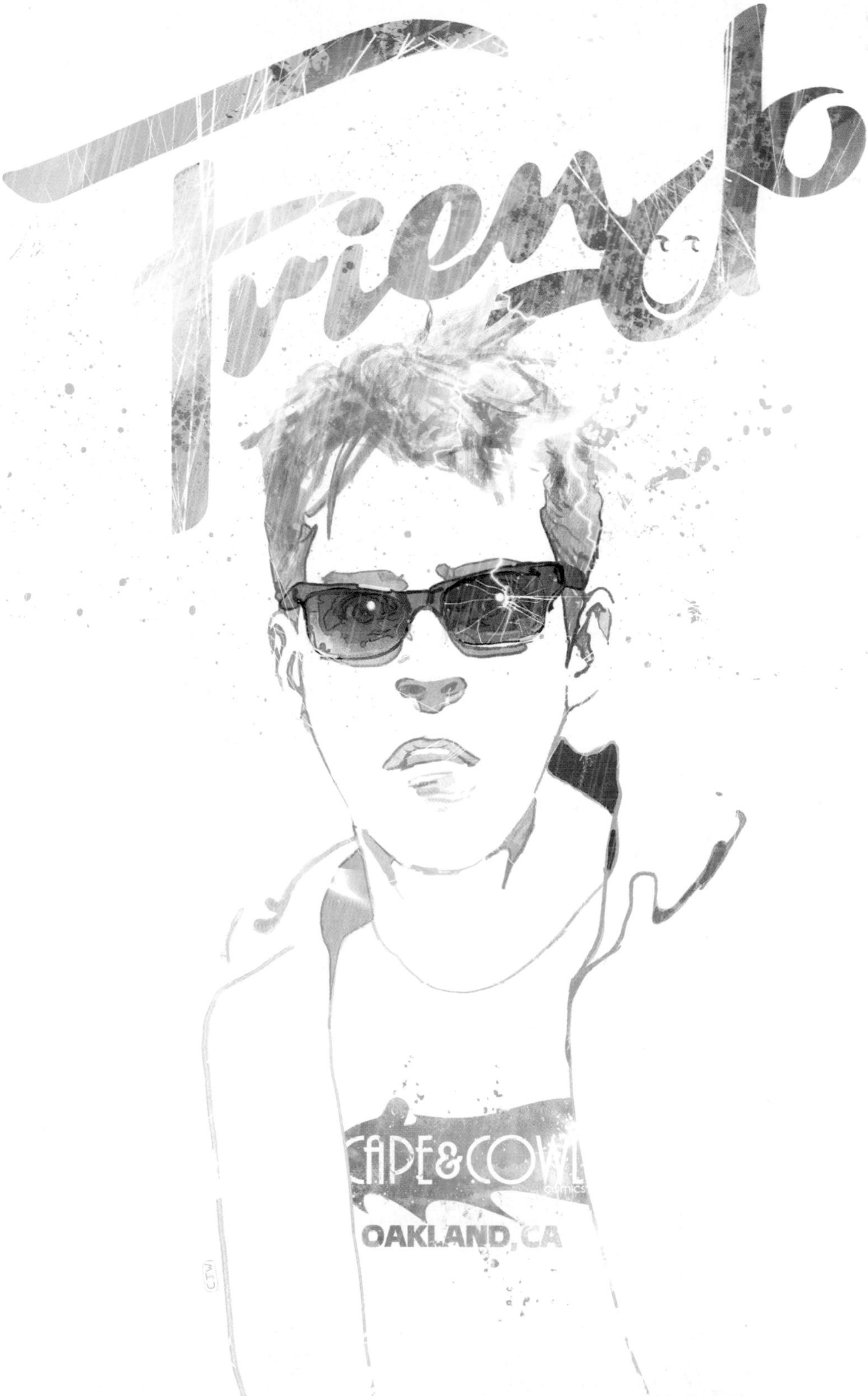
CAPE&COWL
comics
OAKLAND, CA

ICONOGRAPHY

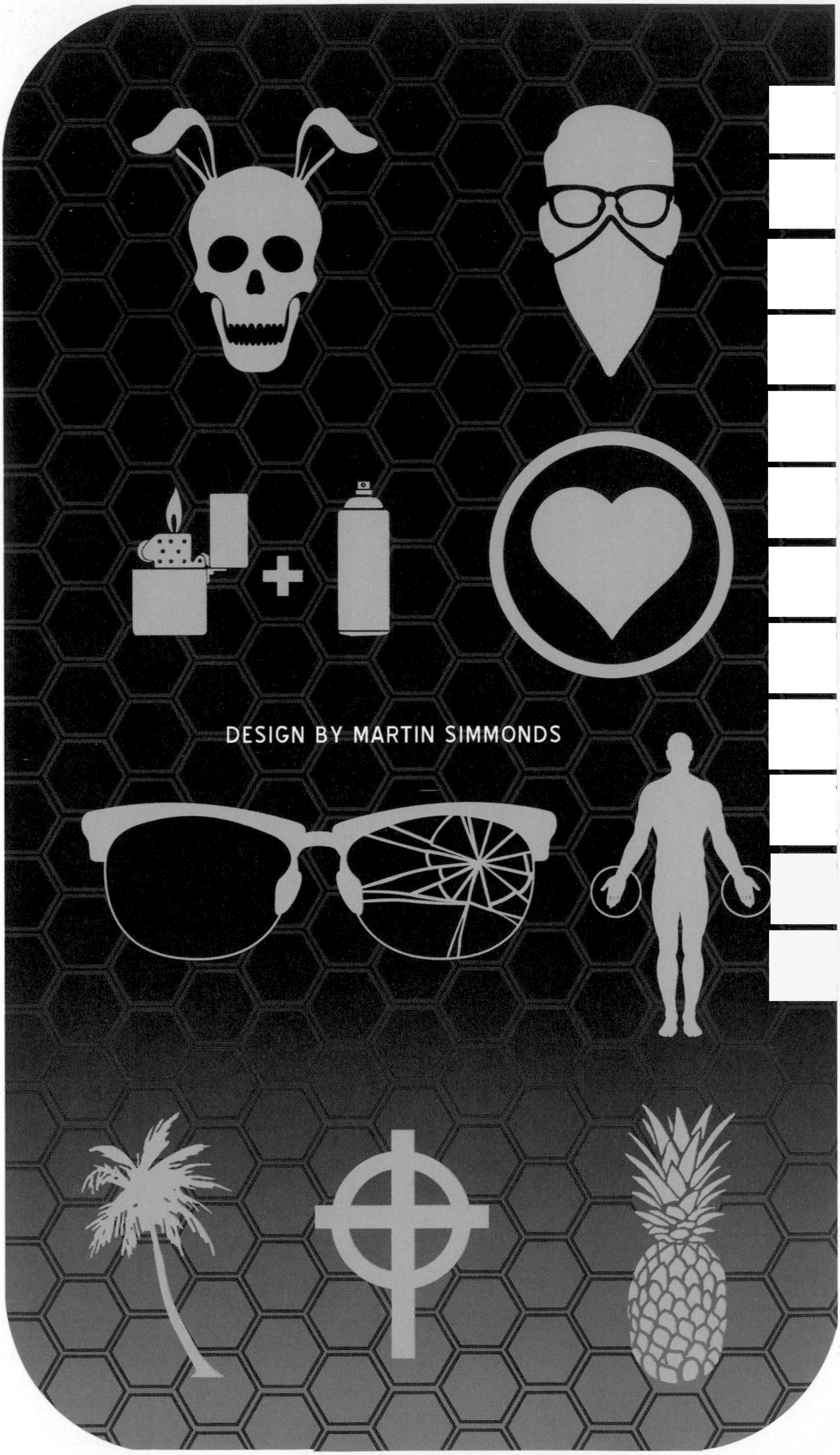
DESIGN BY MARTIN SIMMONDS